W9-ACV-714

# SALADIN

# SALADIN

*Hero of Islam*

## Geoffrey Hindley

Pen & Sword
**MILITARY**

# To my father's memory

First edition published in Great Britain in 1976
This edition published by Pen & Sword Military
an imprint of Pen & Sword Books Ltd
47 Church Street, Barnsley
South Yorkshire S70 2AS

Copyright © Geoffrey Hindley 1976, 2007

ISBN 978 1 84415 499 9

Typeset in Ehrhardt by Phoenix Typesetting, Auldgirth, Dumfriesshire

Printed and bound in England by Biddles Ltd, King's Lynn

Pen & Sword Books Ltd incorporates the Imprints of Pen & Sword Aviation, Pen &
Sword Maritime, Pen & Sword Military, Wharncliffe Local History, Pen & Sword
Select, Pen & Sword Military Classics and Leo Cooper.

For a complete list of Pen & Sword titles please contact
PEN & SWORD BOOKS LIMITED
47 Church Street, Barnsley, South Yorkshire, S70 2AS, England
E-mail: enquiries@pen-and-sword.co.uk
Website: www.pen-and-sword.co.uk

# Contents

# List of Plates

*Plates between pages 112 and 113*

A dramatic monument to Saladin erected in Damascus in twentieth century.

This famous image of Saladin, dating from about 1180, is attributed to an artist of the Fatimid school.

Built between 685 and 691, the Dome of the Rock, sometimes called the Mosque of Omar, is the earliest great architectural monument of Islam.

The interior of the Dome of the Rock.

The Citadel at Jerusalem, showing fortifications from the time of the Crusades.

This nineteenth-century print of Jerusalem depicts the Holy City within its walls much as it must have looked to Saladin preparing to lay siege to the place in 1189.

The interior of the great mosque at Damascus, the Mosque of the Umayyads.

A view of the Mosque of the Umayyads at Damascus, showing the colonnaded courtyard with the city laid out beyond.

A nineteenth-century view of the ruined classical temples at Baalbek overlooking the Beka'a valley.

A watercolour view of Tyre, seen from its isthmus, by the nineteenth-century topographical artist, David Roberts.

The ruins of the crusader castle of Belvoir, known to the Muslims as Kaukab.

The most famous of all crusader castles, Krak des Chevaliers.

The crusaders' castle of Montreal, known to the Muslim forces as ash-Shaubak.

The site of Saladin's great victory of the Christian forces at 'The Horns of Hattin' overlooking the Lake Tiberias (the Sea of Galilee) in 1187.

# Maps

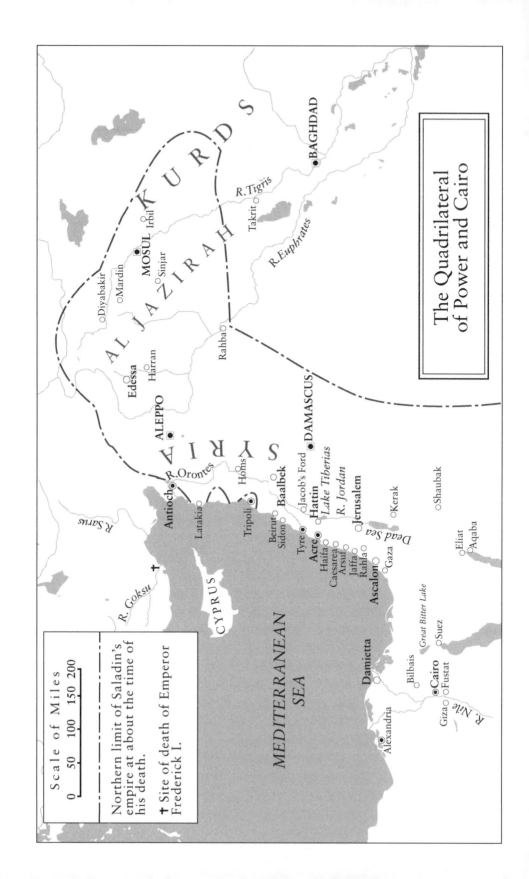

The Quadrilateral
of Power and Cairo

Scale of Miles
0   50   100  150  200

Northern limit of Saladin's
empire at about the time of
his death.

+ Site of death of Emperor
Frederick I.

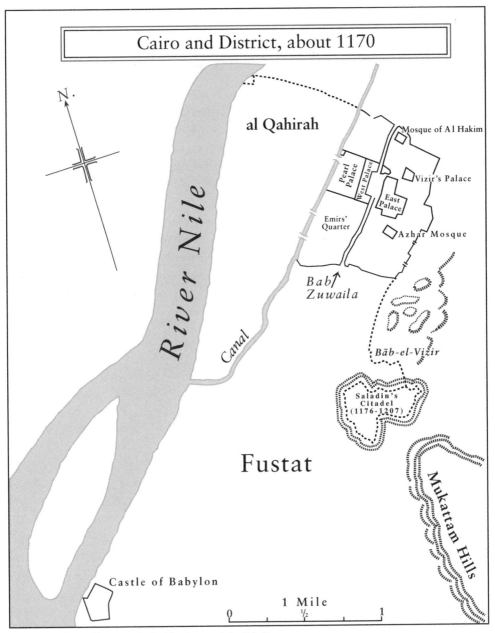

Cairo and District, about 1170

N.

al Qahirah

Mosque of Al Hakim

River Nile

Pearl Palace

West Palace

Vizir's Palace

East Palace

Emirs' Quarter

Azhar Mosque

*Bab Zuwaila*

*Bāb-el-Vizir*

Canal

Saladin's Citadel (1176-1207)

Fustat

Mukattam Hills

Castle of Babylon

1 Mile

0        ½        1

Dotted lines show additions to the fortifications made by Saladin.

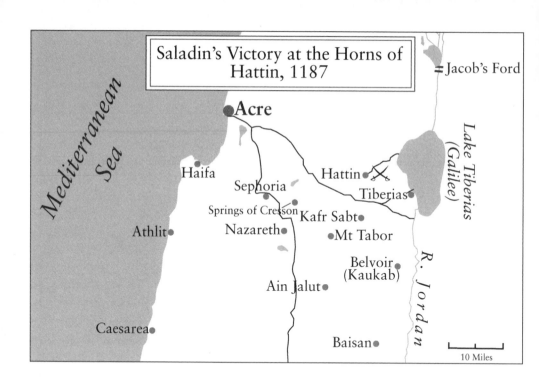

**Saladin's Victory at the Horns of Hattin, 1187**

= Jacob's Ford

Mediterranean Sea

Lake Tiberias (Galilee)

R. Jordan

●Acre

Haifa

Sephoria

Springs of Cresson

Athlit●

Nazareth●

Hattin

Tiberias

Kafr Sabt●

●Mt Tabor

Belvoir (Kaukab)●

Ain Jalut●

Caesarea●

Baisan●

10 Miles

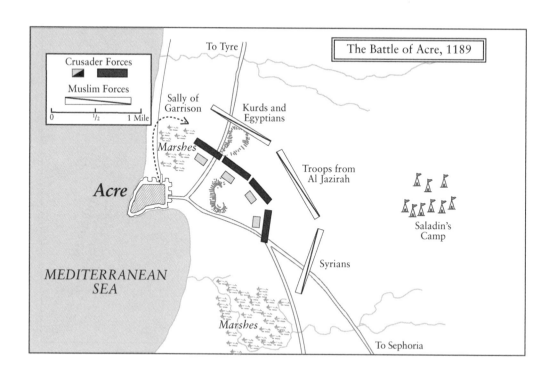

**The Battle of Acre, 1189**

To Tyre

Crusader Forces

Muslim Forces

0      ½      1 Mile

Sally of Garrison

Kurds and Egyptians

Marshes

Acre

Troops from Al Jazirah

Saladin's Camp

Syrians

MEDITERRANEAN SEA

Marshes

To Sephoria

# Introduction

Saladin is one of those rare figures in the long history of confrontation between the Christian West and the world of Islam who earned the respect of his enemies. This alone would make his life worth investigating. For the English-speaking world at least his name is firmly bracketed with that of Richard I the Lionheart, in a context of romantic clichés which form one of the great images of the medieval world of chivalry. The identification began during the lives of the two men and has continued down to the present. Of the two we know very much more about the Muslim hero than about his Christian rival, thanks to the eulogising biographies of his secretary Imad-ad-Din al-Isfahani and his loyal minister Baha'-ad-Din, the numerous but more critical references to him in the *Historical Compendium* of Ibn-al-Athir (1160–1233), the greatest historian of his time, and detailed treatment of aspects of his career in other contemporary Muslim sources. Of these three, the first two began their careers in the service of Selchük Turkish princes who represented the ruling establishment that Saladin was to displace, while the third, although he remained loyal to the Selchük dynasty of Zengi and regarded Saladin as a usurper, was too honest and objective a man to deny his great qualities.

And this brings us to the second fascinating focus of Saladin's career. His father, Aiyub, rose high in the service of Zengi and then of his son Nur-ad-Din, but as a Kurd in a Syrian world then ruled by Turkish dynasties he could hardly hope to win the supreme power. The fact that his son did so is one of the greatest tributes to his abilities and was an unforgivable act of presumption in the eyes of the old-school Turkish officials. After the death of Nur-ad-Din in the year 1174 Saladin was to force his claim to suzerainty throughout Turkish Syria, from Mosul to Damascus, and in his last years was the acknowledged arbiter of the rivalries among the descendants of the great Zengi. For die-hards it was bitter proof of the decadence of the world, epitomised in a story told to Ibn-al-Athir by one of his friends. In the autumn of 1191 the Zengid prince Moizz-ad-Din had come to Saladin to beg his mediation in a family land dispute. When the young man came to take his leave of the great king, he got down from his horse. 'Saladin did the same to say his farewells. But when he prepared to mount his horse again, Moizz-ad-Din helped him and held the stirrup for him. It was Ala-ad-Din Khorrem Shah, son of Izz-ad-Din prince of Mosul (another Zengid), who arranged the robes of the sultan. I was astonished.' Then Ibn-al-Athir's friend concluded his horrified account with an invocation. 'Oh son of Aiyub, you will rest easy whatever manner of death you may die. You for whom the son of a Selchük king held the stirrup.'

To hold the stirrup was one of the most potent symbols of submission throughout the contemporary world, Christian West as well as Muslim. Admiring contemporaries noted when a pope was powerful enough to exact such tribute from an emperor. Yet it is surely remarkable that after a decade in which he had ruled from Aleppo to Cairo and had led the armies of Islam in the Holy War against the Infidel, Saladin's Kurdish ancestry and his triumph over the disunited Zengids still rankled with his opponents. When the great ruler died his doctor noted that in his experience it was the first time a king had been truly mourned by his subjects. His justice and gentleness were recognised by all those who came into contact with him, but his success was jealously watched by the caliphs of Baghdad, nominal heads of the Islamic community, and dourly resisted by the Zengid rulers he eventually overcame. Seen from the West Saladin was the great champion of the *jihad* in succession to Nur-ad-Din; to his opponents in Syria his espousal of the Holy War seemed an impertinent usurpation. The Third Crusade, which came so close to recovering Jerusalem for Christendom, drew its contingents from France, Germany and England – to oppose it Saladin had only troops from the territories he had forced to acknowledge him.

But despite the jealousy and opposition he provoked in the Islamic community there were few, even among his enemies, who denied Saladin's generosity, religious conviction and evenness of temper. There were those who accused him of assumed piety for political reasons, but then both Zengi and Nur-ad-Din had had such charges levelled against them. It may be that Saladin's strict observance of orthodox Sunnite Islam was in part caused by the wish to emulate the dour and extreme religiosity of Nur-ad-Din. His treatment of his Jewish subjects offers a good illustration of his meticulous adherence to the letter of Islamic law. Before he came to power in Egypt as vizir in 1169 the Shi'ite caliphs of Cairo (considered heretics by Baghdad) had often used Jewish and Christian advisers in preference to their Sunnite Muslim subjects. In consequence they had relaxed some of the restrictions on non-believers. Saladin reimposed many of these regulations, such as the one that forbade Jews from riding horses. But he scrupulously upheld their right to present petitions for the redress of wrongs under the law and their right to have disputes between Jews tried by Jewish judges 'as in former times'.

Saladin's genuine if legalistic tolerance in religious matters is confirmed by the German Dominican Burkhard, who visited Egypt in 1175 and observed that people there seemed free to follow their religious persuasions. To the Jews indeed Saladin's later career seemed to foreshadow great things. The 1170s and 1180s were a period of strong Messianic hopes and Saladin's crushing victory over the Christians at the battle of Hattin in 1187 seemed to herald marvellous things to come. A modern biographer of the great Jewish philosopher Maimonides even suggested that his digest of the law, the Mishna Torah, may have been written as the constitution of the new Jewish state then being predicted. When Saladin proclaimed the right of Jews to return to Jerusalem and settle there after his conquest of the city at least one observer, Y'hudah-al-Harizi, compared the decree to the reestablishment of Jewish Jerusalem by the Persian emperor, Cyrus the Great.

Few figures in the whole history of the Middle East have earned the admiration of Jews, Christians and Muslims, and it is, of course, because of his association with this ancient and historic zone of conflict that Saladin has special interest for a modern writer. For all but one of twenty years he ruled Egypt and Damascene Syria as provinces of a single empire; for much of that time he was also overlord of the western seaboard of Arabia, northern Syria, with its capital at Aleppo, and the North African coast as far west as Tunisia, while his authority was recognised in the distant north-east at Mosul. For these critical decades then Saladin achieved a united Islamic state fleetingly paralleled in our time by the United Arab Republic. The last six years of his arduous and ambitious career harnessed the combined resources of these wide territories in a campaign which shattered the Christian Latin states established in Palestine in the wake of the First Crusade. Most dramatic of all he recovered the holy city of Jerusalem for Islam.

Because of this great victory and because of the heady rhetoric of the Holy War which so obsessed Christian and Islamic thinking during the later part of the twelfth century, it was often supposed at the time and has been supposed since that the conquest of Jerusalem was the only objective of Saladin's career. His biographers have too often ignored the realities of power in the region and the pressures they put on him. Saladin came at the end of a period in the history of the Middle East during which the Sunnite caliphs of Baghdad had been working unrelentingly but with slight success to establish their supremacy in the heretical Shi'ite capital of Cairo; and he operated in a world where the crucial centres of power were the cities of Damascus, Aleppo, Mosul and, to a lesser extent, Baghdad. These were the formative factors behind his own slow yet inexorable drive against Christian Palestine.

The first edition of this book was one of just two biographies of its subject in the English language for many decades; new research and a number of new biographical studies since are outlined in the revised bibliography. I have corrected errors in the first edition. I retain the word 'Saracen' as a useful general term used in the West for the various peoples, Arab, Turk, Turkoman etc., recruited to his armies by Saladin. Conventions on the transliteration of Arabic and other Middle Eastern languages have changed over the years; usage has also changed from 'Moslem' to 'Muslim' and 'Qur'an' is increasingly common for 'Koran'.

By and large, however, the book has stood the test of time fairly well – in particular, its contention that in 1188 Saladin did right to concentrate his energies on the threat posed by the advancing German army of the Emperor Frederick Barbarossa rather than on the capture of the city of Tyre. The collapse of the German crusade could not have been foreseen, while Tyre had never been significant in previous European campaigns. My analysis of Saladin's strategy to lure the Christian army into the campaign that ended in its defeat at Hattin is now generally accepted.

I presented the book as part of a survey I had in mind of the encounter of religious cultures in the twelfth century Middle East: Sunni Islam, Shia Islam, Orthodox Christianity and Roman Catholic Christianity. I was invited to prepare an outline for a projected part-work publication on the world cultural importance of Islam in its early centuries. In the 1970s, such 'multi-cultural studies' were ahead of their time. Teaching a course in European civilization at the University of Le Havre in the 1990s I devoted an element to the contribution made by the Islamic world to the medieval West – in the context of the upsurge of 'Islamism' at that time very topical in Franco-Algerian relations. Events of recent years have brought such studies a higher profile in the Western world.

Saladin should be central to an understanding of Islamic religious attitudes of his time, being a man of honour and integrity who, even if able to respect his Christian enemies, was implacably hostile to them as agents of irreligion – a man for whom *jihad* was very much an armed struggle against the 'infidels' (*al-Kuffar*). In the twenty-first century, this term *jihad* has powerful resonance outside the Islamic world. Although the word is not found in the Qur'an, it was in use from a very early date and the concept evolved in the work of Islamic legalists. Two types are distinguished: 'the greater', *al jihad al-akbar*, which is the struggle against the self to establish the way of Islam in one's own life; and 'the lesser' *al-asghar*, which is struggle or warfare in the way of God.

In a famous personal testament, Saladin set out his dedication to the *jihad* and summed up all his early achievements as means for the recovery of Jerusalem, i.e. al-Quds. In the view of some historians, he took power in Egypt (Chapter 6) to provide himself with a purely dynastic power base. It certainly served that purpose, but he himself pointed out that as soon as he was established there he began regular incursions against the infidels, recovering from them strongholds lost to Islam. Among these he lists the fortress at Aila (Eilat, modern Israel) on the Gulf of Aqaba, built by Baldwin I of Jerusalem back in 1116, giving the Crusader kingdom a strategic base against the roads from Damascus to Egypt and against Mecca and Medina.

Critics have accused Saladin of conducting wars of self aggrandisement as he battled against Muslim rivals simply to build a personal empire: from this point of view the recapture of Jerusalem was, apparently, more a lucky break than the outcome of a careful strategy to bring the army of the kingdom to its knees. But Saladin's claim that his campaigns were essential to the consolidation of Muslim strength for that conquest was utterly justified. Thereafter it was, reports his secretary, adviser and biographer, Ibn Shaddad Baha-ad-Din, his heart's desire to fight the infidels until there was not one left upon the face of the earth.

For generations of admirers, Saladin has represented the intriguing paradox of a man of personal humility, honest purpose and warm humanity who nevertheless won and held great political power and who died an ornament to his religion, loved by his friends and admired by his enemies. His career significantly shifted the balance of power against the enemies of Islam in the Holy Land of three religions. But in his own estimation, he left this world with the work of Allah barely begun.

Peterborough, June 2006

# Chapter 1

# Jerusalem

On Friday, 4 September 1187, the triumphant army of Saladin stood before the gates of Ascalon. It was the major port of southern Palestine which for forty years had been in Christian hands. Now it was to be handed back to Islam. It was the last in a series of capitulations which had followed a massive Muslim victory at Hattin two months previously. On that fateful field the power of the Christian kingdom of Jerusalem had been broken and its morale entirely shattered. As the Saracen soldiers watched the defeated garrison file out on their way to captivity, they could look back on eight weeks of knife-through-butter conquest. Towns and fortresses throughout the kingdom had opened their gates with barely a struggle. Only Jerusalem and a scattering of castles now remained to the enemy. Defeat was closing in on the Christian cause in Palestine and, ominous of disasters still in store, an eclipse of the sun darkened the sky over Ascalon as Muslim banners broke out on her battlements.

The general of this victorious army, Salah-ad-Din Yusuf ibn-Aiyub, was fifty years of age. He was a shortish man, his round face coming to a trim, now grizzled beard, but the hair beneath the turban was still black. Black too were the eyes, keen and alert. For so great a potentate his clothes were simple and unostentatious, but he sat his horse with the ease of thirty years of soldiering in the saddle and the stylishness of a polo champion. As the eclipse slowly darkened the sun's glare an official approached and announced the arrival of Frankish envoys, summoned from Jerusalem to discuss terms for the surrender of that city.

It was clear to Saladin, as it must surely have been to the defenders of that capital now without a kingdom, that the city's position was hopeless. The nearest Christian forces of any strength were a hundred miles away to the north in the coastal city of Tyre. Behind its walls the shaken survivors from the field of Hattin, together with thousands of refugees from the surrounding countryside, drew what comfort they could from the fact that the Muslim army had abandoned its siege for the time being. But, for the moment, they could be discounted as a military threat.

While Ascalon had held there had been some glimmer of a future for the capital. But now Ascalon had fallen and the Gaza garrison, some twenty miles to the south of it, was also on the verge of capitulation. The Frankish troops in Jerusalem held an island in a hostile Muslim sea and even within the walls there were enemies. Thousands of Eastern Orthodox Syrian Christians looked to a Muslim conquest as a liberation from the rites of the Church of Rome. In fact the citizenry could reasonably hope for clemency. In the lightning campaign that had followed Hattin, town after town had been spared and Saladin's advance had seemed more like the progress of a king through his dominions than the bloody triumph march of a conqueror.

As he faced the Christian embassy the sultan saw the prize of a lifetime within his grasp. For years his declared aim had been the liberation of Islam from the infidel and above all the restoration of Jerusalem, holy city of three religions, to Muslim rule. He wanted a peaceful surrender. This city was not just a prize of war to be plundered and made desolate. 'I believe,' he told the envoys, 'that the city is God's abode, as you believe. It would be much against my will to lay siege to the house of God or to put it to the assault.'

To the Christian leaders the case was somewhat different. They remembered that their predecessors had won back the Holy City for Christendom and that they were now its guardians. They had come at Saladin's command but they had no intention of surrendering the city without a fight. To his offer of terms their reply was brave and uncompromising. 'Our honour lies here and our salvation with the salvation of the city. If we abandon her we shall surely and justly be branded with shame and contempt for here is the place of our Saviour's crucifixion. . . . We shall die in the defence of our Lord's sepulchre, for how could we do otherwise.'

Our reporter for this interview is Imad-ad-Din of Isfahan, Saladin's personal secretary. His style is florid and his commitment to his master complete, but the words he puts into the mouths of the Christian embassy ring true and behind his account lies respect for men who, however misguided, were fighting like him in what they believed to be a Holy War. Saladin had offered generous terms to the beleaguered city 'to obtain it in peace and amity', but now that diplomacy had failed he swore a solemn oath to take the place by the sword, and prepared to march from Ascalon immediately.

Some two weeks later, his army appeared before the walls of Jerusalem. Marching up from Ascalon along the coast road and then striking inland, it had come on the city from the west and, on 20 September, the troops began to deploy against the western walls, expecting to overrun them easily after a barrage of stones and fire canisters laid down by the siege artillery. In general, before launching an attack, Saladin made a meticulous inspection of the lie of the land but, on this occasion, underestimating perhaps the strength and determination of the opposition, he opened operations against the nearest sector. It was a mistake. Sorties from the garrison were able to harass the Saracen engineers as they tried to bring the mangonels into action; missile throwers on the great towers of Tancred and David commanded the western approaches and swept the Muslim ranks. Until the early afternoon each day the attackers were blinded and dazzled by the sun rising slowly up the eastern sky behind the bowmen and the artillery on the battlements.

After five days Saladin called off the action. On the evening of 25 September, the defenders saw the army strike camp and begin to move off northward. That night the sounds of the distant chanting and the wooden prayer clappers of the Christians could be heard across the hillsides. The churches of Jerusalem were filled with worshippers giving thanks for this round-one victory; some apparently even thought that the Saracens had withdrawn entirely.

But Saladin had merely shifted the point of the attack. Seeing that the strong westward defences could hold him to a protracted and costly battle he had personally inspected the rest of the perimeter. On the morning of 26 September the citizens awoke to find that Muslim banners were now on Mount Olivet and that the mangonels were already in position for an attack on the weaker northern and eastern walls.

Given conditions within the city, the defence of Jerusalem was surprisingly tough. In addition to the citizens, the supplies had to feed thousands of refugees, few of them able-bodied men. When the city was preparing for the siege, it had been found that there were only two knights in the garrison. In the twelfth century the knight was the best equipped as well as the most thoroughly trained of all fighting men, not simply a member of a socially privileged group. The new commander knighted all the men of the garrison above the age of sixteen; the gesture may have raised morale but it did little to improve the fighting quality of the force.

In fact the city only had an experienced commander thanks to the generosity of Saladin. He was Balian of Ibelin, one of the finest soldiers in the Christian army. After Hattin he had taken refuge with the remnant of that army at Tyre, but his wife, the Byzantine princess Maria Comnena, and his family were still at Jerusalem; Balian begged a safe conduct from Saladin to travel to the capital and arrange their journey to Tyre. This was granted on condition that Balian stayed only a single night and that he swore never again to bear arms against Saladin. Balian took the solemn oath. Yet when he arrived in Jerusalem the pleas of the people and the pressure of the patriarch persuaded him to stay. A man of honour, he protested he had given his oath, but the patriarch, with the bland disregard for commitments made to the infidel that most Christian clerics shared, absolved the knight from this obligation with the words 'I absolve you from your sin and from your oath which it were a greater sin in you to keep than break'.

For Balian it was a real conflict of loyalties. Knightly honour required that he observe his oath pledged to a noble antagonist; Christian devotion and loyalty to his own people made it virtually impossible for him to refuse the pleas of the citizens. But his family was still not out of danger and he needed the goodwill of Saladin. He wrote to him protesting that he had been forced to break his oath and begging that his loved ones be given protection. Saladin not only did not reproach him but even detached fifty of his finest troops to escort the lady of Ibelin and her children northwards to Tyre.

So it was that when Saladin's army began its siege, Jerusalem was led by a determined and capable general. But under the new attack on the northern walls there was little the defenders could do. In the words of an Arab historian, the arrows were as tooth-picks to the walls, plucking defenders out of the embrasures like unwanted pieces of meat. With the missiles and canisters of Greek fire hurled by the siege engines they forced the defenders back from the battlements. Ten thousand horsemen, drawn up just out of bow-shot of the city walls, watched the gates of Jehoshaphat and St Stephen, dashing in to contain and drive back any attempt at a sortie from the garrison.

Imad-ad-Din describes with obvious relish the fearful havoc wrought by the engines of war, and behind the clangour and the screams of the combatants in his narrative we hear the crack and whirr of the wood and ropes as the clumsy machines crash out their murderous missiles. Still more disturbing for the garrison was the ring of iron on stone coming from the base of the walls. There, protected by the covering fire from their army and by a roof of the shields of their comrades, a group of sappers were steadily working on the lower courses of the masonry, others excavated the foundations, propping them with wood as the work progressed. Within forty-eight hours nearly a hundred feet of wall had been undermined, the masonry weakened and the wooden pit props under the foundations surrounded with brushwood and other combustibles.

Even before the wall fell, those within the city were preparing for defeat. The churches were crowded with penitents seeking forgiveness for their sins; the priests made solemn procession through the streets; mothers shaved their daughters' heads hoping to make them so ugly that they would be ignored in the pillage and rape they feared could follow the capture. Saladin had sworn to take the place by sword and there were many in both armies who had heard reports and memories of the days of blood that had followed the terrible Frankish conquest of the city, eighty-eight years before.

On 29 September the props under the foundations were fired, the weakened wall fell, and a great breach was opened up. The hard-pressed garrison had to man it unaided since the citizen militiamen, who had been prepared to fight from behind the comparative safety of the ramparts, refused to defend the suicidally exposed position on the crumbling stone-work. Public opinion began to clamour for surrender and an appeal to the mercy of Saladin. But the new knights of the garrison were eager for a last glorious sortie, to sell their lives as dearly as possible and to win martyrs' crowns for themselves. The result would have been a disaster for Jerusalem. The laws of war permitted unrestrained rights of pillage to an army that took a city by storm. In fact the plunder from such operations was one of the more valuable profits of war-making for the average soldier and no commander could hope to control his men in the heat and blood of battle. Whatever Saladin might have wished, the outcome of a heroic last-ditch stand by the Franks would have meant slaughter and destruction.

Inside the city, the patriarch Heraclius fully realised the potential threats in the situation, not only to life but also to the priceless treasures and the holy relics in the city's churches. He persuaded the knights to reconsider their decision, pointing out that while the heroes might find themselves in paradise at the end of the day, their wives and children would, in all probability, be brutalised, tortured and enslaved. Balian himself apparently came to share this view, and the following day he led a deputation to Saladin's headquarters in the valley of the Brook Kedron to discuss terms.

The battle raged over the breach in the walls even as the *pourparlers* went forward, and in the midst of the negotiations Saladin pointed out to Balian that Muslim standards were already fluttering on the battlements. 'Does a victor grant terms to a conquered city?' he drily enquired. Soon after, a desperate counter-attack from the garrison pushed the invaders back, but the fall of Jerusalem was only a matter of days, perhaps hours, away, and it is difficult at first sight to see what the Christians could hope for.

Saladin's first instinct was to harden his heart against mercy. 'We shall deal with you just as you dealt with the people of Jerusalem when you conquered the city with murder, enslavement and atrocities.' But there were other factors. Despite his oath, Saladin still preferred that the city return to Islam spared the worst disfigurements of war. His emirs and advisers could see other advantages in a negotiated surrender. In the mayhem of a sack much wealth would be destroyed and more be looted by the common soldiery. But in an orderly transfer of ransom money, supervised of course by officers and gentlemen, a perfectly satisfactory percentage could be creamed off on its way to the official coffers. Their advice was to negotiate from the premise that the enemy were already prisoners and to agree the terms of the ransoms.

But it was Balian who provided the clinching argument. The Frankish garrison had agreed to forgo the glory of martyrdom to save their families – if now the enemy refused terms, their desperation and fanaticism could be relied on to make a shambles of Jerusalem and the shrines it contained. Moreover there were 5,000 Muslim prisoners and slaves within the walls whom Balian now used as hostages. According to the chronicler Ibn-al-Athir, he addressed Saladin in the following words: 'Many of the people in the city are fighting half-heartedly in the hope that you will grant them mercy as you have to other cities – such people fear death and desire life. But for ourselves as soldiers, when we see that death must needs be, by God we will slaughter our sons and women, we will burn our wealth and possessions and leave you neither *dinar* nor *drachma* for plunder, nor man nor woman to enslave. When we have finished that, we will destroy the Rock and the al-Aqsa mosque and the other holy places and we will slay the Muslim slaves who are in our hands. Then we will sally out to fight against you; each man amongst us will take his equal down to death with him so that we shall die gloriously or conquer with honour.'

Whether in fact Balian and his men would have been able to hold the perimeter long enough to complete this scenario of destruction is doubtful. But the possibility was there and neither Saladin nor his emirs wanted to put the issue to the test. There remained the question of the sultan's oath. His religious advisers proposed a formula. If the garrison would make a formal surrender at discretion, this would be considered as the equivalent of conquest by the sword and the oath would be fulfilled.

The terms of the ransom were not over liberal nor were they impossibly harsh. More to the point, once the fighting had stopped, not a single Christian was harmed by the victorious troops. Emirs and officers patrolled the streets to prevent outrages against property or person. As we shall shortly see, they made the administration of the ransom pay, but the fact remains that when the Muslim reconquered Jerusalem the handover was civilised and orderly. The contrast with the First Crusade could hardly have been more complete. It is not surprising that Christian chroniclers and citizens alike blessed the name of Saladin for their lives.

Each man was to be ransomed for ten gold pieces, each woman for five and each child for a single gold piece. Because there were thousands of poor who could not hope to raise this kind of money, Saladin released 7,000 people for 30,000 bezants – raised incidentally from the balance left from the treasure presented to the Hospital some years before by King Henry II of England. The ransoming of so vast a population – estimates range from 60,000 to 100,000 – was clearly going to take time. Forty days were allowed; anyone who after that time had still not found the money should be sold into slavery – the normal fate of a defeated population. In fact many Syrian Christians preferred to stay and pay the Muslim tax for the right to practise their own religion.

Payments and releases were controlled as closely as possible. The great gates of the city were closed and at the posterns of each gate stood a Muslim official collecting the ransom money from each head of family as he left. Those freed were to carry with them as much of their personal belongings as they could. This applied from the lowest to the highest. The Muslim camp was furious that the Patriarch Heraclius, though he paid only the standard capitation fee for his personal liberty, left the city accompanied by pack animals and porters carrying off the treasures of the city's churches, the gold plate from the Holy Sepulchre and a vast hoard of his own wealth. Urged by his emirs to stop this flagrant breach of the treaty spirit Saladin refused to 'break faith with them' even though they might take advantage of him at the expense of their own honour.

Many Christians too were outraged at the patriarch's behaviour. After the 7,000 poor had been released for the 30,000 bezants there were still thousands hardly able to ransom themselves, while they could easily have been bought with the Church's wealth. As it was they sold their few possessions at rock-bottom prices to the enemy soldiery to raise the price of their bare freedom and left the city destitute. Below them came thousands of beggars and labourers. Yet many of these found mercy at the hands of the conquerors. Saladin's brother, al-Adil, touched by the misery of the refugees and the plight of those left inside the city, begged a gift of a thousand slaves from Saladin in return for his service in the wars. When they were made over to him he freed them at once. The patriarch, seeing the chance of cheap altruism, asked a similar boon and was granted 500 to release, while Balian begged the freedom of a similar number. When these arrangements were completed Saladin said to his courtiers: 'My brother has made his alms and the patriarch and Balian have made theirs; now would I fain make mine.' And he then ordered that all the old and infirm and poor still left in the city should be liberated. In the words of the Christian chronicler Ernoul, 'they came forth from the rising of the sun until night fell. Such was the charity of which Saladin did to poor people without number.'

When the great exodus was complete, it was found that there were still some 15,000 able-bodied poor men and women who were divided as slaves among the conquerors or sent into their harems. Saladin's war chest had received, it was calculated, 100,000 dinars, and his reputation an invaluable lift. But while all the chroniclers, friend and foe alike, sang the generosity of the high command in their dealing with the defeated city, some Arab commentators described in bitter terms the fraud that was practised by many of the emirs in charge of the ransoms. Imad-ad-Din describes just how one of the tricks was worked.

Saladin had set up offices which issued receipts for full ransom payments. These receipts were valid at the exit points in lieu of cash payments, but a clerk working in one of the offices, 'a person whose word I do not doubt', told Imad-ad-Din just how things were done there: 'often they would write a receipt for someone whose money went into their own pockets and their deceit went undiscovered'. Those outside the civil service, unable to conduct their fraud in the privacy of their own office, developed other techniques. A favourite one was to smuggle a Christian out of the city disguised as a Muslim and then take him for all he had under threat of reporting him to the authorities for evading the ransom collection. This kind of petty fraud was overshadowed by the manoeuvres of the big operators. Emirs claimed hundreds of the inhabitants by right as escaped slaves – there were many refugees in Jerusalem from the surrounding districts and claims like these would have been difficult to check. They then liberated these slaves with apparent generosity, though in fact at the standard ransom rate, or more, which went straight into their own pockets.

Self-interest no doubt prompted the emirs to agree with Saladin's plans for ransoming the city and speculation played a large part in their carrying out of those plans. However there is no indication that Saladin himself had any ulterior motives and much to show that his behaviour was as uncomplicated and honourable as it appears. Ernoul, the Frankish chronicler in Balian's entourage, had no doubt at all about the nobility of the Muslim general. He concludes his account of the surrender with an example of the 'great courtesy which Saladin showed to the wives and daughters of the knights who had to flee Jerusalem when their lords were killed or made prisoners in battle'. They were naturally able to find their ransom money of five gold pieces a head, but the Muslim reconquest of the lands formerly held by their menfolk meant they were now disinherited. They had ransomed themselves from slavery – were they now to become paupers? They begged the conqueror to 'counsel and to help them'. Those whose men were still alive as prisoners piteously begged to be told where they were. Saladin promised to trace as many of the prisoners as he could and return them to their families. In addition, and from his own treasury, he distributed cash grants calculated according to each lady's status. 'They gave praise to God' and 'published abroad the kindness and honour he had done them'. This could of course be construed as some kind of public relations exercise. Certainly the towns of the Frankish kingdom had capitulated easily to Saladin because of his reputation for clemency. But this generosity was on an unheard-of scale; the enemy was virtually finished and in any case it is difficult to see just what advantage Saladin hoped to buy. The fact is that accounts of his career, whether by friend or enemy, described acts both generous and honourable which it is hard to discount. The possibility must be entertained that Saladin was a good, honest and humane man, although in a position of great power.

Whatever his motives, Jerusalem had been spared the destruction and misery proper to war and the celebrations on her return to Islam were not marred by memories of any brutality. But there remained the job of cleansing the city and the Holy Places of Islam of all traces of the Christian defilement. Even while the forty-day process of the ransom was going on, the golden cross over the Dome of the Rock had been brought down and broken up. Christian church furniture was unceremoniously cleared out of the building as well as from the al-Aqsa mosque. The Rock itself, from which Muslims believe Muhammad made his mystical ascent to heaven, had been built over with a Christian chapel, and on the place where the prophet's foot was believed to have rested there now stood a shrine embellished with marble to honour it as a place where Christ had stood before his Passion. The Rock had been sheathed in marble slabs which seem to have been put in place to protect it from relic hunters. It appears that portions had been cut from it and sold by its Christian guardians to be housed in the altars of newly dedicated churches in Europe. Saladin ordered that the marble be removed and the sacred site be once more exposed to the view of the faithful. The mihrab in the al-Aqsa mosque had been covered over and this too was laid bare. The outside of the mosque was obscured by living quarters, a granary and even a latrine built by the Templars who had been the custodians of the place. All these buildings were demolished and the interior of the mosque richly carpeted, in place of the rush-matting that the Christians had used; magnificent candelabra were hung from the roof and illuminated texts from the Koran hung in places of honour round the walls. Finally Saladin had brought from Aleppo an exquisitely carved pulpit which had been commissioned by Nur-ad-Din twenty years before for the Mosque of Umar at Jerusalem when he himself was planning the conquest of the city.

Jerusalem capitulated on Friday 2 October / 27 Rajab, by Tradition the anniversary of the Prophet's mystic ascent to heaven from the Sacred Rock. In the ensuing days religious sites were cleansed of defilement and rededicated for the ceremony of thanksgiving that took place at the Friday prayers on 9 October in the al-Aqsa mosque. At the completion of the formal prayers the vast congregation heard a sermon preached by the chief *qadi* of Aleppo. His sermon was a nice blend of veneration for the holy city and eulogy of the son of Aiyub who had returned it to

Islam. 'With God's help you have brought this strayed camel back from the profane hands of the Infidel. It was the home of our father Abraham, and the spot whence the Prophet Muhammad, God's blessings on him, ascended into heaven. It was the *qibla* to which men turned to pray in the early days of Islam and the place where all mankind will gather on the Day of Resurrection and of Judgement.'

On the day that the capitulation of Jerusalem had been assured, the scribes and clerks in the sultan's chancellery had worked into the small hours writing dispatches to every part of the Muslim world. Imad-ad-Din had written no fewer than seventy to various emirs and city governors before he turned in that night. When the news reached Baghdad the rejoicing was spontaneous and exuberant and the caliph was to send the victorious hero rich gifts and signs of his favour. The whole Muslim world rang with the praises of the noble Saladin, and even opponents who had long been suspicious of his ambitions grudgingly conceded that it was a magnificent achievement. Ibn-al-Athir, loyal to the Zengid dynasty which Saladin had replaced, comments simply, at the end of his account of the fall of Jerusalem, 'This noble act of conquest was achieved by no one after Omar but Saladin, sufficient title to glory and honour.' After nearly ninety years of Christian occupation the recovery of the holy city of Jerusalem seemed to most Muslims an historic achievement of self-evident importance. But this had not always been the view, and it is time to leave Saladin with his triumph and to investigate a little why he came to be in Jerusalem, and the developments in middle eastern history that had led to its becoming his talisman of success. What was the exact importance of the city to Islam? How long had it been revered?

Jerusalem can make many claims to veneration by the Muslims. First as the capital of David and Solomon, respected by Muslims as well as Jews. Second as the home of prophets of the Old Testament and the scene of Christ's death – all regarded as the predecessors of Muhammad. It was the first *qibla* or direction of prayer for the faithful and even when it had been replaced in that honour by Mecca it was still revered as the second house of God upon earth after the Kaaba at Mecca. The Prophet had also named it as one of the three directions of prayer in which the horseman should face before mounting. Anyone who passed through the Gate of Mercy (known to Christians as the Golden Gate) in the Temple precincts was assured of an eternity in Paradise. It was also believed by many that Jerusalem would be the site of the Last Judgement. But more important than all else it was here that the Prophet had made his mysterious ascent into heaven. For the Koran tells that while praying in the mosque at Mecca Muhammad was transported in spirit to Jerusalem and there, mounting the charger Buraq on the Rock, had been carried to the regions beyond the tomb.

Naturally enough such beliefs were very much to the fore in the fervour that followed the recapture of the city. Koranic doctors and Muslim divines flocked to Jerusalem to take part in the festival of liberation. Yet in the previous century the claim that it ranked third among the holy cities after Mecca and Medina had been dismissed by some doctors of religion as a mystical error derived from Judaic-Christian perversions. The claim that the dead should be judged there was said to rest on one of the sayings of Muhammad, but it too was discounted by some as an apocryphal tradition 'invented by the people of Syria, for Allah would resurrect the dead wherever it pleased him'. Even after Saladin's triumph and the final restoration of the city to the Faith thirteenth- and fourteenth-century writers are found belittling the supposed sanctity of Jerusalem and Palestine. One bluntly accusing the local inhabitants of fabricating any 'tradition' that would attract pilgrims.

Modern scholarship adds its own doubts. The French scholar Emanuel Sivan finds the earliest mention of Jerusalem in the context of Holy War exhortations occurring as late as 1144, nearly half a century after the city had fallen. In fact he proposes the view that the whole notion of Jerusalem as specially sacred to Islam was deliberately built up by propagandists as a conscious counterweight to the importance placed on it by the Christians. Yet undoubtedly the city had always had sacred associations for Muslims. It is referred to as the Holy Land even in the Koran and in early Islamic literature, and the mystical sect of Sufism was convinced of its sanctity. In public statements and private comments and in a famous letter to Richard I of England Saladin repeatedly committed himself to the belief in Jerusalem as one of the three great cities of Islam. Of course there was special pleading and much ardent propaganda behind the claims for the city which flowered so strongly in the mid-twelfth century. But the soil from which they grew was fertile, waiting only to be watered.

By the end of the eleventh century religious fervour had waned in the traditional heartlands of Islam. When Jerusalem fell to the First Crusade in 1099, Muslims were more shocked by the massacre which followed in the streets of the Holy City than by the religious implications of its loss. It was to be more than a generation before the rulers of Syria and

Palestine were to see the expulsion of the Franks as a priority overriding their own political objectives. Yet, just as the motive power for the First Crusade had been built up by pilgrims' tales and priestly exhortation in eleventh-century Europe, so gradually, from the early 1100s, the fires of faith began to burn up more brightly in Syria, fuelled by the passion of religious leaders.

The crusaders had won their success through the disunity of the enemy; religion was the only thing that could restore unity to Islam. As it began to do its work, three great leaders were to emerge to use the fire for forging a hammer to smash the invader. The last and most glorious of them was Saladin. His capture of Jerusalem set the seal on a struggle that had for sixty years flowed across the frontiers of religion and rival cultures. To understand his motivation, his achievement, and indeed his personality, we must first investigate a little the world he was born into.

In the 1930s, in his monumental *History of the Crusades and the Frankish kingdom of Jerusalem*, the French historian René Grousset summarised the historical developments in Palestine and the Middle East from the 1090s to the 1290s in his volume titles: Volume I, 'Muslim anarchy and the Frankish monarchy'; II, 'Frankish monarchy and Muslim monarchy: the Equilibrium'; III, 'Muslim Monarchy and Frankish anarchy'.

'In 1092, that is five years before the preaching of the First Crusade,' he wrote, 'virtually the whole of Muslim Asia . . . still constituted a vast, unitary empire from the frontiers of Afghanistan to the sea of Marmora; from Turkestan to the frontiers of [Abbasid, Shia] Egypt: a Muslim empire in which a Selchük Turkish sultanate was superimposed upon the Arab caliphate, .... to form a united Sunni empire. But in 1092 the great Sultan Malik Shah died and the empire was divided among his family.' The rivalry that followed was finally to be brought to a new unity by Saladin. Arab historians, Grousset thought, conferred upon him the posthumous title of 'sultan' as if looking among the records of earlier Turkish rulers for a title worthy of his stature. In fact, like Alexander the Great, the Kurdish conqueror surpassed all precedents. Like Alexander in his era, Saladin embodied the consequence of cause and effect in his, personifying the irresistible force of the counter-crusade.

# Chapter 2

# Across the Battle Lines

For seven hundred years European folk memory has ringed the name of Saladin with a double aura of martial brilliance and soft-toned chivalry. In his book *Islam and the West: the making of an Image*, N. A. Daniel wrote, 'The legend of the true Saladin has been known over a wider area and for a longer time than any figure in western memory than perhaps St Francis.' That claim really is rather a startling one. Yet still more remarkable than the wide currency of his name is his good reputation. After all, by destroying the achievements of the First Crusade and conquering again for Islam the holy city less than a century after it had been won for Christendom, he struck a harder blow at Europe's self-esteem than any Asian warrior since Attila the Hun. Nevertheless, within years of his death, romance and rumour in the West were claiming that there were great men in Europe who could trace their ancestry from the amours of the famous sultan. Centuries later, in his *Notable History of the Saracens*, published in London in 1575, Thomas Newton described the hero of Islam as 'a man of surpassing and politic wit, stoute valyant and of nature frank and liberal. A man very prudent and wise, one for excellent actes, moderation and valiantness greatly renowned.'

Just why Saladin, although he decisively trounced Christian armies and drove them from the Holy Places, has never been pigeon-holed with the other monsters of nursery history is one of the many intriguing facts about the man. The encounter between Christians and their enemies was close and continuing. A number of Europeans met Saladin and many more saw his conduct of affairs at close quarters. They had fine opportunities for verifying the hoary legends of the bestiality of Muhammad and his followers. In fact European attitudes to him switched during his lifetime from stereotyped abuse to poorly concealed eulogy.

Perhaps it was merely a matter of saving face. Europe could not ignore the fact of defeat, and some Christians thought it well deserved. Muslims naturally believed that the Franks had been humiliated by the will of God for their wickedness and corruption and the view is echoed in Europe. From the south of France, friars reported that as they preached their open-air sermons bystanders ostentatiously gave alms to beggars on the fringes of the congregation with the words: 'Take this in the name of Muhammad for he is more powerful than Christ.'

In fact voices had been raised against the Crusading movement for some time before the loss of the kingdom. Summing up the Second Crusade of 1147–8, the anonymous author of the *Annales Herbipolenses*, writing in Würzburg, concluded that the enterprise had been directly inspired by the devil. But the writer also probed the motives of the Crusaders and found them sadly inadequate. 'With difficulty, a few could have been found who . . . were kindled by love of Divine Majesty.' But many more, he went on, only simulated religious zeal while they hurried off to join the army for a variety of discreditable reasons. 'Some, eager for novelty, went for the sake merely of learning about strange lands; others, driven by want and suffering from hardship at home, were ready to fight not only against the enemies of the Cross of Christ but even their fellow Christians, if this seemed to offer a chance of plunder. Others were weighed down by debt or thought to evade the service they owed their lords while some were even known criminals flying from the deserved penalties of their crimes.'

No doubt it was all very reprehensible, but there were respectable authorities to support their attitude. Fulcher of Chartres, the historian of the First Crusade had written: 'Every day our relations and friends follow us willingly, abandoning whatever they possessed in the West. For those who were poor there, God has made rich here. Those who had a few pence there have numberless gold pieces here; he who had a village there, possesses, with God as giver, a whole town here. Why then return to the West when the East suits us so well?'

Being a churchman Fulcher no doubt felt it right to mention the name of God from time to time, but without overstraining the imagination one can almost hear the explosion of disgust that this passage must have touched off in the library at Würzburg. It was not only the more honest Christian observers who commented on these wordly ambitions, their Muslim enemies recognised the facts easily enough.

Before beginning the siege of Lisbon in the year of 1147, the Anglo-Flemish leaders called on the Moorish commander of the town to

capitulate. In his speech rejecting his enemies' demand he poured scorn
on the high-sounding principles that they pretended to. 'By calling your
ambition zeal for righteousness, you misrepresent vices as virtues,' he
cried from the walls. 'It is not the want of possessions but ambition of
the mind that drives you on.'

The Crusades foreshadow the European imperial impulse, 'the ambition of the mind', that began in the fifteenth century. But in this first
venture Europe had to retire before an opponent that was militarily
superior and materially more advanced. The Muslims classed the
Franks quite simply as barbarians. At the end of the eleventh century
European culture could offer little in the arts, in science, or in scholarship to match the sophisticated and mature civilisation of the Abbasid
caliphate. To us it seems obvious that this once great culture was due to
be superseded, but to contemporary Arabs it was by no means obvious.
What was quite apparent was that the rough, tough soldiers of Christ
who came out of the West were neither literate, courtly nor humane.
The barbaric sack of Jerusalem by the Crusaders brought a new dimension to warfare in the Middle East. For three days the Christian army
had run amuck; sober eye-witnesses recalled wading through streets up
to the knees in blood and severed human remains. It would require a
powerful act of imagination for an Arab to treat these newcomers as
civilised.

But as the Frankish settlement in Palestine consolidated itself, and as
the newcomers increasingly adapted themselves to the facts of their new
situation, Frankish and Muslim rulers came to look on each other in
political terms first, with religion generally a poor second. Even the
original crusading army had been divided by the self-interested policies
of ambitious men. But while the simple overriding objective was the
conquest of Jerusalem conflict had remained more or less submerged.
However, during the twelfth century Palestine and western Syria were
divided between four Christian rulers. To the north-east the County of
Edessa lying across the upper Euphrates encompassed some ten
thousand square miles of what is now Turkey. West and south of it was
the Principality of Antioch called after its capital, now Antakya in
Turkey. To the east it bordered the lands of the Muslim ruler of Aleppo
while southwards it shared a frontier with the third Frankish state, the
County of Tripoli. Taking its name from its capital city it stretched
about a hundred miles along the coast to Jabala in the south, occupying
the modern Syrian coastal province of Latakia and the northern territory
of modern Lebanon. Across its borders it faced the Muslim Arab rulers

of Shaiza, Hamah and, most important, Homs. Standing sentinel against these was the site known as the Castle of the Kurds which the Knights of the Hospital refortified as the seemingly impregnable castle of Krak des Chevaliers. South from Tripoli lay the kingdom of Jerusalem. Its southern frontier with Egypt, from the gulf of Aqaba and the Gaza strip, was almost identical with the frontier established by the State of Israel in 1948, but eastwards the kingdom of Jerusalem extended beyond the Dead Sea to Petra and Karak. It included the whole of the territories west of the river Jordan now disputed between the Israelis and the Jordanians. Northwards the kingdom enclosed the southern half of modern Lebanon with the Lebanese port of Beirut as its northernmost city. These frontiers were achieved during the first twenty years of the twelfth century by and large, thanks to the momentum of the Crusade and the disunity of the Muslims. The first state to suffer from the Muslim reaction was Edessa. After barely half a century it was over-whelmed by forces from the great city of Mosul in northern Iraq. Its capture in 1144 sent shock waves across Christian Europe and prompted the mobilisation of the Second Crusade. This disastrous expedition did nothing to stop the gradual recrudescence of Muslim power and the remaining Frankish states were under growing pressure. Aleppo, Shaizar, Hamah, Homs and eventually Damascus became engrossed in the war to expel the Franks. Southwards, Egypt, governed by the Fatimid caliphs and once supreme throughout the Syrian coastlands, still mounted threatening expeditions against the kings at Jerusalem. Sometimes the kings had to fend off skirmishing attacks from the Bedouin of the Jordan desert.

Ancient traditions complicated society and religion within the new Christian states. Before the explosion of Islam in the seventh century, the region had been within the frontiers of the Byzantine empire and owed allegiance to the rites of the Eastern Church. In the centuries since the Arab occupation the population had been allowed freedom of worship on the payment of the standard tax levied on unbelievers. Many found the intolerant single-mindedness of the Frankish rulers an un-welcome change from the *modus vivendi* worked out with the pragmatic Islamic rulers of former times. The Latin Church moved into the organ-isational structure of the former Eastern Orthodox Church. The Patriarchs of Antioch and Jerusalem, once great dignitaries of the Eastern Church, now owed allegiance to Rome; the Holy Places in Jerusalem were in the custody of Catholic priests and the churches in Jerusalem celebrated Catholic rites. Many native Christians belonged to the Jacobite Church of Syria. Its doctrine on the single divine nature of Christ was considered heretical by Latins and Orthodox alike and the language of its liturgy was ancient Syriac. The other chief native Churches were the Armenian Church and the Maronite Church, which held that although the nature of Christ was dual – both human and divine – it was governed by but a single divine will. These groups, all of which survive to this day, were more angered by the supremacy of the Catholic Church than they had been by the Muslim. They were potential fifth columnists should the Franks ever find themselves under pressure.

As the century advanced a growing number of the intruders themselves came to terms with the ancient civilisation they had disturbed. Many learnt to speak Arabic, dressed in eastern fashion – if only because such dress was more practicable than European fashions in the climate – and revelled in the luxuries of eastern hygiene and cooking. Visitors from Europe looked on them askance just as during the nineteenth century members of the British imperial administration frowned on those of their colleagues who 'went native'.

Such visitors included thousands of pilgrims to the Holy Places, some of whom stayed on for a year or two to fight in the armies of the kingdom. In fact the Christians depended heavily on manpower from Europe, since the climate, exotic diseases, as well as the wastage of war, drastically arrested the natural growth of the population. It was in this situation that the orders of the Temple and the Hospital, founded to provide accommodation and medical care for pilgrims to the Holy Places, rapidly grew into military orders. In fact the Temple had from its beginnings undertaken to protect the traffic on the roads from brigands and marauding bands of Muslims. The orders maintained discipline and their *esprit de corps* by vows and a life-style modelled on the obedience and vocation of the monastery. These soldiers of Christ soon became the crack troops of the kingdom of Jerusalem. They also became, thanks to vast endowments from Europe, the richest institutions in Frankish Palestine.

With the advantage of hindsight we can see that the expulsion of the Franks from Palestine was only a matter of time. The time it took for their Muslim enemies to find a leader under whom they could unite. But, so strong is the inevitability of the present, so strong is the belief of most people that things will always remain much as they are, and so engrossing is the day-to-day business of one's own life and ambitions, that very few among the Franks themselves regarded the Christian states in the Middle East as historical anomalies. Knowing nothing about the politics of the land before their arrival they assumed reasonably enough that the divided rule of city by city and the rivalries of the various potentates was a permanent feature. They may have been aware of the large claims to universal authority made by the caliphs at Baghdad, but then there were similar claims made on behalf of the German emperor who, as the self-styled heir of Rome, was supposed to be the overlord of even the kings of France and England. In any case most of the Crusaders were themselves the feudal subordinates of the French king and so were quite familiar with a polity headed by a ruler of large theoretical authority but little practical power. The counts of Flanders and the dukes of Burgundy and Aquitaine all owed allegiance to Paris but ran their affairs independently. Their cousins who joined the First Crusade discovered that even beyond the remote frontiers of Christendom things were run on much the same lines. Just as the Christian kings of England and France were prepared to fight one another for gain so were the Muslim rulers of Damascus or Aleppo. The newcomers were soon allying themselves to suit their political advantage.

The king of Jerusalem claimed supremacy over the other Christian states in the Middle East, over Edessa, Antioch and Tripoli. He found it an authority hard to exert. Edessa fell to the Infidel at least in part because her coreligionists were unable or unwilling to come to her aid. Even within the kingdom itself rivalry and insubordination ran deep. The vast estates of the Templars and the Hospitallers were outside the royal control, being endowments to a spiritual corporation. As for the knights themselves, the finest soldiers in Palestine, they jealously guarded their independence of action and could not be relied upon to take orders of the king as high commander.

The divisions within the Christian lands were matched at first by the rivalries in Islam. The two traditional centres of Muslim authority in the Middle East were Baghdad and Cairo. Baghdad, a capital of learning and culture, had been founded by the Abbasid caliphs who during the eighth and ninth centuries had claimed supremacy throughout the Muslim world. That power had declined but the claims remained. They rested not only in a once real political and military force but also in religion, for the Abbasids headed the orthodox or Sunnite branch of Islam. In the tenth century their weakened position had come under heavy challenge when the Shi'ite sect, the chief rival to Sunnite orthodoxy, found powerful champions in a North African dynasty who rapidly established their power along the whole

North African coast, and then in 973, after an easy conquest of Egypt, set up their capital at the new city and palace complex of Cairo. Tracing their descent from Fatima, daughter of Muhammad, these Shi'ite Fatimid rulers claimed to be in the true line of succession of the prophet, and the contest between them and the heirs to the Abbasid caliphate overshadowed the politics of the Middle East for the next two centuries.

In modern terms, it was a power struggle between Iraq and Egypt for ultimate hegemony in the heartlands of Islam; control of Palestine was the focus. Seen from Baghdad, Saladin and his two great predecessors Nur-ad-Din and Zengi were the agents of orthodoxy in its age-long attempt to crush the usurping Fatimids. In Cairo the objective was to recover complete control of the Syrian coast as a preliminary to a drive on Baghdad. Palestine was the cockpit of war where the intrusion of the Franks was a regrettable diversion; it and north-western Syria constituted a power vacuum in which the rulers of Aleppo, Homs and Damascus battled for advantage, disregarding the great powers – the Christian states soon joined them. They had a common interest in opposing the encroachments of the 'great powers' and the pattern of alliance often reflected this. Saladin's predecessors had gradually forced unity on the lesser Muslim potentates of the Syrio-Palestine system; when in the 1170s he successfully took control of Egypt and yoked it to the new alliance to the north the outlook for the kingdom of Jerusalem was black.

Saladin's religion was of course central to his life. His biographer Baha ad-Din noted that one of the *Hadith*, the canonical Traditions, attributed these words to the Prophet: 'There are five pillars of Islam: the affirmation that there is no god but God; prayer; the paying of the legal tithe; the fast of Ramadan; and the Pilgrimage to God's Sacred House (at Mecca).' The overriding article of faith is the belief in God as the only creator and lord of the universe, absolute in power, knowledge, glory and perfection, and in his single indivisible nature. It is an uncompromising monotheism; which labelled the Christian belief in the Trinity as polytheistic. Secondly, the Muslim believes in the angels of God, immaculate beings and created from light, below them the Jinn created from smokeless fire, and in devils which are evil Jinn. Third comes belief in the prophets and apostles of God. In order of time these are Adam, Noah, Abraham, Moses, Jesus and Muhammad. Christ holds an honoured place. The greatest prophet before Muhammad, he is believed to have been born of a virgin and a spirit proceeding from God but not sharing in his nature and certainly not to be called the son of God. His revelation has been succeeded by Muhammad who is seen as the last and greatest of the prophets and the most perfect of all God's creatures. Belief in the scriptures of God is the fourth item of faith. These include the first five books of Moses, the Psalms of David and the Gospels, though all these are thought to have been corrupted and degraded from their original inspiration. In any case they are all superseded by the Koran which is the uncreated word of God proceeding directly from him through the mouthpiece of his prophet (the very word koran means recitation). It is not surprising in view of this that the actual text of the Koran has always been held in the greatest reverence by Muslims. The copying of the text is a traditional exercise of piety and the finest examples of Islamic calligraphy are to be found in Korans copied by scholars and cultured laymen. Where the Christians decorated their churches with the statues of saints and earned thereby the additional jibe of idolaters, the mosques of the faithful were embellished with tiles and mosaics bearing inscriptions from the text of the Holy Book.

Fifthly, the Muslim believes in the resurrection of the dead and the Day of Judgement and in a future life of rewards and punishments. But though evil-doers will be punished in the afterlife all Muslims can expect, eventually, to enter a state of happiness. This unbelievers can never hope for. Like Christianity, then, Islam is an exclusive religion and this fact alone does much to explain the bitter conflict between the two. The other great article of faith is in the predestination by God of all events both good and evil. The development of the *jihad* in the conflict in Palestine and its part in the career of Saladin is so important that it will be dealt with at length in Chapter 4.

Born in the late sixth century of the Christian era, in Mecca, a city on the fringes of the late Roman world and with a large Jewish population, Muhammad was inevitably influenced by the two great religions that had preceded him. Like Christians, Muslims believe that the revelation of their prophet supersedes what has gone before. Like Christians too, they hold a faith that has much in common with what went before. To the medieval mind the similarities between Islam and Christianity were a cause of scandal leading to the view that Muhammad was a renegade heretic from the Church and a vile perverter of the true faith. It becomes a little more possible to understand the heat and the fury that goaded the passions of enthusiasts on either side of the religious divide. It is to Saladin's credit that while his commitment to his faith was total it never blinded him to the fact that his opponents were men and the possibility that they might, against all the evidence, be men of honour. For while he held to his oath once it had been pledged, no matter to whom, the Christians made no scruple about breaking their word if it had been given to the infidel.

Besides the articles of the faith the Muslim had also four chief duties. These were the obligation to observe the five daily hours of prayer; to give alms to the poor at least once a year and at least a fortieth part of his wealth; to fast during the hours of daylight in the month of Ramadan, and, if possible, to make the pilgrimage to Mecca – the *Hajj* – at least once in his life. Nur-ad-Din, Aiyub, Shirkuh: all had gone. As to the Ramadan fast, religious dispensation was allowed during illness or time of war. Saladin's spare frame and tired features testified to his frail constitution, while war-making in the cause of Islam was almost his way of life. Even so, his secretaries had a standing instruction to keep a tally of fasting days he missed, so that the arrears might be made good at the first opportunity.

It weighed heavily with Saladin, during the closing years of his life, that he had never made the pilgrimage. But in all other respects he was a model of the faith from that day when, in his thirty-third year, he emerged as the master of Egypt and began his career as the champion of Islam. The glory of the capture of Jerusalem was his, but the triumph had been prepared for by his great predecessors Zengi and Nur-ad-Din.

# Chapter 3

# The Quadrilateral of Power

The world in which the young Saladin grew up was a place of cosmopolitan cities in which Armenians, Kurds and Turks, Syrians, Arabs and Greeks, Christians as well as Muslims competed in commerce and learning and the business of government. It was a world – and Saladin's father and uncle proved the point – where a man of talent, whatever his nationality, could hope to rise in the service of the throne. But, like the Austro-Hungarian empire of the nineteenth century, it was also a world of master races. Islam had exploded from Arabia in the seventh century, but by the mid-twelfth century the Arab dynasties had been displaced by Turkish families, of which the greatest was that of Zengi, tutor or *atabeg* of Mosul, and his son Nur-ad-Din. Their partisans criticised Saladin as a usurper trying to supplant an historic dynasty. But there was a still deeper cause of resentment, because Saladin was a Kurd and the first man for over a century to challenge and then overtop the Turkish ruling classes.

Nevertheless, his career can only be sensibly interpreted in terms of the Turkish world he inherited. Its power struggles were determined by a quadrilateral of cities stretching across the Syrian desert and the headwaters of the Tigris and Euphrates. The terminal points of the base line of this quadrilateral are Damascus and Baghdad, separated by some 420 miles. North of Damascus 170 miles stands Aleppo, and from there, veering slightly northwards of due east and 280 miles distant, lies the city of Mosul on the river Tigris. Baghdad is 230 miles south-east of Mosul. And, in theory, it was Baghdad that was the capital of this quadrilateral of forces. It was one of the fabled cities of the medieval world and also the home of the Abbasid caliphs, the traditional captains of the orthodox throughout Islam and the implacable enemy of the usurping pretensions of the Fatimid self-styled caliphs of Cairo. Long before the birth of Saladin, the power of these caliphs of Baghdad had fallen into the hands of Turkish chief ministers or 'sultans', yet the thrust of their policy in Syria was determined by the Cairo-directed thinking of the traditional caliphate.

In the heady days of the eighth century, when the armies of Islam seemed to be sweeping all before them, even Constantinople had seemed within grasp; but the threat had been repulsed and in the intervening centuries Muslim and Christian had found a *modus vivendi*. Life and politics had settled down either side of the great religious divide and the overriding ideological commitment had become something of the past. Baghdad found Cairo a far more compelling problem than Constantinople, and the sultans followed the conventional wisdom. As might be guessed, they, like the caliphs before them, went through periods of weakness, but though European writers may be tempted to discount the influence of the Baghdad sultans in the western theatre it was in fact quite often significant.

All the Turkish dynasties of the area traced their ancestry from nomad Turkoman tribes converted to Sunnite Islam during the tenth century. The natural consequence of this was to focus the interest of these steppe peoples on the heartlands of their new religion. As the vigour of the Abbasids and the other Arab dynasties weakened, they called in Turkish mercenaries, or bought them in the slave markets to act as palace guards. The newcomers rapidly exploited their position to win increasing power, just as the barbarians called in by the later Roman emperors had gradually usurped control of that imperial machine.

The house of Selchük emerged as the leading dynasty and its head, invested with the grandiose title of 'King of the East and West', was given supreme authority over all the lands that admitted the caliph's spiritual supremacy. The greatest of these early sultans, Alp Arslan, conquered Christian Armenia for the caliphate and then at Manzikert (western modern Turkey) in 1071 dealt the Byzantines a crushing defeat. The empire lay open but, true to the traditions of Baghdad, Alp Arslan had Cairo as his long-term objective and regarded these triumphs against the Christians merely as necessary preparatory moves to secure his position before the decisive campaign in Syria, Palestine and then finally Egypt. The time would no doubt come for a war against the infidel but the first priority was to unite the followers of the Prophet under the orthodox caliph.

The point is worth stressing. For the Christian historian, Manzikert is one of the decisive battles of the world. The emperor Romanus Diogenes had mobilised a great army with which he aimed to crush

Turkish power and halt its encroachments into eastern Anatolia once and for all. These fertile uplands were traditionally the power house of the empire and seemed essential to its survival. The obliteration of the imperial army put an end to such hopes, and, although the day was far in the future, did foreshadow the birth of modern Turkey. But Alp Arslan had no thought of a drive on Constantinople. The victory was important because it left him free to plan a strategy against Egypt. This is the perspective in which we shall have to learn to view the career of Saladin. It started with a Turkish-inspired conquest of Egypt; only when that had been achieved did he turn his attention to Jerusalem.

Alp Arslan died in 1072, one year after his victory, and was succeeded by his son Malik-Shah. At the opening of his sultanate he found himself faced, ironically enough for one of his ancestry, with a nomad problem. New waves of Turkoman tribes were pushing against the northern frontiers and Malik-Shah decided to divert their raids into Anatolia, opened up 'in a fit of absence of mind' by the victory of his father. He commissioned his cousin Sulaiman to mobilise the tribesmen for a systematic conquest of the peninsula for Islam and Baghdad. Sulaiman duly carved out a territory for himself with its capital at the ancient Byzantine city of Nicaea. He continued to acknowledge the writ of Baghdad but was alone in the allegiance. The Turkomans had little interest in grandiose schemes of conquest on behalf of some distant sultan; they set about winning independent statelets for themselves while some even infiltrated the lordships of Syria.

There the authority of Baghdad was strong and rapidly extending. In 1085 treachery brought the great Christian city of Antioch into Turkish hands. Farther south, the forces of Fatimid Egypt, once supreme in Syria, were being pushed back to the Egyptian frontiers by Malik-Shah's brother, Tutush. Pro-Fatimid factions remained in some of the coastal cities, while in exceptional cases Arab dynasties still held sway – but during the 1080s Syria came firmly under Selchük administration.

Under Malik-Shah that administration was tightly organised. Headed by the sultan at Baghdad it was divided into provinces, each headed by a member of the Selchük family bearing the title of king. If he was young or inexperienced the sultan appointed to his court an *atabeg*, responsible for his training in military affairs and administration – the title rapidly became synonymous with 'governor'. Below the king and *atabeg* came district and city governors, responsible, among other things, for raising and maintaining the military forces in their regions. When Malik-Shah died in 1092 things fell apart as his sons struggled for the succession in Iraq and governors throughout the empire mobilised the forces under their command as private armies.

When Tutush died in 1095 the pattern of Iraq was repeated in Syria. His dominions in Syria fell apart during the succession contest between his sons Ridvan and Duqaq; Antioch, Muslim for barely a decade, threw off its allegiance to Aleppo and Jerusalem was retaken by Egyptian armies while an Arab dynasty managed to establish itself at Tripoli. Aleppo under Ridvan, and Damascus under Duqaq, reverted to the status of independent states. To the east Kerbogha, the *atabeg* of Mosul, continued to work for the conquest of Aleppo and now extended his ambition to the whole of Tutush's divided territories; Baghdad was still being contested by the sons of Malik-Shah.

This was the position in the cities of the quadrilateral in 1097, when the crusaders began their trek from Constantinople across Anatolia to Palestine. But first they had to cross the lands of Kilij Arslan, son and heir of Sulaiman of Nicaea. He had usurped the title of sultan and renounced allegiance to Baghdad – he could expect no help from there. The crusaders reconquered Nicaea for the empire and then destroyed his array at the battle of Dorylaeum. The route to the Holy Land was open. Few of the Turkish rulers in Syria mourned the fall of Kilij Arslan and none saw the potential behind the new Christian threat. They had heard that the Franks were marching under the protection of the emperor and assumed that they were also marching, as mercenaries, under his orders.

Since Antioch had been lost by the empire only ten years before, and since the Franks were heading for it, it seemed reasonable to assume that their objective was the recapture of imperial territories recently lost. The Egyptian régime so far misunderstood the state of affairs as to offer the Franks a treaty whereby northern Palestine should return to Christian allegiance while Egypt moved back to its ancient centres in the south. This, of course, would have meant the crusaders agreeing to Egyptian control of Jerusalem. The proposal, which made sense in terms of the political map of Syria before the Turks came, must have struck the crusaders as utterly risible. Yet the Franks themselves reinforced the impression that their aims were limited in a letter to Duqaq of Damascus. Anxious to keep him out of the war they assured him that they were fighting to recover only the lands formerly belonging to the Greeks – all other territorial frontiers would be respected. No one could suspect that the ultimate objective of the mailed knights could be Jerusalem, for that had ceased to be in Greek hands 450 years ago.

Yet in that autumn of 1098, with the Frankish army advancing remorselessly upon the city, the governor of Antioch realised that whatever their ultimate objective might be here and now he desperately needed allies. The bulk of his city's cosmopolitan population was made up of Christians, whether Syrian, Armenian or Greek, and many were summarily expelled. But in addition to potential fifth columnists inside the walls he had managed to antagonise his closest neighbour, Ridvan of Aleppo, by allying with Damascus against him the previous year. As a result he found himself forced to appeal for help to Kerbogha of Mosul. Anxious no doubt to prevent the Christians from recovering Antioch, Kerbogha also calculated that once inside the city as its saviour he could easily make himself its complete master and that then his territories would hold Aleppo like a nut in a nutcracker. He was not alone in seeing how the possession of Antioch would strengthen his power. Duqaq of Damascus and his *atabeg* Tughtigin mobilised an army of relief, though they were thrown back by the Franks. Then Ridvan, revising his short-sighted and vindictive policy, tried to force the Christians back from Antioch, but he too was defeated.

The survival of Antioch as a Muslim city now depended on Kerbogha. Early in the year he set out from Mosul with a large army including contingents from Persia and Iraq, but first laid siege to Edessa, strategically sited some miles north of the Mosul-Aleppo road and recently captured by a Christian force. After three weeks Kerbogha abandoned the attack, but the delay had already given Antioch, also, to the Christians. As it approached the city, the Mosul army was swelled still further by the contingents of Duqaq from Damascus and many others, though Ridvan held back. He feared the impact of a great victory by Kerbogha on his own position in Aleppo. Other allies who had joined the seemingly invincible Mosul army were equally apprehensive. When the decisive battle came they deserted, led by Duqaq. Andoch remained in Christian hands.

It was the first of many occasions when a promising Islamic counter-attack foundered in the shifting sands of Syrian politics. As the crusaders marched south to Jerusalem, the coastal towns of Palestine bought their short-term immunity one by one. When the Holy City had fallen and it was obvious the Franks had come to stay, emirs and governors still attempted piecemeal independent resistance rather than unite against the common enemy. Inevitably they gradually fell to the Christians.

The future lay with the big four and particularly with Mosul, Aleppo and Damascus. But a united front would not be achieved until one had forced the submission of the other two. For most of the century they fought amongst themselves with only intermittent campaigns against the Franks. Ridvan of Aleppo, hemmed in by the Christians at Antioch and Edessa and always wary of the plans of Mosul, never took any consistent initiative against the Christians, content if he could remain master of his own city. He even showed willingness to cooperate with the Franks and so disgusted his subjects that they forced him to permit an appeal to the caliph in Baghdad to launch a war against the infidel. This army was led by Maudud, the new *atabeg* of Mosul. Again it seemed that fate was driving Aleppo into the arms of its traditional enemy. When Maudud brought his force up to the walls of Aleppo, hoping for provisions and accommodation, Ridvan not only closed his gates but even imprisoned leading citizens whom he suspected of pro-Mosul sympathies. He knew that once inside the city Maudud could overthrow him with popular support.

Two years later Maudud, supported by the army of Tughtigin of Damascus, defeated the forces of Baldwin of Jerusalem. Mosul was now the dominant city in the Muslim quadrilateral and Maudud the dominant figure, but in the September of 1113, the year of his victory, he was murdered by an Assassin as he and Tughtigin entered the great mosque of Damascus to celebrate their triumph. Immediately Tughtigin had the murderer executed, but rumour at once accused him. It was said that he too feared that Maudud had designs against his city. The theory was better than plausible. Maudud had come to power in Mosul only six years before under the patronage of the sultan of Baghdad. He found himself ruler of a city with a traditional policy in Syria and he acknowledged the authority of Baghdad where the powers of the sultan were growing again after the troubles that had followed the death of Malik-Shah. Damascus had long been one of the targets of Mosul policy and it was also a vital factor in the Baghdad strategists' long-term designs on Cairo.

In the year that Maudud was assassinated Ridvan of Aleppo died. Five confused years followed there until a faction of citizens deposed Ridvan's successor and called in Il-Ghazi, ruler of Mardin some 180 miles away to the north-east. Almost despite himself, he was to fulfil the dreams of the Aleppans for their city to take the lead in the war against the Franks. Il-Ghazi was delighted to add Aleppo to his already extensive dominions, but would have preferred a peaceful border with the Christians. He was forced to play champion of the Faith, however, by the successes of the army of Antioch. In June 1119, Christian and Muslim met on the plain of Sarmada – the battle that ensued was to be long remembered by the Franks as the Field of Blood. Apart from a troop of a hundred horse who broke through the encircling Muslims early in the battle, hardly a Christian survived. Those not killed on the field died in the aftermath, some being butchered as they tried to escape through the surrounding orchards, others being dragged in chains the fifteen miles to Aleppo to be tortured to death in its streets. Antioch was now defenceless, but Il-Ghazi did not follow up his advantage and preferred to celebrate his victory rather than look for another. He was the hero of the hour, but he soon returned to his capital at Mardin, and died three years later without winning any other triumphs for the cause of Islam.

His brief period of operations from Aleppo nevertheless did pull that city round on to the course that military geography seemed to have set for it. With Mosul it formed the base of a Muslim triangle pushing northwards against the territory of Christian Edessa; it was also the first bastion against Antioch. For eighteen years Ridvan, perhaps naturally enough, had run the city's affairs to ensure his own survival against both Muslim and Christian powers. But for the next half-century it was to be controlled by men whose capitals were elsewhere and whose ambitions lay beyond Aleppo. The trend began with Il-Ghazi and it was strengthened when al-Bursuki, *atabeg* of Mosul and loyal lieutenant of Baghdad, brought it, with the rest of northern Syria, into his dominions. His assassination in November 1126 shattered a threatening build-up of Selchük power and brought a sigh of relief from the Franks. But it was premature. Yet two years later Aleppo fell into the hands of another *atabeg* of Mosul who eventually did yoke the two cities to a single policy.

When, in 1128, Zengi Imad-ad-Din came in triumph to Aleppo, it is doubtful whether nostalgia figured prominently in his emotions. He was a hardened soldier, ostentatiously devoted to pietism when it suited him, as capable of double dealing as he was skilled in diplomacy, ruthless and mightily ambitious. Yet boyhood memories there could have been, since his father had been the governor of the city for the great Malik-Shah. He had died when his son was only ten years old, but his household had rallied round the boy and, more important, the young Zengi had found a powerful protector and patron in Kerbogha of Mosul, another veteran in the service of the sultan and a bosom friend of his father. Accordingly, in 1094, Zengi was called to the court at Mosul. He lived there, a favoured courtier under successive rulers, for thirty years. In their armies he won a reputation for bravery and resource which even the Christians honoured, and he came to the notice of Baghdad.

In 1122, when he was thirty-eight, Baghdad made him governor of Wasit and Basra, the chief Turkish garrison towns in lower Mesopotamia. The following year he played a major role in the defeat of an Arab putsch against the Caliph al-Mustarshid and his Turkish-controlled régime. Hardly had he won the caliph's respect for defending him than Zengi found himself on the orders of the sultan, Mahmud, at war with the caliph's forces. Al-Mustarshid, more vigorous than his predecessors, hoped to re-establish the old authority of his office. But his attempt to oust the sultan Mahmud was foiled by Zengi, whose loyalty to the sultan won him the post of *atabeg* of Mosul when al-Bursuki died in 1127.

Zengi was the first Muslim leader of any stature to present himself as fighting the Holy War on any long-term basis. He was more brutal, less sincere and more politically devious than his son Nur-ad-Din, but men looked back on his reign as the turning point of the tide against the Christians. He and his son brought the Turkish régimes in Syria to the pinnacle of their prestige, and their renown was to overshadow Saladin for years. From Mosul, in accordance with the city's traditional policy, Zengi marched against Aleppo, to be welcomed by citizens eager for strong government and effective leadership against the Franks. From here he forced the submission of Muslim Syria as far south as Homs. Damascus still remained, but Zengi was needed back at Mosul to secure his power base.

In 1131 Sultan Mahmud died. The struggle between his brothers Mas'ud and Tughrul for the succession was joined by the Caliph al-Mustarshid, who hoped to outmanoeuvre both. His army, operating for the time being on behalf of Tughrul, defeated Zengi, who had rallied to the side of Mas'ud, forced him back to Mosul and besieged him there for a few months in 1133. Thus the complications of Iraqi politics had direct bearing on events in Syria if only because they distracted Zengi for a time from his objectives to securing his power base in Mosul. But, early in 1135, he received an appeal from a new régime in Damascus offering the homage of the city in return for his support. A ruler of Mosul who already controlled Aleppo could hardly refuse such an offer.

Although al-Mustarshid was still threateningly strong in Iraq, Zengi set out in haste on the 400-mile march to Damascus. Even as he was *en route*, a coup overthrew his would-be client. Zengi was as able to take advantage of his expedition to force the submission of the town of Hamah, but well-defended Damascus was clearly going to present a tougher problem. As preparations for the siege began Zengi was astonished to receive a notification from the caliph to leave the city in peace. Still more astonishingly, this most powerful Turkish prince obeyed the caliph's request and felt he could do so without losing face. Clearly the Turkish establishment was now facing the possibility that the moribund caliphate, which they had so long controlled, might be on the verge of a genuine renaissance of power.

However Mas'ud, who had been steadily advancing his power, defeated, captured and arranged the murder of the egregiously ambitious caliph. He had little difficulty in providing himself with a compliant puppet more in agreement with Selchük ideas of how a caliph should behave. The only remaining problem for Mas'ud, now firmly established as sultan at Baghdad, was to buy Zengi's support for the new arrangements there. At the end of four tense years, the *atabeg* found himself once more the most powerful lieutenant of the Selchük sultan in the west and free to pursue his ambitions there.

Within two years he had forced King Fulk of Jerusalem to surrender the fortress of Montferrand, which was ideally sited to overlook the doings of the lords of Damascus and the movements of the Franks up and down the valley of the Orontes river. For Zengi still aimed to conquer Damascus. He married the mother of the young ruler, he occupied neighbouring Homs in force and, no doubt hoping to terrify the Damascenes into submission, he slaughtered the garrison of Baalbek, after having promised them their safety on the most solemn oaths known to Islam. But the city refused to yield either to diplomacy or violent threats, instead it allied with Fulk of Jerusalem, who had as little interest as they in seeing Damascus fall to Mosul. The combined forces were enough to persuade Zengi to withdraw to Baalbek, and there was a new threat to him from Iraq.

Mas'ud now felt sure enough of his position to discipline even the powerful *atabeg*. It is really rather remarkable that Zengi, now a man approaching sixty, lord of a large province, once the chief agent of

Mas'ud's rise to power and regarded as the greatest potentate in Syria, found it expedient to make a show of submission. The tie with Iraq was still effective and inhibiting on his policies.

Two years after this improbable humiliation, Zengi had sailed clear of all censure, to become the most renowned figure in Islam. Because of the magic that surrounds the name of Jerusalem, it is easy to lose sight of the full extent of Frankish penetration in the Middle East. The first major achievement of the original crusaders had been the capture of the great town of Edessa. Under successive counts it constituted a vital buffer province on the Franks' northern frontier and a constant source of harassment to Aleppo and Mosul. While it was held, the strategic balance favoured the Christians. But the city had emotional as well as military significance. It had been established as a Christian common-wealth even before Constantine the Great made Christianity the official religion of the Roman empire. The Edessenes boasted themselves the oldest Christian polity anywhere in the world and, even though the place had been conquered for Islam in the seventh century, there was still a large, mainly Armenian, Christian community there at the time of the Crusade.

In the autumn of 1144, Zengi launched a feint attack on the city of Diyar-Bakr some eighty miles to the north-east of Edessa. Its ruler had recently formed an alliance with Joscelin of Edessa and, as Zengi calcu-lated, the count left his capital in force to harass the *atabeg*'s lines of communication with Aleppo. Immediately the Mosul army turned back and by forced marches reached the city, now shorn of its best defending troops. Christians were to blame Joscelin bitterly for what happened next. Instead of marching at once to relieve his capital he retired to another city, confident that the massive fortifications of Edessa could hold out. The force he had led out made a powerful garrison behind the walls but was too small to defeat the massive army of Zengi. Now he had to wait for Christian reinforcements from Jerusalem, 300 miles distant.

Having outmanoeuvred the enemy, Zengi now prepared for the siege. He had a large siege train and an army at a pitch of religious fervour after months of *jihad* propaganda. The reduced garrison, led by the Catholic and Armenian bishops, held out doggedly for four weeks; but when the Muslim engineers breached a massive section of the walls the end was only hours away. The city was sacked with a ruthlessness that threatened to equal the Christian atrocities at Jerusalem. But when he made his formal entry Zengi was so impressed by the beauty and the riches of the place that he ordered an end to the destruction. Within years the whole county of Edessa, 10,000 square miles of vital strategic territory, was once more Muslim.

The fall of Edessa is one of the great events of twelfth-century history. If the Franks in Syria were numbed by the shock, the effect in Europe was little short of traumatic. For decades men had been warned that without continuing aid from Europe the Holy Land would be lost to Christendom, now the warnings struck home. St Bernard led the call for an expedition and his fervent preaching precipitated the Second Crusade.

In Islam the victory was greeted with jubilation from Baghdad to North Africa. The poet al-Qaysarani wrote: 'Tell the rulers of the infidels to flee the territories they pretend to hold, for this land is the land of Zengi. Men said that the *atabeg* would be pardoned all his sins for this one deed and would be admitted at once to the joys of paradise. During his reign, fervour for the *jihad* had grown by the year, and the capture of Edessa was seen as its first great triumph and Zengi its greatest hero. He had knocked the coping-stone from the Christian edifice in Palestine – it seemed only a matter of moments before the whole building should crumble.

But two years later Zengi was dead, murdered by a servant he had insulted; it was a weighty blow to the hopes of the faithful. Yet he was to be followed by one more glorious, for his son Nur-ad-Din was to prove a still more noble warrior in the Holy War.

On Zengi's death the ruler of Damascus reclaimed the city of Baalbek. But Aiyub retained his command. In addition, he was granted a mansion in Damascus and the taxation from ten villages as an *iqta*, the revenue base for an official income. Baalbek, some 4,800 feet above sea level, was dominated by the great Roman temples to Jupiter and Bacchus. Massive columns still survive – before the huge earthquake of 1170, the buildings were virtually intact and fortified with towers and ramparts. Below stretches the Beka'a valley, rich in cereal crops and orchards of fig, apricot and mulberry trees, even vineyards. (It was said that the teenage Saladin would indulge in wine.)

Aged eight Saladin moved to the family house in Damascus. No doubt the privileged youth and his friends would be seen of an evening riding and taking archery practice or playing polo, as would his own children. His father, Aiyub ibn-Shadi Naim ad-Din (i.e. 'Star of the Faith') enjoyed respect from Nur-ad-Din, but it was Saladin's uncle, Shirkuh, who kept the family name prominent at the court in Aleppo.

# Chapter 4

# Nur-ad-Din and the Propaganda
# of the Jihad

At a time when war not only was, but was accepted as being, common-place, the ideal of the Holy War offered men a noble motive. The prevailing modern orthodoxy holds war at best to be a disgusting neces-sity but more usually simply disgusting. It regards the concept of a Holy War with particular contempt. Murder and brutality, it is argued, are neither excused nor elevated because they are committed in the name of the ultimate good. Religious conviction is that much the worse if it leads men to kill one another, and the word 'fanaticism', which derives from the Latin meaning 'divine inspiration', is used of such apparently warped conviction. Our society does not of course live by these lofty beliefs – witness the fascination with books, magazines and television programmes on war, to say nothing of our massive armaments indus-tries. Neither medieval Christianity nor Islam held them.

For them warfare and violence were not only facts of normal life, as they are with us, they were also legitimate tools of God's purpose. If we are to understand Saladin, we must live for a time in a world where war can be good and Holy War the highest ideal a man can aim at. It was the fanaticism of the crusaders which inspired the slow swell of sympathy for the Holy War, or *jihad*, in Syria; by the time of Saladin, it had burgeoned into a powerful popular movement, thanks to a good deal of careful propaganda during the reign of Nur-ad-Din.

At first, only a few men saw the long-term threat that the success of the Crusade posed Islam. Even before Jerusalem fell, a shrewd old imam from Damascus was sizing up the pattern of the future, as it took shape in the hard-fought siege of Antioch. 'No single town will be strong enough to check the advance of the Infidel but all the Muslims of Syria must come to its aid – and if that be not sufficient the obligation to help will lie on the Muslims of the neighbouring lands.' But this analysis was far ahead of contemporary thinking.

Rulers lost little time in coming to terms with the Christians where it suited their purposes. Tughtigin of Damascus settled his boundary disputes with the king of Jerusalem with the greatest amicability and to the disadvantage only of the peasants of each side. In 1108 a battle was fought between two armies each of which comprised Christian and Muslim contingents – the outcome was a victory for Ridvan of Aleppo and his ally Tancred of Antioch over the army of the Turk, Chavali of Mosul, and the Frank, Baldwin of Edessa.

Only a few of the imam's immediate disciples took heed of his warnings. Among them was 'Ali ibn Takir al-Sularni who determined to awake public opinion to the Christian menace. In 1105 he completed his *Book of the Jihad*, subtitled *A Call to the Holy War, the Duty to Wage It and Its Rules, together with a Eulogy of Syria and the Frontier Territories*, and in the spring of that year gave a public reading of the first half in the mosque of a Damascus suburb. It seems to have made some impact, for the reading of the second half, in the autumn, was held at the great mosque of the Umayyads in the centre of the city. The following year al-Sulami died, but eight years later the work was given a second reading in the mosque of the Umayyads and *jihad* agitation seems to have continued for a time among activist groups of the city's intellectuals.

Al-Sulami inveighed against the inaction of Syria's rulers. 'How can the princes carry on their pursuit of high living after such a catastrophe?' he demanded. It is for them to unite in a *jihad* to 'exterminate these Franks and recover all the territories they have conquered'. Yet far from doing this, he went on, they seemed to be paralysed with fear at the very mention of the name of the Franks. Though it was bitterly resented, the charge of cowardice came near the mark. At their first impact the mailed knights of Europe made a deep and terrifying impression on the Islamic rulers and their armies, so that years later in his Syriac *Chronography* Bishop Bar Hebraeus reckoned that 'in those days all the Arabs in Syria trembled before the Franks'.

The evidence of early *jihad* advocacy in Damascus is of special interest since it was in this town that Saladin spent his formative years. But in Aleppo, too, isolated and sometimes influential voices were raised against the prince's too easy acceptance of the Frankish presence. The *qadi*, Abu-l-Hassan used his considerable prestige to force Ridvan to take a tougher line and pressure mounted from other quarters until the prince reluctantly gave permission for a party of pietists to seek aid from the caliph in Baghdad for the Holy War. An army was dispatched from Baghdad; but when it arrived before Aleppo it found the gates locked against it. Ridvan had no intention of admitting a caliphal army to his city where the pietists would be a willing party of revolutionists.

For twenty years or more the cause of the *jihad* rested with ardent but isolated intellectuals and holy men, until the politicians found themselves gradually forced into the arena. Often enough their motives were self-interested. In 1118 the Turkoman prince Il-Ghazi came to power in Aleppo with popular backing as a supposed champion of the Holy War. But in fact the humiliation of the infidel was the kind of diversion he could well do without, and a peaceful border with the principality of Antioch would have left him conveniently free to extend his power among the squabbling states of Muslim Syria. But successful campaigning by Roger of Antioch threatened to encircle Aleppo entirely.

Even so Il-Ghazi moved carefully and in June 1119 was in the plain of Sarmada awaiting the army of Tughtigin of Damascus rather than risk a single-handed encounter with the Christians. In the event, battle was forced on Il-Ghazi by the impetuosity of Roger and by the urging of his own Turkoman free lances. They were in the business of soldiering to win booty and ransoms and were quite innocent of any ideological commitments, but before the battle started Abu-l-Fadl of Aleppo, one of the moving spirits behind Il-Ghazi's rise to power there, gained his permission to preach the *jihad* through the army. His ardour soon infected even these sceptical mercenaries; strong men wept openly, and a force of professional soldiers was transformed into a body of fiery fanatics. The battle was long remembered by the Franks as the Field of Blood. The Turkomans won a rich booty, but the massacre of the prisoners, carried out in the heat of religious fanaticism, robbed them and Il-Ghazi of the huge profits in ransoms and slaves. Antioch was now defenceless, but, as we saw, Il-Ghazi did not follow up his advantage.

The impetus of the *jihad* faded in Aleppo, but Muslim morale soared. The Field of Blood had been won in the name of the Holy War and was a triumph for the Faith. The death of Roger of Antioch in the battle took on a deep symbolic meaning, for he had been killed at the very foot of the great jewelled cross that had been the Christians' standard. The victor received a robe of honour and the title of Star of Religion from the caliph and basked in the eulogies of the poets.

'This Roger,' sang one of them, 'has been cast into hell, but thou hast won the eternity of paradise. Thanks to thee the pillars of Infidelity have been shattered and the seat of monotheism has been once more set up its place.' For a time, the 'terrifying sound of the Franks' had been exorcised.

The scholars – once the pioneers of the *jihad* – were now becoming the agents of princely propaganda. Tughtigin of Damascus, for example, was presented by his chroniclers, not entirely accurately, as a devout champion of Islam. His letters to the caliph were full of talk about the *jihad*, but in earlier days the *atabeg* had seemed less inspired by religious zeal. In 1110, threatened by the Franks, the port of Sidon had won his protection only by offering the sizeable fee of 30,000 bezants. When the Sidonese refused to pay up once the danger was passed Tughtigin threatened to call back the Christians. A year later it was the turn of Tyre to face the infidel – it offered to surrender itself to Tughtigin if he saved them. In fact the siege was raised by the Tyrians themselves and the governor refused to submit the town to the rule of Damascus. Tughtigin thought it wiser not to press the point since the town had proved itself too tough for the Christians and they were more skilled in siege warfare than his own forces. Concealing his weakness under a show of virtue, Tughtigin proved himself an expert in the vocabulary of the political *jihad*. Bridling at the suggestion that he had any designs on the town he protested, 'I did what I did for the love of God and his Muslims, not in the hope of money or power', according to Damascus's historian Ibn al-Qalanisi.

Tughtigin's sincerity may at times have been in doubt but Damascus was at the heart of the growing movement. Religious fervour reached a peak in 1129 when a determined Christian attack nearly captured the city. The defence, led by Tughtigin's son, was inspired by the preaching of the Abd-al-Wahhab al-Sirazi who was encouraged to journey to Baghdad to win the caliph's support.

During the 1130s ardent protestations of loyalty to the Holy War became an important part of a Syrian ruler's repertoire. The fierce piety of the early days, reinforced by encouragement from the political establishment, was being transformed into a popular movement with a momentum of its own. Leaders often exploited it. The town of Hamah fell to one of Zengi's armies while its governor was with him and another army supposedly on a *jihad* campaign. Nevertheless it was Zengi who really put the *jihad* on the political map with the capture of Edessa. Short of Jerusalem no target held a higher place in Muslim hopes, and in calling up his allies Zengi made explicit appeal to their obligations to wage the Holy War. From the fall of Edessa writer after writer advocated a war to the death against the Franks and their expulsion from the coast of Palestine or 'Sahil'.

Yet if the capture of Edessa opened up a rich vein of rhetoric, it did not herald the massive and unrelenting drive against the Christians that ardent devotees looked for. When Zengi died his lands were parcelled out between his sons, the elder, Saif-ad-Din, taking Mosul and its territories, while Aleppo and the Syrian domains went to Nur-ad-Din. This arrangement cut the younger brother off from al-Jazirah, the great region between the upper waters of the Euphrates and Tigris, dominated by Mosul and a valuable reservoir of manpower to his father. But it also freed him from the in-fighting of Iraqi politics that had so often distracted Zengi from his Syrian ambitions.

Furthermore, the fall of Edessa eliminated Aleppo's chief northern rival and left Nur-ad-Din able to conduct an orderly expansionist policy: first against the neighbouring Christian state of Antioch and then southwards to Damascus. The prize of Jerusalem, which was later to seem so important, was left to a future in which the Zengid house should have completed its destiny and become master of Muslim Syria. When Nur-ad-Din died, Christian princes still ruled at Antioch and Tripoli; the great fortress of Krak des Chevaliers still held the armies of Islam at bay; in the south, al-Karak and ash-Shaubak (Montreal) still plundered the rich caravans which led up from the Red Sea port of al-Aqaba to Damascus; the Holy City was still held by unbelievers, its sacred al-Aqsa mosque still defiled by their rites.

As the years passed, a few isolated voices began to question whether the champion of Syria might not have lost sight of his priorities. The same criticisms were to be levelled at Saladin, with much greater force, by adherents of the old régime outraged that this Kurdish upstart should have entered on the Zengid inheritance and overthrown a Turkish mastery that had lasted a hundred years. Why did he not turn his might against the Christians? Why did he desert the sacred cause of *jihad* proclaimed by Nur-ad-Din? The answers should emerge in a later chapter. Here, because Saladin was to model himself so closely on his great predecessor, we must take a look at the actual record of Nur-ad-Din.

He was a fine soldier and won many a brilliant victory against the Christians. Yet no single feat could equal the taking of Edessa or Saladin's triumph at Jerusalem. After fending off an attempt by the Christians to reclaim Edessa, he set about the methodical elimination of the whole county from the political map. Next, turning to Antioch, he launched a series of sieges which stripped it of half its strong points and pushed the frontiers back to the Orontes river, reducing the once immense principality to a coastal strip. In 1149, at the glorious battle of Inab, Raymond of Antioch was defeated and slain and his skull, encrusted in silver, dispatched to the caliph – a publicity exercise well calculated to appeal to contemporaries and ornately boost the prestige of the conqueror. A year later, Joscelin, titular count of Edessa, was captured, blinded and sent to end his days in captivity. Yet another year had barely passed when the city of Turbessel was snatched from the hands of the emperor at Constantinople.

It was a brilliant commencement to the reign and the chancellery at Aleppo ensured that its master's victories were the talk of Islam, by a stream of proclamations dispatched throughout Syria and beyond. Yet in a way these Christian defeats were merely the gratifying and prestigious by-products of a policy directed first and foremost to the expansion of Aleppan power along the natural lines determined by the strategic geography of its position. They were followed not by the proclamation of *jihad* against the great city of Antioch herself but by a dogged three-year manoeuvre to overthrow the ruler of Muslim Damascus. There were good reasons no doubt. The city showed an unfortunate readiness to ally with the Christians to preserve its independence from Aleppo. Though one might observe in passing that had Nur-ad-Din concentrated on the common enemy Damascus might not have felt the need for its unnatural friendship. The fact was that the logic of Aleppan expansion pointed south, and in pursuing it Nur-ad-Din was only realising an ambition that had directed his father's policy.

If proof were needed that Nur-ad-Din placed the requirements of his evolving Syrian hegemony before the strategy of the *jihad*, it came in 1164. In that year, at the battle of Artah, he won a crushing victory which laid Antioch wide open to his armies. Bohemond, its prince, Raymond, count of Tripoli, Hugh of Lusignan, and a procession of other Christian notables were led in chains to Aleppo, while Nur-ad-Din found himself surrounded by a council urging him to deliver the coup de grâce. The capitulation of Antioch would have been a Muslim triumph to match Edessa, and its skeleton garrison girded itself for an heroic defence. Yet the blow did not fall. The city was still viewed from Constantinople as an imperial dominion, and the 1160s were a time of great Byzantine strength. Nur-ad-Din calculated that to hold Antioch against imperial counter-attack might well stretch his resources to their limits, and he had no wish to give the Byzantines cause to interfere in his affairs. So long as it could be contained against the coast, as it undoubtedly could be, the state of Antioch posed no immediate threat. Whatever the expectations of the *jihad* enthusiasts, the Destroyer of the Infidels and Polytheists now directed his power not against the Franks but against the heretic caliphs who ruled the rich and strategically important land of Egypt.

It was, of course, virtually impossible for any ruler to give the single-minded devotion to the Holy War looked for by the extreme pietists. The whole concept had been born in simpler days when the stormtroopers of Islam were fanatical, military adventurers with fortunes to make in the vast Christian heathendom north and west of Arabia. By the twelfth century the territories conquered by the early caliphs had settled into a pattern of long-established, wealthy and sophisticated states where the strident idealism of earlier times inevitably jarred against complex political reality. In any case, the Zengids, as the self-proclaimed agents of Baghdad, were the heirs of a traditional policy that antedated the revived enthusiasm for the Holy War. Long before Christians had arrived in Palestine, Turkish sultans had been viewing Syria as the power base from which to oust the heretical Fatimids from Cairo. The force of history, as well as the pricks of ambition, drove Nur-ad-Din and then Saladin to look first for mastery in the Muslim world before turning their might on the Christians. To charge them with carving out great personal dominion at the expense of co-religionists is right in a way which is quite irrelevant.

Good Muslims themselves, both men wanted to see the extirpation of the Franks; as strategists they fully recognised the threat that could come from their beach-head kingdom and its principalities. But as hard-headed politicians they also recognised that the enemy, perennially short of men and funds, at odds with the native population, repetitively quarrelling amongst themselves, and with their wealthy ports controlled by Italians who would as lief deal with Muslims as Christians for profit, was the least of their worries. While Syrian power continued in full and confident spate, the Christians seemed almost a side-show contingent, to be contained on the defensive and dealt with at leisure.

The French scholar Emanuel Sivan develops the convincing thesis that Nur-ad-Din encouraged the preaching of the *jihad* as a tool of propaganda. The aim was to force unity on Syria, Iraq and then Egypt, so that their massive resources could be combined against the

Unbelievers. But there were to be emirs and others who learnt that this military evangelism could be used equally well to subvert their authority over their own subjects who might be urged to transfer allegiance to Nur-ad-Din in the common effort against the Christians.

The revival of *jihad* teachings began in the work of isolated pietists and enthusiastic scholars and the leaders of the orthodox religious establishment had little interest in it at first. They were more concerned with the struggle against heresy and the triumph of Sunni Islam. But the twelfth century also saw a notable revival in popular religious feeling and it was this which, harnessed to the idea of the *jihad* by Nur-ad-Din and his propagandists, changed an esoteric enthusiasm into a popular mass movement.

An important factor in Nur-ad-Din's success was his personal religiosity. His enemy, Kilij Arslan of Konya, accused him of hypocrisy, though he could not fault his meticulous observance of the faith. Even at this distance in time one is willing to refute the charge of hypocrisy and to accept as something more than flattery the words of a courtier that 'he led a double *jihad*, against the infidel and against his own soul, to deliver himself from the snares of evil.' His austerity impressed contemporaries. Unlike most Muslim rulers of his day he strictly observed the injunction against drink and imposed almost puritanical regulations both against it and against all frivolous entertainments. He founded innumerable colleges for orthodox scholarship, he abolished the non-canonical taxes that others, less scrupulous than he, had levied, while his ardent campaign against heresy, which for an orthodox Sunni at that time meant principally Shi'ism, won him the title of Subduer of Heretics.

Yet, in thirty years, his actual achievements against the Franks were neither so numerous nor so overwhelming as might have been expected. His court eulogists, who dubbed him 'Guardian and Clarion of the Muslims', also urged him, 'in the name of God do not expose yourself to danger. Were you overcome in battle not a man in all Islam but will go in peril of the sword.' But such protestations were a necessary part of the image presented by the court of Aleppo to the world at large. We know the names of eleven poets who wrote elaborate eulogies of the ruler and also tracts and treatises on the Holy War, one of which was commissioned by Nur-ad-Din himself. While the chancellery dispatched its news of triumphs and its exhortations to others to shoulder their responsibilities, the encomiums of the poets were given publicity throughout Syria. And when, at last, his lieutenant Saladin overthrew the Fatimid caliphate, Nur-ad-Din sent a proud embassy to Baghdad with instructions to read the proclamation of the great event in the towns and villages on the road.

At the beginning of the reign this kind of propaganda had been used to good effect against Damascus. There the ruler's policy of shifty friendship with the Christians was already being viewed by a growing section of the populace as a shameful expedient when, in 1148, by a decision of incredible folly, the Christians threw the *atabeg*'s overtures back in his teeth.

The European armies that had descended on Palestine in response to the preaching of the Second Crusade understood nothing of the subtleties of local politics. Their uncomplicated creed was to fight the Infidel wherever he might be found, and amongst the lords of the crusader states there were those who looked enviously towards the rich lands of Damascus. Nur-ad-Din had not yet fully established himself, but it could already have been clear to thoughtful men that he was the greatest threat to the Christian cause. By politic alliance with Damascus they stood the chance of strangling the growing power of Aleppo at birth. Instead, the Christians marched against Damascus and forced it to appeal to the man it most feared.

The siege was a fiasco which spelt the end of the Crusade, but in the city it fired a fresh surge of enthusiasm for the *jihad* that was to be a vital help to Nur-ad-Din in the years ahead. The Damascenes fought off attack after attack, rejoicing to play their part in the sacred war. Heroic episodes in the defence were circulating generations after. 'Among the soldiers was the aged lawyer, al-Findalawi. When the general saw him marching on foot he went to meet him and said: "Sir, your age is a sufficient dispensation from this battle. I will concern myself with the defence of Islam," and he begged the virtuous old man to retire. But he refused, saying: "I have offered myself for sale and God has bought me; I have not asked that the contract be annulled." By this he was alluding to the words [in the Koran] "God has bought the faithful, both them and their possessions and has given them paradise in exchange." He went on to fight the Franks and was killed not far from the walls of the city.'

This kind of thing became part of the popular folklore of Damascus, and the sacrifices of the people in the day of their trial by the Infidel were recounted with increasing bitterness as their ruler relapsed into his old policy of alliance with them. Moreover the Christians had withdrawn from the siege when news of Nur-ad-Din's approach reached them and the average Damascene was convinced that the lord of Aleppo had been their true saviour even though he had not joined battle. For the next six years Nur-ad-Din was constantly on the lookout for his chance. His agents trumpeted his victories through the streets of Damascus and his ministers reproved its ruler, protesting that their master had no thought of conquest but wished only for an alliance to drive out the Franks once and for all. Usamah, the secretary of Nur-ad-Din, reproached Unur of Damascus with the charge that he wished 'only to please the Franks, those who anger God with their acts'. While Ibn-Munir, the poet, lamented: 'Ah, Damascus, Damascus, is it not high time that Jerusalem was freed?'

Duly publicised, such exhortations had their intended effect and the rift between ruler and people widened. Discontent in the city reached a climax when, in 1154, Mujir-ad-Din Abak, the new *atabeg*, agreed to a yearly tribute to Jerusalem. The ground had been laboriously prepared for the idea of a change in régime and now opened a calculated manoeuvre which combined high moral talk with political chicanery.

The misery of the citizens had been increased for some weeks past by food shortages and Nur-ad-Din seized the opportunity. He halted the relief convoys coming down from the north while his agents in the town spread the rumour that the approaching famine was the direct outcome of the ruler's irreligious policies. Other fifth columnists persuaded Mujir-ad-Din that a group of his own nobles were plotting to overthrow him (at least one, Aiyub, former governor of Baalbek, and now in high command in the Damascene army, probably was). The panic measures the distracted *atabeg* took against them isolated him from his few remaining supporters. The army of Nur-ad-Din approached slowly to allow disaffection to do its work and on 25 April, thanks to treachery, his troops entered the city to jubilant demonstrations. The take-over was bloodless. Looting was forbidden and when the delayed food convoys arrived admiration for Nur-ad-Din the Deliverer was, at least among the more naive sections of the population, boundless.

Aleppan propaganda had described the Damascus-Jerusalem entente as the one remaining bar to a conquest of the Franks. And yet Nur-ad-Din's first act was to reaffirm the truce and then to pay a further instalment of the tribute money. When he died, twenty years later, the balance in Syria between Franks and Muslims was hardly altered. Though during that time Zengid power had won a further massive extension with the conquest of Egypt.

In these circumstances, it comes as no surprise to find a vizir of Egypt questioning Nur-ad-Din's motives. 'Say to your lord,' he wrote to

Usamah the secretary, 'how many more times will you delay the fulfil-
ment of your promises to religion! Attack Jerusalem.' The vizir,
Tala'i-ibn-Ruzzayak, was well aware of Nur-ad-Din's designs on Egypt
and hoped to defuse them by using the kind of propaganda that so far
had been the monopoly of Aleppo. In 1160 he even went so far as to
appeal to Aleppo and distant Konya to sink their differences and join
him in a communal enterprise against the Franks. 'Does neither of you
fear the one God? Is there none among your subjects who is a true
Muslim? Perhaps God will lend a hand in this matter if we three take up
arms together.' It was a daring manoeuvre to upstage Nur-ad-Din, the
vaunted champion of Islam, but it drew only vague generalities in reply
and the following year the vizir died.

Ibn-Ruzzayak's allusion to Jerusalem was neatly ironical since it seems
to have been largely Aleppan propaganda that had brought the city to the
focus of *jihad* thought. Before the conquest of Edessa in 1144, when
Muslims tended to think of the war against the Franks in defensive
terms, al-Sulami's had been the only influential voice to call for the
liberation of Jerusalem. Afterwards, it began to be realised that much of
the impetus of the Crusading movement had derived from the Franks'
devotion to the Holy City. Under Nur-ad-Din's patronage more and
more writers began to stress the important place the city held in Islamic
belief as a counterbalance to its Christian reputation.

The orthodox men of religion proved powerful agents of Aleppo *jihad*
doctrines, especially in al-Jazirah. In 1164, the year of Artah and of the
capture of the city of Banyas, Nur-ad-Din imperiously commanded
the cities of al-Jazirah to send him troops. Appeals to religious zeal alone
were reinforced by more persuasive pressure which decided at least one
emir, the lord of Hisn Kaifa, to answer the summons. At first he had
refused, but second thoughts led to a change of policy which he
explained to his council with a certain wry bitterness:

It is likely that if I do not support the *jihad* proclaimed by the lord
of Aleppo he will relieve me of my realm. For he has written to the
holy men of our country asking their help in prayer and urging
them to fire the Muslims with enthusiasm for the Holy War. Each
one of these divines is, at this moment, surrounded by his disciples
and a host of followers reading the letters of Nur-ad-Din, weeping
tears of devotion and ranting against me. I greatly fear that if I did
not accede to the request for troops these men of religion would
unite to excommunicate me from the community of Islam.

During the 1160s, all but Nur-ad-Din's most fervid admirers began to observe that his actions did not completely square with his protestations. In 1159 he found it expedient to sign another truce with a Christian, this time Manuel of Byzantium. In 1162, when Baldwin III of Jerusalem died, he held back, despite advice that the opportunity was ideal for an attack on the mourning kingdom. He was unwilling, he said, to go to war on a people lamenting so great a king. Unquestionably it was chivalrous, but not in the spirit of the *jihad*, and we have already seen the equally puzzling decision not to attack Antioch after the victory of Artah.

Yet if his policy against the Christians lacked incisiveness the sixties did witness a series of determined campaigns which culminated in the mastery of Egypt. When the long-promised assault on Jerusalem still held fire, even loyal admirers became restive. Just after the Egyptian triumph, 'Imad-ad-Din urged his master to 'purify Jerusalem of the ordure of the cross . . . now that you have won Syria and Egypt for the glory of Islam.' From one who as a client of the court depended on its patronage, this mild remonstrance was a sign of real dissatisfaction. Ibn-Asakir of Damascus, a man of independent means and exalted rank, was forthright to the verge of bluntness. 'There can be no excuse,' he wrote, 'for you to neglect the *jihad*, now that you rule from Egypt to Aleppo and now that even the sovereigns of Mosul obey your orders.'

But Nur-ad-Din was once again consolidating his position. This time against the threat he suspected of an independent Egypt under the young Saladin. Once more the well-tried plea went out for reinforcements for the Holy War and Ibn-al-Athir, a chronicler generally sympathetic, tartly observed that though 'he wrote to Mosul, Diyar-Bakr and to al-Jazirah, demanding troops for the Holy War, his true design was quite different.' The task was left to Saladin. Criticised by the caliph for being dilatory when he finally did take Jerusalem, Saladin would protest: 'For nearly a hundred years . . . the desire for its reconquest did not come to any sovereign, until . . . God called me.' Imad-ad-Din, Saladin's secretary who penned this letter, had served Nur-ad-Din; no doubt, he too had become dubious as to his sincerity of purpose.

# Chapter 5

# The Family of Aiyub

We know almost nothing about the personal life of Saladin before, in his twenty-eighth year, he took his first major command in the forces of Nur-ad-Din. Even the year of his birth is uncertain in the Christian calendar. He was born in the year 532 of the Muslim Hegira but the month is not known. The year 532 A.H. ran from 19 September A.D. 1137 to 8 September 1138. The statistical probability therefore places Saladin's birth in the latter year. But if information on the young Saladin is scanty, the careers of his distinguished father and uncle are comparatively well documented.

He was descended from the Kurdish Rawadiya clan. His grandfather, Shadhi ibn-Marwan, launched the family fortunes through the good offices of a friend, Bihruz, who, from humble beginnings, had risen to become governor of Baghdad. He placed his old friend's eldest son Aiyub as commander of the important city of Takrit about half-way between Baghdad and Mosul on the River Tigris. By a combination of luck, good judgement and influential contacts, Aiyub was to go far. In the year 1132 the watchmen on his fortress's walls saw a troop of horsemen flying across the plain towards the river. Its general was the young Zengi, carving a distinguished career for himself in the tangled woods of Baghdad politics, but just at this moment on the verge of catastrophe. He had been defeated by the armies of the caliph and if his pursuers caught him his career was liable to come to an abrupt halt. He needed transport desperately and Aiyub sent a boat across.

Since Zengi and Bihruz had long been enemies this was a puzzling but outright act of betrayal. Not long after Aiyub again crossed his superior, refusing to order the execution of an important political prisoner committed to his custody. One supposes that there were reasons for these daring acts of insubordination, and the fact that he continued in his post shows that he calculated the political probabilities correctly. That at least is in tune with what we know of the man in later life. It is possible too that Bihruz was not entirely sure of his own position and that Aiyub had other, even more influential patrons in the capital. However, in 1138 Bihruz became military commander in Baghdad and when, in that year, news reached him that Shirkuh, Aiyub's brother, had killed a man in an affray he finally relieved him of his command. Apparently the brothers and their families had to make their escape under cover of darkness; probably they had enemies enough by this time to make their fall from favour a signal for the settling of old scores. It was on this very night, so runs the tradition, that Aiyub's third son, Salah-ad-Din Yusuf, was born.

Both probability and historical opinion are against the tale, but Saladin was not the first nor the last great man whose nativity received the attention of the myth makers. Within a year of their humiliation the family of Aiyub were notabilities at Zengi's court in Mosul. The great man's star was firmly in the ascendant and he had not forgotten that day on the Tigris, six years before. In 1138 he went on campaign against Damascus and took Aiyub with him. The city held out but its dependant, Baalbek, fell to the armies of Mosul and as we have seen Aiyub ibn-Shadhi was left there as commander. Zengi was too hard-nosed to consign such a vital strongpoint – an advance post in Damascene territory established for the next attack – on friendship alone. Clearly Aiyub was a man of considerable ability. He was also a man of unconventional piety and founded a college for the Sufi sect of mystics in the town.

For the next seven years he held Baalbek for Zengi. When his patron was murdered in 1146 he rapidly adjusted to the new situation. After a resistance determined enough to establish his bona fides as a loyal servant to the house of his patron, he surrendered the place back to Damascus. His new masters recognised his value and he remained in his post, rising in time to a high place in the Damascus administration. It seems that, although he was patently unable to relieve the siege of Baalbek, Nur-ad-Din resented Aiyub's defection, and it was his brother, Shirkuh, who now maintained the family's standing at the Syrian court. After their father's death Nur-ad-Din and Saif-ad-Din hurried to secure themselves in the power bases bequeathed them – Saif-ad-Din to Mosul with his father's vizir and Nur-ad-Din to Aleppo where he was proclaimed by Shirkuh.

He was a very different man from his brother. Aiyub emerges as a shrewd, calculating and circumspect character, wily in politics but decisive in action. Shirkuh, by contrast, was boisterous and impetuous. But he shared his brother's ability for political manoeuvre and his persistence and was to become Nur-ad-Din's right-hand man. He was short, with a cast in one eye, and, according to contemporaries, had the 'coarse features of the low born'. Even in an age when gluttony was commonplace for those who could afford it, Shirkuh won a reputation for excess and, it is starkly recorded, died of over-eating. Yet this paunchy, unprepossessing little soldier, could look back on a battle career of real distinction. At the battle of Inab in 1149 he killed Raymond of Antioch in single combat, the greatest feat of arms that day. Loud mouthed and truculent, tough and courageous, Shirkuh was, more often than not, victorious, and was a thoroughly professional soldier with a careful eye for details of supply and the tactician's feeling for terrain.

After Nur-ad-Din's capture of Damascus in 1154, the brothers once again found themselves serving the same master. In fact the capitulation of the city smacks of a cosy family arrangement. Sent ahead of the main army as an 'ambassador', with an impressive force at his back, Shirkuh appeared before the walls to negotiate the terms for the alliance of Damascus and Aleppo. The ruler of the city refused to let him within the walls, or to go out to meet him. He had good reason to be wary. While his heralds argued with one brother across the fortifications, the agents of the other were fomenting discontent amongst the populace. As at Baalbek eight years before, Aiyub (now in the Damascus military high command) correctly sized up the drift of events. The populace was near rebellion and the massive army of Aleppo was bound to overcome the demoralised defenders sooner rather than later. He played the game of turncoat with his accustomed aplomb and he won a large prize. His part in the bloodless victory was acknowledged by the unparalleled privilege that he alone was allowed to sit in the presence of Nur-ad-Din when the king gave audience. When he returned to Aleppo, Aiyub was left as governor of Damascus. Saladin, now sixteen, grew to manhood a member of the ruling family of the richest and the second most important city in Syria.

Saladin's education would have followed the traditional lines for an Arab gentleman. By an admonition of the prophet, the search for knowledge was incumbent on every man and woman. The worlds of learning, philosophy, science and religion were seen as an integrated whole, but central to *adab*, a gentleman's education, was the concept of *zarf* – of elegance and refinement. *Adab* was founded in Koranic studies, Arabic grammar, rhetoric and poetry. In later life Saladin showed a passion and proficiency for theological debate. His father being a patron of Sufi mysticism, it has been suggested that Saladin was brought up in the Sufi tradition of renunciation of the world and the self. But these facts do not support the idea, put forward by many of Saladin's biographers since Stanley Lane-Poole's classic of the 1890s, that he led the life of a recluse and even, according to the French scholar Champdor, was a timid young man. Saladin may have had more than the nodding familiarity with theological debate expected of a gentleman, but he was no stranger to the social refinements of *zarf*. He was described as the perfect companion and conversationalist, being 'well acquainted with the genealogies of the old families and the details of their victories and a master of all traditional lore; he had the pedigrees of the great Arab horses at his fingertips.'

He entered army service at the age of fourteen, when in 1152 he left Damascus to join his uncle at Aleppo; here he received a military 'fief' or *iqta* in the service of Nur-ad-Din. Four years later, aged eighteen, he was appointed to a post in the administration of Damascus and shortly after that entered the personal entourage of Nur-ad-Din as a liaison officer 'never leaving him whether on the march or at court'.

There is nothing to suggest that he was notably pious during this period, and indeed some rather conclusive evidence that he was not. Between 1157 and 1161, when he was twenty-three, his father and uncle between them led three of the pilgrim caravans to Mecca. On the last occasion Nur-ad-Din took part. But Saladin did not. Why is not recorded, though there is no hint that he was ill. The pilgrimage is binding on all Muslims able to perform it; Saladin's chief made time for it, despite a heavy official schedule; the fact that he, a young courtier with, one presumes, time on his hands, did not might suggest that there were more engagements on the social calendar. In his forties, he told his secretary Baha'-ad-Din that when he became vizir of Egypt, 'in recognition of the blessings that God had vouchsafed to him, he gave up wine and the pleasures of the world'. Until that time he seems to have indulged them freely. His passion for hunting never left him, and as a young man he had been a renowned polo player.

This game had a special prestige in a military society as a peacetime sport that kept men and horses fit – it could also be highly dangerous. Many an oriental prince met his death in the mêlée as teams of ten or twenty riders clashed in the battle for the *tchogan* or ball. (A French traveller in the seventeenth century even recorded a Persian match involving three hundred riders with two or three balls in play simultaneously.)

One medieval Syrian aristocrat had this advice for his son: 'I shall have no objection if you wish to play polo once or twice a year, but even then, to avoid accidents, do not play in a crowded field. Six players on each side are quite sufficient.'

Such caution would have been despised by the young bloods at court. The *tchogandar*, or polo master, was a highly respected officer. As in any aristocratic society, diversions and etiquette were part of politics, so that when Saladin was invited by Nur-ad-Din to join his side in a polo match it was a sign of high favour.

During his life at Damascus and Aleppo, his father's and his uncle's stock continued to rise so that when, in 1157, Nur-ad-Din fell desperately ill, he deputed Shirkuh to mobilise Damascus against possible crusader attacks. Two years later the Syrian king again fell ill and the two brothers were once again to the fore – a hostile commentator even accused Shirkuh of planning a coup. Although probably a slander it indicates the ambitions of Shirkuh; in the autumn of 1163 a new theatre of opportunity seemed to open for them in Egypt.

In one of the periodic upheavals in Cairo the vizir, Shavar, had been ousted after a rule of only eight months. He made his way to Damascus and there offered Nur-ad-Din a third of the annual revenue of Egypt plus the costs of the expedition in return for his reinstatement. The reply was not immediate, though many of Nur-ad-Din's advisers, among them Shirkuh, urged him to seize the opportunity. Then, any reservations he may have had about Shavar's reliability were cut short when he heard that Amalric of Jerusalem, taking advantage of the chaos in Egypt, had invaded and won a large annual tribute plus a promise of indefinite truce from the Egyptians. Immediately the Syrian king prepared an expedition under the command of Shirkuh and in the following spring Dirgam, the new ruler in Cairo, was defeated at Bilbais. With the powerful Damascene army at the gates of Cairo he found himself deserted by the caliph and attempted to escape, but he was thrown from his horse and killed by the mob.

Shavar was back in power, but Shirkuh appears to have consulted Sunnite theologians in Cairo on the feasibility of ousting the heretical Fatimid régime. They advised against the attempt. Unaware of these machinations, Shavar now made it clear that he had no intention of keeping to the extravagant bargain he had struck with Nur-ad-Din. Very possibly he doubted whether he could. Committing a third of the caliph's revenues to a foreign power was easy enough in Damascus, but to force that commitment through council was a different matter. Even if he succeeded, his responsibility for such a drain on the national resources would be a strong argument in the hands of any rival looking to supplant him. Taking the dilemma by the horns, Shavar denied Shirkuh and his troops entry to the walled city of Cairo and refused the indemnity. It was a sizeable piece of bravado and provoked an immediate response. On 18 July, the Syrian forces, swelled by large numbers of Bedouin, defeated a force of Egyptians and Shavar himself was almost lynched in the mêlée. He and his cause were saved only at the last moment when the caliph threw in the palace guard against the Syrians.

Shavar had already appealed for help to Amalric of Jerusalem. Unnerved by the prospect of Nur-ad-Din controlling both Egypt and Syria he responded with alacrity. By early August the Franks had forced Shirkuh back on to the defence in the fortress of Bilbais which Saladin had already garrisoned as a potential fall-back point. The combined armies of himself and his uncle were besieged there for three months. The pressure was released by events in Syria. Taking advantage of Amalric's absence, Nur-ad-Din had struck against Antioch and won his triumph at Artah. Amalric was soon looking for terms which Shirkuh, his forces too weakened and exhausted to take advantage of Shavar once his protector had withdrawn, was willing to settle.

This Egyptian expedition, undertaken against Nur-ad-Din's better judgement, had achieved nothing except to expose Shavar's opportunism and to give Shirkuh the opportunity to size up the country and establish contact with some of the elements opposed to the régime. He was convinced that with better preparation and a larger investment in men and resources Egypt could easily be taken. He not only argued his case in Damascus but wrote to the caliph's court at Baghdad, describing the situation in Egypt, the country's immense potential wealth and the numerous orthodox Muslims there, subjects of the heretical Fatimid rule.

Baghdad's enthusiasm for the Egyptian campaign, which it elevated to the status of a Holy War, was a big factor in Nur-ad-Din's decision to venture south once more. In the interim, moreover, Shavar was faced with further unrest among the Bedouin. A general persecution of the malcontents in Cairo followed, and some escaped to the court at Damascus. In January 1167 a well-found force of Kurds, Turkomans and Bedouin set out for Egypt with Shirkuh in command and Saladin once more on the staff. Shavar, with ample warning of the invasion, sent for help to Amalric. At a meeting of the barons at Nablus it was decided to mobilise the whole force of the kingdom. Once again the Franks saw themselves faced with the threat of encirclement, but, remembering Nur-ad-Din's triumphs in 1164 when the army was in Egypt, the kingdom was to be put on full defensive alert. Even as the mobilisation proceeded news came that Shirkuh's force was entering Sinai. An attempted interception failed.

The Syrians were on a desert route specifically chosen to avoid the possibility of Frankish attack. A few days' journey from the isthmus of Suez the army was struck by a tearing sandstorm. Given the time of year this was probably whipped up by the fierce south wind known in Syria as the simoom ('evil' or 'polluted') and feared as a carrier of infection. Some of the troops seem to have died in the ordeal while many more were probably weakened by inflammation of the nose and throat and resulting infections. In view of the convoluted campaign that was to follow it looks as though Nur-ad-Din had underestimated the strength of the Christian response and his expedition may have been under strength for the work it now had to do. If, as seems likely, the unexpected disaster of the sandstorm had weakened it still further then Shirkuh's strategy in the weeks ahead, otherwise rather puzzling, can perhaps be explained.

After crossing the Suez isthmus Shirkuh took a line of march which, while ensuring him against Christian harassment, brought him to the Nile some forty miles south of Cairo. If the expedition's objective was the overthrow of the Fatimid caliphate then it is difficult to see why the army did not march directly on the capital. Once at the Nile Shirkuh immediately crossed the river to the west bank. Since the caliphal palace was on the east bank, and since, of course, the river widened in its journey north and became increasingly difficult to cross, one is forced to conclude that Shirkuh was more concerned to put an effective barrier between himself and his enemies than to make an immediate strike against them. He probably knew that the combined Frankish and Egyptian armies heavily outnumbered his own.

He made camp at Giza, across the river from Cairo, and awaited developments. The most promising was that his enemies would fall out. At Shavar's headquarters the atmosphere was tense. By involving Cairo in shameful dealings with the Christians he was risking isolation from court, yet it was the court party which controlled the purse strings and he needed money to pay his unpopular allies. King Amalric had once said that Egypt should be the milch cow of Jerusalem and now, persuaded by his barons, he was threatening to withdraw unless extravagantly well paid. If he did, Egypt would have to face Shirkuh alone and Shavar's policy would be utterly discredited. While he argued terms with the Christians his tottering position was undermined by a message from the Syrian camp, proposing a joint Muslim alliance against them.

Perhaps Shirkuh had scented a whiff of desperation in the air wafting across the river from Fustat, where Shavar had his headquarters. His proposal ended with a persuasive plea for joint action in the Holy War: 'I do not think,' he concluded, 'that Islam will ever have such a good opportunity as this.' The implied criticism of a politician willing to ally with the infidel, followed up with a lofty appeal to the *jihad*, was in the best traditions of Aleppan diplomatic technique. But in the context the ploy seems faintly ridiculous. The commander, who six weeks before had set out with the avowed intention of deposing the heretical Fatimid vizir now appeals to him, and in the name of religion, to fight the allies he had called in to protect him – who were, in any case, virtually in control of the capital.

Shavar's reply to this charade was a tetchy 'What is wrong with the Franks?' After all, Nur-ad-Din had allied with them on occasion. Unwisely the Syrian ambassador lingered at Fustat, awaiting another opportunity to reopen the subject. While he was there, a delegation of palace officials arrived, with the crucial down-payment on the terms negotiated with the Christian king. Before he and Amalric got into their final discussions, Shavar ordered the execution of the Syrian, to demonstrate good faith to Amalric and rejection of the Shirkuh alliance. What followed is reported only by William of Tyre.

William says that Amalric insisted on dealing direct with the caliph. To the horror of the court, the infidel was allowed into the sacred precincts and then, still more outrageous, the caliph himself clinched the treaty by shaking the Christian envoy's hand with his own, ungloved, hand. A bargain had been struck which promised to bring Amalric 400,000 dinars, and in return he agreed to fight. But it was not so easy to come to grips with the enemy. For weeks the armies faced one another across the broad waters of the Nile until Amalric found a crossing down stream where a large island divided the river into two branches. The combined Egyptian and Frankish forces made the crossing in good order and Shirkuh now began a long retreat south up the river. Eventually he called a halt more than a hundred miles south of Cairo and was, apparently, preparing to cross the river. The majority of his officers advised against a fight. But one, who had formerly been a slave of

Nur-ad-Din's, pointed out that if the expedition returned without
victory and without even having done battle with the enemy its leaders
would be dispossessed of their lands and humiliated. Saladin was among
those convinced by this combination, and the council decided, after all,
in favour of making a stand.

Amalric was also hesitant. He was quite confident of extracting money
from Egypt, one of his principal reasons for being there, and if his enemy
seemed likely to slink off without further persuasion there seemed little
grounds for a fight. The kingdom of Jerusalem was not so full of soldiers
that it could afford to squander its fighting strength. However,
according to the Christian historian William of Tyre, the king was
visited by a vision of St Bernard, the preacher of the Second Crusade,
who accused him of cowardice in the face of the Infidel. Thus, the
commanders who had both been at first reluctant to fight found themselves locked in battle on 18 March 1167. In a conventional Turkish
battle tactic, Shirkuh placed the baggage behind the centre of the army.
Saladin was given command here with orders to retreat before the
Frankish cavalry so as to lure it away from its allies. The baggage wagons
provided a natural fall-back position round which the retiring troops
could re-form if need be. The battle went according to plan. The
general's nephew executed his manoeuvre efficiently, giving Shirkuh
and his picked cavalry ample time to scatter the Egyptians on the right
wing. When the Frankish horse returned from their pursuit it was to
find their allies routed and themselves in danger of encirclement. King
Amalric barely escaped with his life. Despite this decisive victory
Shirkuh did not feel strong enough to follow it up with an attack on
Cairo. Instead he marched rapidly to Alexandria.

It was the second city of Egypt, an immensely rich trading port and
currently the haven of Naim-ad-Din, a refugee from Shavar's régime in
Cairo. He had already promised funds and supplies to Shirkuh and the
general found them waiting for him. Having supervised the organisation
of the defences of Alexandria, he left Saladin in command of the city,
with a garrison of a thousand troops, while he himself set out for the
south to recruit support among the Bedouin and to plunder.

This new command was an important step in Saladin's career. His
part in the April battle had been effective, but the text-book tactics had
demanded neither initiative nor improvisation. He owed his place in the
high command primarily to his family connections and that was enough.
But he was already in his thirtieth year and if he had any ambition to
reach the top of his profession he would have to prove outstanding

ability. So far he had done little more than conduct a routine set-piece manoeuvre in which failure would have been ridiculous and success was no more than to be expected. His competent garrisoning at Bilbais had shown some administrative talent in war but now, commanding a great city against superior forces, he faced a different and much more testing situation. Soon after Shirkuh had quitted the city Shavar and Amalric came up and prepared for a methodical siege, ignoring Shirkuh's diversionary expedition to the south in favour of re-taking the rich prize of Alexandria. As the siege lengthened, conditions in the city rapidly worsened, and the enthusiasm which had greeted the Syrian army soon evaporated. Only Saladin's firm command and inspiring leadership held the place long enough for his uncle to return from the south and even to threaten a siege of Cairo. The Frankish-Egyptian high command decided to seek terms.

Saladin had emerged as the second most influential and competent man on the expedition. Having held Alexandria brilliantly, he was left to organise its terms of surrender. With characteristic concern for his troops and subordinates he forced Shavar to guarantee immunity to all the citizens who had helped the Syrians and an arrangement with Amalric to transport the Syrian wounded to Acre in his ships to save them from the rigours of the long desert march. Unfortunately neither provision held for long. Shavar quickly forgot his assurances and Saladin had to intervene with Amalric to persuade his ally to stop his reprisals against collaborators. As to the wounded, those who had recovered on the passage were put to work in the sugar plantations round Acre and were only freed when King Amalric reached the port.

During the negotiation, Saladin made friends in the Christian camp and was entertained there for several days. The first elements in the western picture of him are sketched around this episode. Later a Christian writer told how Saladin, the chivalrous infidel, was knighted by Humphrey II of Toron. Fraternisation across the battle lines was not unusual and William of Tyre specifically refers to one friendship of Humphrey and a Saracen emir. Possibly, during some banquet or formal reception the Frankish knights honoured their chivalrous opponent with some ceremony from the ritual of knighthood, though of course, as he was not a Christian, the oath could not be administered.

After these courtly diversions he marched back with his uncle to Damascus – Shirkuh with 50,000 dinars as the price of his withdrawal. Once again a campaign had ended inconclusively. But so long as Egypt's rulers were too weak to resist ambitious interference, the country would remain at the centre of the fight between Christian and Muslim.

Politics comes next to religion for an understanding of the place of Egypt and above all Cairo in Saladin's world. Cairo, standing about fifteen miles north-east of the ancient Egyptian city of Memphis, originated with the military base set up at al-Fustat by the Arab army that conquered Egypt from the Byzantine Empire in the 640s. Under Egypt's Fatimid Shi'ite regime (from 969) a new walled city, al-Qahirah, was built north of Fustat as the dynasty's capital. The native Egyptians or Copts, practising their own variant of Christianity and paying the official religious tax, remained important in the bureaucracy, sometimes becoming vizirs. Saladin would continue this tradition of toleration (a tradition in decline, it seems, in our own day). It was in Egypt that the Jewish philosopher and polymath, Maimonides, a fugitive from the intolerant Almohad regime of his native Cordoba, settled in the 1160s. Here he wrote his famous *Guide for the Perplexed* and in Cairo he entered the service of Saladin as physician, later serving his son.

Trade, favourite theme of the tales from the famous 'Arabian Nights' collection (many with Egyptian settings), was central to the Islamic world. The *Hajj* made Mecca a hub of routes from the Red Sea; one powerful Adeni trading family, whose branches and agencies dominated those routes, had its own commercial enclave in Cairo. The Fatimid caliphs, trading on their own behalf and creaming taxes from other traders, were Egypt's most active merchants; the profits fed the opulence of their court. Saladin continued the pattern through his commercial agents but channelled the proceeds to the public purse, above all to his military programme. Egyptians would grumble that he used the country's wealth to win mastery in Syria, but no one would doubt that he had restored her influence.

# Chapter 6

# Vizir of Egypt

The Kurdish commanders had extricated themselves from near disaster, but the expedition had not even approached its objectives, The 50,000 gold pieces said to have been paid to Shirkuh were offset by large Christian gains. They installed a resident prefect at Cairo and a garrison which controlled the city's gates – they also forced the Egyptians to double their annual tribute to 100,000 dinars. On his return Saladin devoted himself to politics and the diversions of the court. Two expeditions to Egypt had brought his family little success, and he put the whole episode behind him.

But the situation in Egypt could not be so easily dismissed. Shavar, began to lose influence. The Frankish garrison in Cairo was a standing indictment of his policies and the heavy tribute still owing fed the growing opposition to him. To placate it he let the payments fall behind, but this merely infuriated his erstwhile allies and Amalric was soon under pressure to invade Egypt in earnest. The king opposed an immediate expedition. He had recently concluded an alliance with the Byzantines and wanted time to involve them. He also had more fundamental doubts. Egyptian tribute money, even if delayed, was a valuable addition to Jerusalem's war chest against Syria. He warned the hawks in the council, 'if we invade with the intention of taking possession, the sovereign, the army, the cities and the peasants will unite against us and will fly into the arms of Nur-ad-Din. If he should come to their aid it will be the worse for us.'

The fact that he listed the 'sovereign' as a power to be reckoned with shows that Amalric, who had refused to ratify his treaty with Shavar until it had been approved in direct negotiation with the caliph, accepted that the Egyptian court still influenced events. Perhaps Shavar's position was weakening, but the air was thick with strange rumours – one remarkable story going the rounds claimed that Kamil, the son of Shavar, was trying to arrange the marriage of his daughter and Saladin.

Whether true or not it implied a move towards rapprochement between Syria and Egypt which could harden into alliance if the Christians acted precipitately. Twice they had had to withdraw from Egypt because of Syrian threats to the kingdom. If they now broke faith with their party in Cairo they might force the union of Muslims which was the most serious long-term danger. Amalric conceded that something would have to be done, but he was overruled in the matter of timing. In October 1168 the Franks moved south, this time as the invaders, not the allies, of Egypt. They were met in the desert by an ambassador from Shavar and answered his tirade with the bland suggestion that another two million dinars might perhaps buy them off. Shavar ordered the garrison of Bilbais to resist.

It was under the command of his son Taiy, and the stubborn defence surprised the Christians, who generally despised Egyptian troops. It also infuriated the soldiery, which, once inside the city, ran amuck and slaughtered the population, the Coptic Christians along with the Muslims. This massacre united Egypt against the invader even more completely than Amalric had feared. Malcontent Muslims might have welcomed the fall of Shavar, the Copts would almost certainly have provided a Frankish fifth column. Bilbais crushed any such hopes. On 12 November Shavar ordered the destruction of Fustat old city where Amalric had encamped on his earlier expedition.

Amalric had marched on to surround Cairo and Shavar had settled down to the congenial manoeuvres of bribery; his son, taken prisoner at Bilbais, was ransomed for a sizeable figure and it seemed possible that even at this stage the Franks could be bought off without the need to call in the dangerous support of Syria. Frankish councils were as ever divided. The warmongers who had urged the invasion in the first place wanted first and foremost to get their hands on the plunder and tribute money which, during peace, went direct into the royal coffers. Now that the vizir seemed willing and able to disgorge vast sums to the army in the field, they urged withdrawal a few miles from Cairo so that negotiations could proceed without duress on Shavar. The fact that the Franks were only in Egypt to secure long-term advantages seems to have been forgotten. The arrangements suited Shavar well enough, but his son Kamil, who was in close touch with the court, agreed that the time had come to call in Nur-ad-Din to finish the Frankish menace once and for all, and forced his father to concur in the caliph's initiative.

The palace enthusiastically made the proposal its own. During the first weeks of the Frankish campaign Shavar's chancellery had been depicting him in the glowing imagery of the Holy War, as the champion of Islam. Now that he had been forced to turn once again to bribery the rhetoric died, yet even so he had supporters among the religious establishment and the administration where some realised that Syrian intervention would mean the end of the Fatimid régime. Others despised the Syrian forces for their motley ancestry as Turks, Kurds, Armenians and so forth and opined that 'it would be better to pay tribute to the Franks than to let in the Ghuzz'. But popular feeling was running so strong after the massacre at Bilbais that negotiations with the Christians had become dangerous as well as humiliating.

The appeal to Nur-ad-Din was reinforced by a letter from the caliph himself. This was accompanied by a lock of his wife's hair, to show that the Syrian king could hope to share the favours of his still more cherished bride – the realm of Egypt. A letter written in the caliph's own hand was remarkable enough in itself – the eloquent token he sent with it and its potent symbolism emphasised the invitation in the strongest possible way.

Nur-ad-Din's immediate response to the embassy was to send for Shirkuh. He mobilised a force of 8,000 men, comprising 2,000 troops from his personal bodyguard plus 6,000 Turkomans and Kurds, officered by Kurds and Turks. In addition to a war chest of 200,000 gold pieces he gave each man twenty pieces as a bonus. He also ordered Saladin to accompany his uncle. The reply was a surprising refusal: 'By God! even were the sovereignty of Egypt offered me I would not go.' Yet eventually the pleas of his uncle and the orders of his sovereign, who showered him with horses and arms, forced Saladin to reconsider. Later he claimed that he went to Egypt 'like one driven to his death'.

This reluctance is one of the best attested episodes in Saladin's career and it is a puzzle. The '67 campaign had been less than triumphant and quite possibly he had no wish to be associated with another failure; there were also bad memories of the siege of Alexandria. Yet by now he was a veteran soldier and no speculation can fill out the skimpy contemporary accounts of the affair satisfactorily. The army set out on 17 December 1168 and as soon as he heard the news Shavar, hoping to solve his dilemma by having Frank and Syrian exhaust themselves far from his capital, warned Amalric of the advance. The king withdrew from Cairo in a half-hearted attempt to intercept the Syrian army at Suez, but the two forces did not meet and Amalric's withdrawal became a retreat.

His aim had been to secure the Christians' hold on Egypt. Before he invaded they had their prefect in Cairo and a garrison there, and good chances even though the times had been uncertain. Now things had hardened beyond recall in favour of Syria. The atrocity at Bilbais had much to answer for. In '67, faced by a firm Franco-Egyptian front, Shirkuh had been forced to waste his powers in a hazardous holding fight at Alexandria and fruitless raiding. Now, the Syrians were no longer outsiders but the favoured guests of the caliph; now Amalric found himself allied to a weak vizir and robbed of any Egyptian friendship by the brutality of his own troops. He had to quit the field and for a time the palace held the initiative – -for Shavar the writing was on the wall.

On 9 January Shirkuh entered Cairo to a great welcome as Deliverer of the Muslims. He had audience with the caliph and received from him a robe of honour which he proudly showed to his troops. For the moment Shavar could do nothing but concur in the general enthusiasm and made daily visits to the camp of his unwanted ally with all the pomp and panoply he could muster. At the same time he tried to involve his son in a plot to assassinate Shirkuh at a banquet, pointing out quite rightly that if they did not dispose of the Syrian and his officers he would shortly put an end to them and to all the Fatimid leaders. According to Ibn-al-Athir, Kamil replied: 'What you say may well be right. But in my view it is better to be killed leaving Egypt to the Muslims, than by the Franks who will certainly return and deal with us once Shirkuh is dead.' In the event Shavar, the veteran plotter, was outplotted. On 18 January, making a pilgrimage to a mosque on the outskirts of Cairo, he was arrested by a Syrian guard commanded by Saladin and beheaded on the orders of the caliph. The same day Shirkuh was installed as vizir. To pacify the mob and win their support, he permitted them to loot the palace of the deposed vizir, keeping none of the treasures for himself or his troops. But he permitted his emirs to seize the estates of Shavar's officers. The palace sent a letter to Nur-ad-Din to inform him that henceforth the Egyptian military would be commanded by his lieutenant, Shirkuh. The reaction from Damascus was immediate and angry. The caliph was urged to order Shirkuh back to his master and when this failed Nur-ad-Din confiscated the commander's holdings in Syria.

It is hardly surprising that Nur-ad-Din was suspicious. Only two years previously Shirkuh had argued him into a campaign blessed by Baghdad as a holy war to overthrow the Fatimids. But now that the Egyptians' allies were driven from the field and he himself was in full control of the capital, Shirkuh not only did not depose the caliph but even recognised his authority by accepting the appointment as his chief minister. From Damascus it looked as though once free of his master a loyal servant had seized the moment to turn rebel. The analysis may very well have been right, but since two months after his appointment Shirkuh died of his excesses we can never know how he would have used his position. The situation in Cairo was not simple. The people hailed Shirkuh as liberator from the Christians, the palace still held the political initiative. The caliph and his advisers were delighted to have Shavar removed for them, but could be expected to oppose any attempt by Shurkuh to displace the Fatimid régime. Shirkuh was not strong enough to force the issue, and had little inducement. While he meticulously observed Egyptian independence and permitted the observance of Shi'ite rites he had the real power of vizir and the cooperation of the establishment.

His death on 23 March 1169 meant the appointment of a new vizir, It also meant the election of a new commander of the Syrian army in Egypt; the two posts need not necessarily be held by the same man. One palace faction proposed that the Syrian troops be settled in Egypt as a powerful addition to the caliph's forces but that the vizirate be given to an Egyptian army officer. The caliph and his advisers, however, recognised that although they held the balance of power the new vizir must be acceptable to the 'army of liberation'.

Saladin had been designated by his uncle to succeed him as commander and he could count on the support of the Kurdish contingent, but he had strong rivals among a group of Turkish officers, aggressively loyal to Nur-ad-Din, who dubbed themselves Nuriyah. The pro-Saladin lobby was led by 'Isa al-Hakkari, who had risen in the service of Nur-ad-Din. He had been named as the chief negotiator in the rumoured marriage between Saladin and Shavar's daughter in 1168, which at least shows he was popularly considered a loyal friend to Saladin. Largely thanks to him Saladin won the army command. But the decision was not unanimous, and the leading Nuriyah returned with his troops to Damascus, where he accused Saladin of disloyalty and self-seeking. Meanwhile, Saladin was invited by the caliph to follow his uncle as vizir. The palace may have hoped to spark off further Syrian defections. Immediately the news reached Aleppo, Nur-ad-Din confirmed the confiscation of Saladin's and Shirkuh's estates and offices in Syria, including the town of Homs, and slightingly ignored the office of vizir and the titles granted by the Cairo régime, referring to Saladin simply as 'commander-in-chief'.

By including Nur-ad-Din's name among those mentioned in the official Friday prayers at Cairo and by other gestures of submission Saladin did his best to soften Aleppo's attitude. At the same time, owing his appointment to the palace, he was a regular attendant at court and companion of the caliph in ceremonial duties. The two were seen heading the Ramadan processions and each Friday made joint pilgrimage to some mosque. The Kurdish vizir trod carefully between his Sunnite overlord and Shi'ite master, gradually allaying the suspicions of the one and becoming strong enough to override the other. If the caliph had hoped for a pliant subordinate he soon found his mistake.

By the summer of 1169 Saladin had formed a personal bodyguard; in July of the same year his position was further strengthened by the arrival of his brother Turan Shah. Even before Shirkuh's death his nephew had had to do a good deal of the administrative work since the vizir was generally drunk and incapable. When Saladin took the office he showed the powers it might have in efficient hands and reinforced by the arrival of his family he began to build a strong position. Worried, the court party decided to call in the Christians once more. But Saladin learnt of the plot before Amalric. An alert agent, intrigued by the unusual design of the sandals of a court messenger, had them unstitched and discovered the dispatch addressed to Amalric. A detachment of Saladin's guards was ordered to the country villa of the chief plotter, the black eunuch, Moutamen, and killed him before he had a chance to rally his own troops.

Saladin now dismissed all the palace servants loyal to the caliph and also installed his own ministers. For a moment it looked as though he had overreached himself. The displaced ministers stirred up trouble among the Nubian palace guard who were already furious at the death of the great black minister; they attacked Saladin's troops in the palace area and the caliph looked on at the seething struggle. The overwhelming numbers of the black guard found themselves congested in the streets and courtyards but even so things were looking dangerous for the Syrians. At this point Saladin callously ordered that the barracks housing the guards' families and also a contingent of Armenians be set on fire. The mutinous troops streamed back to rescue their wives and children from the flames; many were cut down in cold blood on Saladin's orders while most of the Armenians perished in the fire.

Resistance continued for a further two days in some quarters and the rebel remnant was given a safe conduct out of Cairo, but this too was violated and in bloody and ruthless fashion Saladin had put an end to the threat of rebellion in Cairo. The caliph, we are informed, hastened to assure Saladin of his loyalty.

News of the Cairo crisis had by now reached the Christians. Embassies to Europe urging immediate reinforcements while the enemy was in disarray found no support, but Constantinople did agree to a joint expedition with Amalric. On 10 July a Byzantine fleet headed south. However, the kingdom had been unsettled by the '68 campaign and Amalric was not ready to leave until the middle of October, crossing into Egypt on the 25th. Saladin had had ample warning of the invasion and had concentrated his army at Bilbais. Unexpectedly, the Christians laid siege to Damietta.

Perhaps a rapid assault would have won the place, but the Frankish command intimidated by the massive fortifications prepared for a methodical siege. Their caution was utterly mistaken. Saladin had been thrown temporarily off balance by the Christians' choice of target so that they still had some slight advantage of surprise. The defenders had been able to block the entrance to the river with a heavy boom so that while Amalric was deprived of the support he expected from the fleet Saladin was able to pour reinforcements into the town down the open branch of the Nile. Day by day the Greek commander watched the enemy garrison growing stronger in men and provisions, while his own men who had set out in July with provisions for only a three-month campaign grew weaker and more mutinous. He urged Amalric to risk an all-out attack. But still Amalric held off, and it gradually became obvious that the expedition had failed. In mid-December, for the second time that year, the Christians withdrew with nothing achieved.

It was the end of an eventful year. During the nine months since he had taken office as vizir, Saladin had proved himself a master in politics and war. Despite the open antagonism of Nur-ad-Din his troops in Egypt had remained loyal to him; a dangerous plot had been foiled and a revival of palace influence nipped in the bud; a threatening mutiny had been crushed and an army of invaders comprehensively routed. Finally, and perhaps most interesting, Nur-ad-Din's prompt reply to the appeals for reinforcements had shown that, however suspicious he might be, Nur-ad-Din dared not abandon Saladin to the risk of a Christian take-over.

The way Saladin weathered these early troubles revealed a powerful political talent. The vizirate of Egypt was probably the most insecure job in the contemporary Muslim world. In the years to come he was to show still more impressive administrative skills which were to bring the country its longest period of untroubled government for half a century. Just now, however, there was more stormy weather ahead.

Nur-ad-Din was increasing the pressure for the dissolution of the Fatimid caliphate. But before this could be done, and before the name of al-Mustadi of Baghdad could be substituted for that of al-Adid, there were powerful vested interests that had to be negotiated. Once it had been done, Saladin's only title to legitimate authority in Egypt would be in question. He moved carefully to secure his position, and began to replace key figures in the military and administrative establishment with his own nominees. In the early summer of 1170 he won an important new ally when his father, having at last received Nur-ad-Din's permission, came to join him at Cairo. The occasion revealed the measure of Saladin's ascendancy. Conferring an honour which no previous caliph had bestowed on a subject, al-Adid rode out to greet Aiyub in person at the outskirts of the capital.

With a suitable gesture of filial obedience Saladin offered to resign the vizirate to his father. Even if the offer was genuine it was not practical politics. Refusing the proposal, Aiyub remarked that God would not have chosen his son for so great an office had he not been worthy of it and added that it was never wise to play with one's luck. But he did accept the treasurership and Alexandria and Damietta as *iqtas*, while Saladin's brother, Turan-Shah, was granted Upper Egypt, a section of Cairo and the district of Giza. With his brothers in vital commands and the family patriarch, veteran in politics and master of administration, in a key post, Saladin began to move with ever more assurance. In June his first son, Ali al-Afdal, was born to his wife, Umm al-Afdal.

In the last months of 1170 he took the offensive against the Christians. Merely carrying the war into the enemy territory would raise Egyptian morale considerably. Leaving Cairo on 26 November he marched for the Templar fortress of Darum on the southern frontier of the Christian kingdom. The attack was launched on 10 December, but the Templars were able to hold out while the main Christian army under King Amalric came up. The Egyptians slipped away under cover of darkness and marched on the city of Gaza, putting it to the sack. The fortress there was too strong for them, but the operation had served notice that Egypt was once again a force to be reckoned with. More important, it concentrated Christian attention on the Mediterranean frontiers of the kingdom while Saladin's forces were mounting a surprise and elaborate operation further south.

A flotilla of prefabricated ships had been transported by camel from Cairo to the Gulf of Suez, where they were launched for the voyage round Sinai. By the end of December they were in position in the waters of the Gulf of al-Aqaba and on 31 December cooperated with the land forces from Saladin's field headquarters for a successful combined land and sea attack on the port. The recovery of this rich trading port and key staging post in the pilgrimage route to Mecca was a major victory for Islam. It was also a brilliant triumph for an army which for years had been satisfied if it could defend its own frontiers – generally with the help of infidel allies. In rather less than two years, by efficient, well-planned military reform, Saladin had made the Egyptian army a fighting force.

He had also moved steadily to strengthen his position as vizir. In the summer of 1170 'Isa al-Hakkari was appointed chief judge in Cairo; in March 1171 the Kurdish *qadi*, al-Fadil, was made head of the country's judiciary. A few months later more purges of the military seemed to give him unassailable control of the Egyptian establishment. The moves were watched with cold suspicion from Damascus and in August 1171 Nur-ad-Din sent a direct command that the Fatimid government and caliph were to be overturned forthwith, and threatened that if nothing was done he would come in person. Saladin ignored the caliph's protests against the purge and soon after ordered more army units to the capital. At about this time al-Adid fell ill. On Friday, 10 September 1171, the first Friday of the year 567 A.H., the bidding prayer in the chief mosque of Fustat omitted the name of the Fatimid caliph for the first time in two centuries. A week later al-Mustadi was named in the prayers of the chief mosque of Cairo, and as the orthodox invocation was echoed throughout the capital the palace grounds were being methodically taken over by Saladin's troops. The royal family and its retinue were rounded up and placed under house arrest.

The constitutional arrangements of two centuries had been over-turned without a murmur of protest. There were to be repercussions later, but the only immediate result was an enquiry on behalf of the dead caliph's ten-year-old son as to when he was to be installed as successor. Saladin calmly replied that the boy's father had given him personally no authority in the matters of the succession and that was that. Barely a week after the caliph's death in the night of 12 September and but a few days after the solemn, religious proclamation of the Abbasid house, Saladin marched out of Cairo to a new campaign.

The objective was the strategic Christian strongpoint of ash-Shaubak (Montreal). About twenty-five miles to the south of the Dead Sea, it overlooked the route from Syria to the Gulf of al-Aqaba, and the communications between Syria and Egypt. Amalric, caught off guard, could not come at once to the relief of the garrison and the commander begged a ten-day truce. Nur-ad-Din was marching south from Damascus with a large army, and the fall of ash-Shaubak seemed certain. But a few days before the truce was due to expire the defenders saw in astonishment that the Egyptian force was striking camp. They were not the only ones surprised by the withdrawal. Even in Saladin's own entourage it was whispered that he was retiring to avoid a face-to-face encounter. If they did meet, the speculation ran, the vizir of Egypt would be forced to accept the post of second-in-command in the field army and might even be relieved of his offices in Cairo.

To Syrian noses the whole thing smelt rankly of treason, and there can be little doubt that political self-interest was an important factor in Saladin's decision. The given reason was that news had just reached the camp of a rising in Upper Egypt which threatened the whole Syrian position in the country. But Saladin's brother was handling the rebellion effectively and it is unlikely Saladin really believed his own presence was needed. However, he did have grounds to be angry and worried both with Nur-ad-Din's attitude and about his own situation in Egypt. Acting on instructions from Damascus, he had deposed the heretical caliph – and incidentally seen Nur-ad-Din receive the first congratulations from Baghdad for the action – and, again ordered by Damascus, he had left his own capital within days of the coup, when unrest was most to be feared, to make an attack deep into enemy territory. His withdrawal from ash-Shaubak may have been calculating but there were reasons for a return to Cairo. News soon came that Nur-ad-Din was planning a punitive expedition.

Saladin called an urgent conference of his family and advisers. Reaction was mixed but generally defiant, summed up in passionate words by one of the younger cousins Taqi-ad-Din 'Umar – 'If the king of Syria comes, we will fight him and force him back.' Saladin's father, always the diplomat and now perturbed at the kind of effect such hotheaded talk would have in Damascus, brought the proceedings sternly to order. 'Know that should Nur-ad-Din come nothing would stop me or your uncle here from dismounting and kissing the ground at his feet,' he said to the young hot-head. Then turning to Saladin he went on, 'Even if he ordered us to take your life we should do it. If we would act thus how do you think others would? For all the army and all your council here owe their homage to Nur-ad-Din should he come. This is his land and if it pleased him to depose you we would immediately obey him. We are all Nur-ad-Din's mamluks and slaves and he may do with us as he chooses.' Aiyub's advice was to conciliate the king with an offer of total submission: 'News has reached us that you intend to lead an expedition to Egypt; but what need is there? My Lord need but send a courtier on a camel to lead me back to Syria by a turban cloth about my neck – not one of my people would attempt to resist him.'

After the council had dispersed Aiyub warned Saladin against yielding to ambitious talk. There would always be an informer willing to report back to Nur-ad-Din, and provocation was pointless since time was on the side of the younger man. If Nur-ad-Din could be placated there need be little fear of any Syrian invasion, but if things should reach that point Aiyub swore he would fight to the death rather than the king should take even a single sugar cane of the rich crops of Egypt from his son. For the next three years Saladin followed his father's advice. In April the following year a caravan left for Aleppo carrying much treasure from the Fatimid palace including a valuable antique ceremonial robe and turban belonging to one of the early caliphs and, more to Nur-ad-Din's liking, 100,000 dinars. In 1173 this Egyptian tribute consisted of more rich treasure and a further 60,000 dinars. Nur-ad-Din's name was added to the invocations in the mosques at Cairo, and in his dealings with his overlord Saladin maintained the most correct protocol. But nothing could dispel Nur-ad-Din's suspicions or satisfy his expectations for cash return from the Egyptian venture.

Saladin was indeed determined not to lose Egypt. In the summer of 1173 he was ordered up to besiege Karak in Moab, a few miles south of the Dead Sea. He obeyed but, as in 1171, retired on news that Nur-ad-Din was coming to join him. This time he could show good reason however; his loved and respected father. The aged Aiyub had been thrown from his horse and in fact died before his son reached Cairo.

But while he complained bitterly against Saladin, Nur-ad-Din, who had the resources to take ash-Shaubak unaided, dissipated his strength with campaigns against the sultanate of the Selchük Turks of Konya. The real charge against Saladin was not so much that he was using Egypt in his own interests as that he was not prepared to subordinate the country to the interests of Syrian policy. Popular enthusiasm for his régime flowed from the fact that it was beginning to restore Egypt to great-power status. Nur-ad-Din had hoped that Egypt would provide a rich and docile province. But Saladin, who had secured his position at Cairo virtually unaided, saw no reason to comply.

The capture of al-Aqaba and the attack on ash-Shaubak, while they demonstrated the effectiveness of Egyptian arms, were operations of equal advantage to Syria. In 1173 Egyptian armies were driving westward along the North African coast into territories that had not known rule from Cairo for a century and a half. This revival of the glories of the Fatimid past brought new sources of revenue for the financing of the vizir's new army and fleet and appealed still more powerfully to the Egyptian public. Commanded by Sharaf-ad-Din Karakush, a member of the staff of Saladin's nephew Taqi-ad-Din, the array advanced through Tripolitania, took Tripoli itself, and even pushed into the territories of Tunis. An important part of the Mediterranean littoral was won back for Egypt.

The following year, 1174, saw Saladin presiding over the recovery of yet more territories of the former Fatimid empire. Early in February his brother Turan-Shah crossed the Red Sea to al-Hijaz. Then he marched south into the Yemen taking Aden and other major strongholds. These conquests remained with the Aiyubid house for fifty years. With the North African gains they brought Egypt to a position she had not known for generations and, added to her command of al-Aqaba, restored her to the prestigious position of protector of the pilgrim routes to Mecca. In the popular imagination Saladin the conqueror was now Saladin Protector of the Faith.

The people of Egypt had reason to approve the Kurdish vizir, who, in five years, had brought the country so far back on the road to glory. The comparison with the devious and cloistered intrigues of the Shavar régime was startling. Of course many ministers of the old régime were incensed by the revolution and plots were gathering force to a countercoup. Upper Egypt, traditionally the base for campaigns against a too-successful vizir, had been temporarily pacified by Turan-Shah before his Red Sea expedition. In 1172 he had repulsed an invasion from Nubia and compelled its ruler to sue for terms. The brunt of that invasion had fallen on Aswan, where the governor had fortunately held loyal to Cairo. But in 1174 he decided to join the members of the displaced judiciary, administration and military now plotting the overthrow of Saladin. They were led by the son and grandson of two former vizirs. Remarkably, they judged it safe to involve two men high in favour with the Aiyubid régime. These were Ibn-Massal, who held a senior post in the administration and Zain-ad-Din, a leading divine of the Sunnite establishment. It is difficult now to know why such men should have been thought open to subversion – in the light of what was to happen it seems at least possible that the whole plot was set up by Saladin's secret service to smoke out opposition.

Following Egyptian tradition in these matters the conspirators contacted the Christians, and the Normans of Sicily agreed to launch an attack on Alexandria to coincide with a rising in Cairo; this was planned for harvest time, the most vulnerable period for any medieval military establishment, when commanders and troops alike tended to be away on the estates. Saladin's situation was potentially very dangerous. Following the North African campaigns of the previous year a sizeable body of troops had been detached for garrison duties in the new provinces while the Yemeni expedition of February had drawn further forces off from the capital. Possibly this was no coincidence. The campaign into the Yemen had been planned and decided on largely thanks to the urgings of a Yemeni poet and historian, Umarah, a prominent figure of the earlier régime. It was he who had persuaded Saladin that the region was ripe for conquest and so had ensured that the vizir's elder brother, one of his strongest lieutenants, would be out of Egypt when the rebellion broke. Umarah was also one of the chief plotters.

It was an elaborate plan, coordinating attacks on the northern coast and a rebellion in the far south at Aswan with a rising in the capital. But it was betrayed from the first. Zain-ad-Din, the Sunnite divine, either because he foresaw failure or, as been suggested above, because he was an *agent provocateur*, made contact with Saladin's chief secretary al-Fadil and offered to betray his fellow conspirators in exchange for their confiscated estates. The fact that he was able to bargain with the administration is in itself suspicious – as a self-confessed traitor he should have been in no very strong position to negotiate. Whatever the secrets behind the comings and goings, Saladin moved with precision and speed. On 12 March the remaining royal family members were put under close house arrest, and early in April a wave of arrests brought in the conspirators. A special tribunal condemned them to death by crucifixion and, beginning on 6 April, they were publicly executed in Cairo.

The rising had aborted, and with it the most serious threat of subversion. But there were consequences still to follow. King Amalric, who had also agreed to lead an army against Saladin, died early in July shortly before the plot should have matured. But King William II of Sicily sent a fleet under his renowned admiral Margaritus. In late July it was seen standing in to Alexandria. The force consisted of 200 galleys carrying 30,000 men and 80 freighters loaded with horses, equipment and armaments. But the Christians had hopelessly miscalculated. Not only had the Egyptian uprising been quashed months before but the defences of Alexandria were in excellent repair and the harbour mouth blocked with sunken ships. Saladin was close at hand, with a large army. After three inglorious days during which the garrison had harried them with audacious sorties and night attacks the Normans took to their ships and fled, leaving 300 men stranded on the hostile shore. The Sicilians headed north.

Within days of the Christian rout messengers posting up from Aswan reported that the region was being terrorised by rebels led by the town's governor. Saladin sent his young brother al-Adil to put down the rebellion, and early in September the trouble was over. The contemporary records do not specifically link the Aswan rising with the main plot but the timing could hardly have been coincidence. Had the Norman invasion not evaporated so quickly the régime would have been faced with simultaneous attacks north and south; a situation avoided by only a few days. But those few days were enough for Saladin to deal with the threats piecemeal. During the summer, news had reached Cairo of the death of Nur-ad-Din on 15 May; Syria was wide open with possibilities for Saladin, but it was not until October, with the last murmur of rebellion silenced, that he could set out for Damascus. Then, however, so complete had been the pacification of Egypt that he was able to leave his capital in the hands of his brother al-Adil and not return for seven more years.

Brutal when necessary, but always decisive and bold, Saladin had solved the Egyptian problem. For generations vizirs had come and gone in a turgid succession of faction fights. The pieces on the board were the vizir, the palace party, Syrian or Christian intruders fishing in the troubled waters and, as often as not, the governor of Upper Egypt. As each pawn successively 'queened' (it is thought the original of the modern chess 'queen' was the 'vizir') the pieces were set up and the game begun again. By outmanoeuvring his enemies and at need liquidating them Saladin had called a halt to the game for a generation. He had, moreover, brought better and more enlightened government to the country than it had known since the days of the great caliphs. The treachery and killings that kept him in power tell against him in a modern evaluation. But the death of courtiers was too commonplace to be of much concern to the citizenry of Egypt, while the ending of the seemingly endless feuds was accompanied by Egypt's return to power, prosperity and influence in the world. Biographers of Saladin anxious to hurry on to the grand and chivalrous doings of the Holy War have traditionally glossed over the early years of his Egyptian rule. Yet the fact is that these were formative to his career and reveal qualities of decision and tenacity that were vital in the years ahead.

In *Saladin in his Time* (1983), P.H. Newby noted that at the height of his career Saladin (vizir, later called sultan, of Egypt) would be known to his contemporaries as al-Malik al-Nasir Salah al-Din Abu 'l-Muzaffer Yusuf ibn Aiyub ibn Shadi. The Arabic 'al-Malik' is usually translated as 'king'; 'al-Nasir' as 'defender of' or 'victorious in (the Faith)'. It has been claimed that the great man, son of Aiyub who was son of Shadi and generally called 'the honour' (Salah) 'of religion' (al-Din), never himself adopted the title of king. Maybe not, but his contemporaries had no hesitation in awarding it to him.

His fortifications at Cairo, his capital from 1169 to 1176, still testify to his stature as a potentate. The result of the works he ordered was to consolidate the city's defences. First the existing walls were reinforced, but then a new circuit was constructed for the capital and old Fustat while the immense works were crowned with the majestic citadel on the rocky promontory of the Muqattam hills. The expenditure in materials and resources was of course huge, even if the use of slave labour in the form of Christian prisoners of war is taken into account.

The restoration of Sunni rule in the city of the heretical Fatimids meant the return of Egyptian patronage of the holiest sites in Islam. When Saladin abolished the toll charges levied on the pilgrims to Mecca and compensated the authorities there for their loss in revenues, he had restored something of the ancient prestige of Muslim Egypt. He would also ruffle feathers in Baghdad, where the caliph was jealous of a possible challenge to his standing in the community of Islam.

# Chapter 7

# The Critical Years

The period from May 1174 to September 1176 was a decisive one. It opened with the deaths of Nur-ad-Din, his suspicious and menacing overlord, and King Amalric, Islam's last dangerous competitor on the throne of Jerusalem. It closed on the distant battlefield of Myriocephalum where the sultan of Konya destroyed the military capability of the Byzantine empire. During the two and a half years that lay between, Saladin, against difficult and shifting odds, made himself master of southern Syria; after that he could turn against his remaining rivals in the Muslim world knowing that the coastline kingdom of the Christians could expect no more help from the north.

At the beginning of 1174 the future had looked gloomy. The threatened domestic rebellion had been crushed but during the spring Egypt and her ruler were facing up to almost certain invasion from Syria. Nur-ad-Din's suspicions of Saladin, fed by his leading advisers who had come to hate and fear the Kurdish upstart, had come to a head. The king's nephew, the ruler of Mosul, had been ordered to bring an army to the war and in April was already on the move. On 6 May, Nur-ad-Din moved south to Damascus from his chief capital at Aleppo to plan the final details of the expedition against Egypt. Although in his sixtieth year he was still vigorous, the undisputed lord of Syria, and determined to bring Egypt under his direct rule. He had threatened intervention before, but this time the threat was to be implemented.

A man of deep though conventional piety, Nur-ad-Din was given to philosophising, and one May morning, riding through the orchards about Damascus with his entourage, he might have been heard debating the uncertainty of life and human ambitions. Soon it was to seem a prophetic episode, for within days the king was brought to his sick bed with an acute infection of the throat. A suppurating ulcer made his breathing painful and brought on a fever, of which, on 15 May, he died.

He had been a good Muslim and a great and just ruler. His reputation, won in earlier days, as the terror of the infidels, and his austere piety had won the respect of his subjects and his love of justice their gratitude. More important still, the king's firm and shrewd management of men and events had brought a generation of orderly stable and centralised government to an area that had been divided for centuries. The quadrilateral of power was at last firmly based. Nur-ad-Din had enjoyed the recognition and blessing of Baghdad; he was the ruler of Aleppo and Damascus and had installed his nephew at Mosul. Thanks almost entirely to him, the great prize of Muslim unity seemed to have been won and the days of the Infidel to be numbered. To his admirers his death was a body blow to Islam. But, as will be argued, it came just in time to save the community of the faithful from a new period of destructive civil war.

For all his wisdom and experience Nur-ad-Din was never able to establish a trusting *modus vivendi* with Saladin, his most brilliant and powerful subordinate. The ambitions of the younger man were obvious enough, and there was, perhaps, some justice in the charge that he had not remitted as large a tribute as Aleppo had a right to expect from the rich province he governed. And yet he had brought Egypt back to Sunnite obedience, the age-old objective of the strategists of Baghdad, and this had decisively tilted the power balance in the Holy War. The ambitions that Nur-ad-Din so much feared had been turned to the reconquest of territories in Africa and Arabia that Egypt could legitimately claim, and so had further strengthened the southern state without encroaching on Syria's sphere of interest. Saladin was too clearheaded to risk a trial of strength with Nur-ad-Din, even had he wished to, and there is nothing to suggest that he did.

In 1171 Saladin's father had advised him against open defiance. At that time, outside the Aiyubid family even the most loyal of Saladin's commanders would probably have deserted him if the king of Syria had come in person to Cairo, while the numerous displaced members of the Fatimid régime would willingly have abetted his overthrow. Had Nur-ad-Din acted then on his first impulse he could no doubt have put an end to Saladin's career and with it what he and his advisers increasingly regarded as a threat to the dynasty. Three years on, however, Saladin had won success and acclaim in Egypt, he had strengthened his resources and secured his authority. The time had passed for a Syrian walk-over; invasion now would almost certainly have sparked off a war to shatter the unity of Islam in the Middle East for generations.

Throughout this book we find the geography and politics of power clouded by a rhetoric of the Holy War, so eagerly employed by the chief contestants that it has coloured the view of historians as it did that of contemporaries. When Nur-ad-Din or Saladin pursued policies to extend and consolidate their own power – the traditional concern of rulers – they were accused by opponents of betraying the cause of Islam. Nur-ad-Din's projected campaign against Egypt was just such a project, but, given his suspicions of Saladin and his obligation to his dynasty, it is hard to see what alternative was open to him. So long as he lived, Egypt and Syria were certain to be at odds, and as his son, eleven in 1174, grew into manhood and inherited the quarrel, the rift in Islam would widen. Paradoxically, for Nur-ad-Din to die when he did was to the long-term disadvantage of the Christians. It offered Saladin a chance to combine Syria with Egypt under his rule while Aleppo and Damascus were distracted by the power struggle around the boy heir.

The young king of Syria was the focus of that struggle, but the real issue was the traditional contest for Syrian supremacy between the two great cities. Six days before his unexpected death, Nur-ad-Din had given a boost to the prestige of Damascus when he held the ceremony of his son's circumcision there and had him proclaimed heir in the traditional way, walking before the boy as he rode through the streets and bearing before him the *ghasiyah*, the banner of office. A week later the young heir was proclaimed king and the star of Damascus was clearly in the ascendant. The régime there appointed the regent, Ibn-al-Muqaddam, who also became commander-in-chief of the armed forces. The news of the old king's death was sent to Aleppo by pigeon post where the governor of the citadel swore the emirs to the new allegiance, and it seemed that Aleppo was going to accept the lead which Damascus had assumed.

As described by the Aleppan historian, Kamal-ad-Din, the swearing of the new allegiance was deftly handled by the citadel governor, Jamal-ad-Din. The news of Nur-ad-Din's proclamation of his heir in Damascus had only just arrived and had not yet been officially announced in Aleppo. Realising the turmoil that might follow the announcement of the king's death, Jamal-ad-Din accordingly preceded it with a proclamation of the succession ceremony. 'He immediately ordered that the drums be beaten and the cymbals and trumpets sounded; he convened the superior officers and the notables at Aleppo, the men of law and the emirs, and said to them: "Our master has just circumcised his son and installed him as his heir. . . ." All expressed their joy at the news and addressed their praise to god most high. Then the commander said: "Take the oath to the son of our master . . . as . . . he ordained. . . ." Then the different classes of people took the oath.' The way was prepared for a smooth transfer of power in the city to the powerful family of Ibn-ad-Dayah, formerly one of Nur-ad-Din's chief advisers. The eldest son, Shams-ad-Din, assumed the position of governor of the city and took up his residence with Jamal-ad-Din in the citadel; his brother, Badr-ad-Din Hassan Ibn-ad-Dayah, was named chief of police. Meanwhile Shihab-ad-Din Ibn-al-Ajami, formerly an official of the treasury, was named the new vizir to the young king. Damascus's claims on the regency were not to go unchallenged. But nor were the ambitions of the Dayah family.

It is reported that as he lay dying Nur-ad-Din said: 'Only one thing causes me unhappiness, the thought of what will befall my family at the hands of Yusuf, son of Aiyub.' Shortly after his kingdom was indeed being plundered, but the aggressor was his own nephew. Saif-ad-Din of Mosul was marching with his army commander, Gümüshtigin, to join his uncle's Egyptian expedition when the news of his death reached him. The army at once divided, a detachment under Gümüshtigin, pushing on to Aleppo to win control of affairs there for Mosul while Saif-ad-Din turned away from the remote prospect of Egypt to the congenial busi-ness of conquest in the now leaderless lands of northern Syria. Sweeping westward, he took Nisibin, Edessa and ar-Raqqa. At Aleppo Gümüshtigin soon established himself among the ruling clique and in June he was made the leader of the delegation to Damascus to bring as-Salih back to Aleppo.

From the moment they had secured themselves the Dayah family had been determined to recover the young king. Shams-ad-Din had written to him, urging him to return to the capital, to supervise the operations against his cousin in al-Jazirah. It seems that the boy, prompted by his mother, favoured the move. Damascus was obliged to recognise Shams-ad-Din as regent and to surrender the heir. In the escort, headed by Gümüshtigin, which took him to Aleppo, were numerous Aleppan nobles who had feared to return before, expecting reprisals from the régime of the Dayah clan. They had no need to worry. Once back with the king firmly in his keeping, Gümüshtigin promptly had the brothers thrown into the city's dungeons. The new régime at Aleppo began to look menacing to Damascus, and the city's rulers looked about for new allies.

At first they, like Nur-ad-Din, had considered Saladin the chief threat to the Zengid establishment. Before evening fell on 15 May a messenger was riding post to Cairo to demand that Saladin recognise as-Salih as suzerain in Egypt as well as in Syria. Whereas the Zengid, Saif-ad-Din, had renounced his allegiance, Saladin ordered that the name of as-Salih be invoked in all the mosques of Egypt and the North African provinces. These loyal formalities were followed by an embassy to Damascus to do homage to the new king. As a telling earnest of the Egyptian ruler's sincerity, it took with it coinage newly minted in Cairo, bearing the inscription of as-Salih.

As Saladin's embassy was being prepared, the rulers of Damascus were reverting to traditional policy and negotiating with the Franks. Immediately the news of Nur-ad-Din's death had reached Jerusalem, King Amalric had seized his chance to march on Banyas, the frontier fortress between the kingdom and Damascus. Ibn-al-Muqaddam hastened to meet the invaders and offered to buy them off handsomely and to release all Frankish prisoners in Damascus. He also pointed out the danger which Egypt could pose to both Syria and Jerusalem and proposed an alliance. The terms suited Amalric's strategy – it seems likely that the campaign had been primarily intended to extract danegeld rather than conquer Damascus – they also suited his inclinations. He was a desperately sick man, dying on 11 July of dysentery, at the age of thirty-eight. Thus by mid-summer, barely two months after the death of the great king of Syria, his dominions were reverting to their constituent parts. Mosul was plundering the territories of Aleppo; Aleppo was preparing to force subjection on Damascus; Damascus was in alliance with the infidels. The death of Amalric, almost miraculously opportune, freed Saladin of the fear of Christian intervention as he prepared to intervene in the crumbling situation in Syria. The interest of Islam required that he put a stop to the opening rivalries; his own interests required that he establish himself before those rivalries should be settled. The rulers of Mosul, Aleppo and Damascus, members of the traditional Turkish ruling class, were agreed on one thing, if on nothing else: that the inheritance of Zengi and Nur-ad-Din should never fall to a mere Kurd, if they could prevent it. As things turned out, their divisions and suspicions were too deep, but to take advantage of their disunity Saladin had to take the initiative on every possible occasion.

When news reached him of Saif-ad-Din's northern conquests he wrote immediately to Damascus demanding to know why he had not been officially informed and his help asked for. He also wrote to 'Imad-ad-Din Zengi, who was the brother of the ruler of Mosul and whom Nur-ad-Din had placed in charge of the neighbouring city of Sinjar. Playing on the young man's jealousy of his brother's conquests, Saladin was able to open a split in the ranks of the Zengid family, which was to prove highly advantageous. In letters to other Syrian towns Saladin deplored the alliance struck between Damascus and Amalric, protesting his own total commitment to the Holy War. It was a propaganda line which had been well used by Nur-ad-Din; few people in Syria would have been unfamiliar with it, and the more cynical must have wondered how long it would last this time. Saladin's *jihad* propaganda was a development of themes first sketched out by Nur-ad-Din's apologists, but they were to be used to greater effect.

In a letter to Damascus he legitimately claimed the right to act as regent. There was no arguing with this – in five years he had proved himself a master in war and politics and was now the greatest figure in the Muslim world. But when he went on to speak of the relations between himself and his overlord, he strained credulity: '. . . if Nur-ad-Din had thought any of you capable of taking my place, or being trusted as he trusted me, he would have appointed that man governor of Egypt, the most important of all his possessions.' But it was precisely Nur-ad-Din's dilemma that although his trust in Saladin had sunk steadily since he became vizir, the king could think of no way of displacing him short of an armed expedition. Still more impudently, the letter continues, 'if death had not prevented him he would have bequeathed to me alone the guardianship and bringing up of his son'. The one thing that death had indisputably prevented Nur-ad-Din doing was to lead an army into Egypt to try conclusions with the man now claiming calmly to have been his most trusted lieutenant and the natural choice for the guardianship. But at this stage in the devolution of Nur-ad-Din's power the focus was the young successor. Isolated still in Egypt by domestic uncertainties, and generally distrusted by the powerful men in Syria, Saladin could do little more for the moment than write letters and protest his loyalty to the Zengid dynasty. Though even now he felt he could risk a few dark hints. 'I perceive that to my hurt you have arrogated to yourselves the care of my master and the son of my master. Assuredly I will come to do him homage and repay the benefits I have received from his father by service which shall be remembered for ever; and I shall deal with each of you according to his work.'

By the end of the summer the rulers of Damascus recognised that the fiery vizir would soon be coming to Syria not just to demonstrate his loyalty to his new king but with the full authority of Nur-ad-Din. Ibn-al-Muqaddam appealed rather desperately to Mosul, but Saif-ad-Din was still pleasantly occupied in securing the provinces he had recently detached from the Syrian kingdom. So, making virtue of necessity, Ibn-al-Muqaddam wrote a formal invitation to Saladin to come to Damascus, and even sent his agents through the city during the preceding weeks to stir up enthusiasm among the populace. This indicates how far out of touch with popular feeling the ruling clique had become, for Saladin's stock stood high with the citizenry at large.

Towards the end of October Saladin set out from Cairo with just 700 picked cavalry, his brother Tughtigin and chancellor al-Fadil. The Franks made no attempt to harass his rapid march through their lands of Transjordan and he was joined on his way by various desert shaikhs and local garrison commanders. Among these were his cousin Nasir-ad-Din, son of Shirkuh, and Sadiq-ibn-Jaulah, master of Busra, who was astonished at the small force the vizir had with him and how little treasure he had brought to bribe the city's officials. But Saladin was travelling light, determined to get to the theatre of action as fast as possible after months of enforced delay. The fact that he was also riding at the direct invitation of the governor of the city was an advantage that he could hardly have hoped for. In these circumstances speed was more important than security, and in any case Saladin was confident of a popular reception. His arrival on 28 October was something of a love feast, with popular demonstrations of welcome beginning while he was still miles from the city walls.

Perhaps the citizens had not forgotten that the vizir's father, Aiyub, had been their governor. Saladin had no intention that they should: the first night he spent in his father's old house. The next day Ibn-al-Muqaddam ordered the gates of the citadel opened. He was removed from his post in favour of Saladin's brother Tughtigin but assured of a profitable appointment in the future. Tughtigin was installed as governor of the city in the name of the young king as-Salih, and during a whirlwind ten-day visit Saladin found time to win the good graces of the city fathers with a more practical and pointed gesture when he abolished the non-canonical taxes, forbidden during the reign of Nur-ad-Din but reimposed by the régime which had claimed so insistently the right to the guardianship of his son. He also received an embassy from Aleppo.

Saladin had sent envoys ahead to Aleppo with a letter protesting his loyalty to as-Salih. 'I come from Egypt in service to you and to fulfil an obligation to my dead master. I beg you to take no notice of the advisers who surround you at the moment; they do not show you the respect due your status and wield your authority for their own ends.' It is difficult to see what, if anything, Saladin hoped to gain by this. The court at Aleppo included numerous powerful and long-standing enemies of his, and the young king seems to have chosen their protection willingly. He certainly had little to gain by putting himself under Saladin's tutelage. The most powerful man in Syria was unlikely to surrender the absolute authority when the time came to end the minority. Aleppo rejected his protestations of loyalty with calculated contempt. The embassy was led by one of the generals who had left Egypt years before in protest at Saladin's appointment as vizir. After he had delivered the king's formal rejection of Saladin's claim to the regency the ambassador launched into a tirade of insults and invective. Accusing Saladin of having come into Syria to usurp the kingdom outright, he went on: 'The swords that once captured Egypt for you are still in our hands and the spears with which you seized the castles of the Fatimids are ready on our shoulders and the men who once resigned your service will now force you to quit Syria. For your arrogance has overreached itself. You! – You are but one of Nur-ad-Din's boys; who needs people like you to protect his son?' They were words to strain the conventions of diplomatic immunity to breaking point, and the ambassador had perhaps Saladin's renowned chivalry to thank that he escaped with his life.

Within days of this explosive interview the Egyptian and Damascene forces were on the road to Aleppo. On 9 December Saladin took the town of Homs, leaving a detachment of troops to contain the garrison of the citadel. From there he marched on to Hamah. The town's governor had played an important role in setting up the new Aleppan régime during the summer, but now he decided to accept Saladin's claims of loyalty to the young king and agreed to go and put his case at Aleppo. If the régime there refused an accommodation he would surrender Hamah. He was arrested on arrival at Aleppo and his brother, left in charge at Hamah, handed the place over to Saladin. By 30 December Saladin was before the walls of Aleppo, prepared for an extended siege. In desperation Gümüshtigin called for help not only from the Franks but also from Sinan, the leader of the heretical Assassin sect based at castle Masyaf in the mountains to the south and west of his beleaguered city.

Gümüshtigin's appeal to Sinan and the latter's agreement are just one more instance of how politics overrode principles and expediency cancelled tradition in twelfth-century Syria. Saladin was soon to make propaganda out of the fact that the rulers of Aleppo who claimed the right to advise the son of Nur-ad-Din did not scruple to ally with his great enemy. But for the time being Saladin's life was endangered by the alliance. One day during the first week of January 1175 a murder gang made its way to the heart of his camp outside Aleppo. Their disguise was not pierced until the last moment and one of them was cut down at the very entrance to the vizir's tent.

Aleppo made a surprisingly determined resistance to Saladin. The ruling clique paraded the young king through the streets to beg the support of the people; with tears in his eyes he implored them to protect him from his father's rebellious servant who had come to rob him of his inheritance. Aleppans were proud to be loyal to the memory and the heir of Nur-ad-Din, whatever they might think of the men who had succeeded to government, and they fought stubbornly. However, when Gümüshtigin relaxed the restrictions on the Shi'ite sect in the city their loyalty was strained. The revised regulations were no doubt part of the price that had to be paid for the alliance with Sinan, and they did guarantee the support of the communal effort by a religious minority, but they did nothing to improve the popularity of the heretical sect. Having appealed to heretics outside the city and placated heretics inside the walls Gümüshtigin prepared to force Saladin to raise his siege by allying with the infidels.

Like the Syrians, the Christians were in the throes of a royal minority, however the regent, Raymond of Tripoli, enjoyed general support in the kingdom and was a competent ruler and administrator. Following the spirit of the alliance that Amalric had agreed with Ibn-al-Muqaddam of Damascus, he now marched against the city of Homs and, in alliance with the garrison of the citadel which still held for Aleppo, opened a diversionary front to relieve the pressure on Aleppo. The force that Saladin had left at Homs could not hope to hold out against the Christian army and the garrison, and rather than lose the city for the sake of an uncertain siege Saladin hurried south. Raymond immediately withdrew from Homs and in mid-March Saladin forced the citadel as well as the city into submission. He then marched on Baalbek, which also capitulated. By April 1175 Saladin was master of Syria from Hamah southwards, and the worst fears of the Zengid ministers in Aleppo were confirmed.

By this time the Egyptian successes were being taken seriously even at Mosul. In the previous year, Saif-ad-Din had refused appeals from Aleppo and Damascus. He did not trust the régimes and was determined to consolidate his hold on the territories he had taken from Aleppo. But now he realised that the future of the whole dynasty was in jeopardy and sent his brother, 'Izz-ad-Din, with a large force to join the western armies. At the same time he marched with the remainder of his army against Sinjar, where his other brother, 'Imad-ad-Din, had gone over to Saladin. The carefully laid alliance with Sinjar was now paying its dividends by diverting part of the Mosul war effort away from the attack on Saladin. But when the allied forces of Aleppo and Mosul made contact with him at Hamah, where he was waiting anxiously for reinforcements from Egypt, it was obvious that he was far outnumbered.

Despite their advantage, however, the allied commanders decided on negotiations. The concessions he at first offered showed just how conscious Saladin was of his weakness, but his enemies also had some difficult calculations to make. Over the thirty years of Nur-ad-Din's reign Aleppo had reversed the traditional supremacy of Mosul and Gümüshtigin had no intention of crushing Saladin only to find himself once again the subordinate of Saif-ad-Din. If he could persuade the Egyptian ruler to renounce his recent conquests without a fight then the army of Mosul would have served its purpose, without winning the initiative in Syria. At first negotiation seemed to promise a quite dazzling success for Aleppo. Saladin agreed to recognise her supremacy, to restore Homs, Hamah and Baalbek, to retain Damascus only as governor for as-Salih, and even to make restitution for the money he had distributed from the royal treasury there to the populace of the city. It looked like a walk-over, always assuming that the Egyptian vizir would have held to the terms once he felt strong enough to challenge them. But the allies pushed their advantage too far when they insisted on one further condition and demanded the cession of Rahba. This town had been among the holdings of Shirkuh that Nur-ad-Din had confiscated. Saladin had restored it to Shirkuh's son, Nasir-ad-Din, and to surrender it now would not only be a complete acceptance of as-Salih's royal prerogatives but, more importantly, would undermine Saladin's position as the head of the Aiyubid dynasty. He had been spinning out the negotiations and using bribery among the enemy commanders to win time for his own reinforcements, led by his nephews Farrukh-Shah and Taqi-ad-Din, to arrive. But with this last demand the negotiations had to break down.

The battle was fought on 13 April. Occupying a twin-peaked hill known locally as the Horns of Hamah, Saladin had the advantage of terrain, but even so he was hard pressed until the reinforcements came up in the nick of time. The enemy were utterly routed and a massacre was only averted by the orders of Saladin, who rode into the thick of the battle to stop the killing. Now it was his turn to dictate terms, and they were surprisingly moderate. All political prisoners in Aleppo were to be released and the Aleppan army was to march under Saladin against the Franks on request, but the young king was to stay at Aleppo under the guardianship of its rulers. Despite his decisive victory in the field Saladin had neither the time nor the resources for the protracted siege that would have been needed to conquer Aleppo. In any case events were flowing in his favour. As-Salih might still be king in Aleppo but his advisers had been forced to recognise Saladin's independent authority in his own territories. He formally renounced his allegiance to the Zengid house and assumed the title of sovereign in his new Syrian lands – the title was soon to be confirmed by the caliph.

The first round in Syria had been won. It was a victory for the interests of Islam as well as for Saladin himself. Of course the Zengid establishment accused him of self-interested *arrivisme*. Appealing to the people of Aleppo, as-Salih had pilloried him as 'this unjust man who aims to relieve me of my town; who repudiates the benefits which my father showered upon him; who has respect for the rights neither of God nor of Man'. Dispatches from the army of Mosul before its defeat at Hamah referred contemptuously to 'this mad dog barking at his master'. In Aleppo the rulers claimed: 'We have lost only the bodily manifestation of Nur-ad-Din, but his spirit is still with us and the All High God will guard his dynasty.' In reply Saladin poured scorn on Damascus and Aleppo, who had bought the friendship of the Franks: 'the treasure of Allah, meant for his cause and the interests of Islam, has been wickedly dissipated, to the anger of God and of all pious Muslims'. The wealth of Aleppo had been given to the infidels and bought lances to pierce Muslim breasts, men who acted like this had ostracised themselves from the community of the faithful. Still worse was their betrayal of the principles of the Faith itself. In Mosul Saif-ad-Din had repealed Nur-ad-Din's prohibition on wine, while in

Aleppo even heretics found favour with the authorities. 'What an astonishing difference there is between those who carry on the struggle against the infidels and those who prefer the friendship of the impious to true believers and who hand over to them their most precious treasures.'

Saladin was able to turn the most unlikely material to propaganda advantage; but what he had to say rang true to many in Aleppo and Damascus who had been disillusioned by the compromising policies of their rulers. So long as the Zengids ruled in Syria and Saladin in Egypt the chances of a common front against the Christians were remote. Saladin claimed that the only reason for his expedition to Syria was to unite Islam and 'put an end to the calamities inflicted by her enemies.' '. . . if this war against the Franks did not necessitate unity it would not matter to me how many princes ruled in Islam'. There were plenty to contest this claim at the time and many who have done so since, but there can be no question that had Saladin not won control of the whole of Nur-ad-Din's inheritance the war against the Franks would have been crippled.

Having now won a de facto authority in Syria Saladin needed it confirmed. He had written to Baghdad to request a diploma recognising his conquests and conferring the title of king, and in the letter set out his credentials as a champion of Islam. He listed his mastery of Egypt and its return to Sunnite allegiance, his victories over the Franks and the recovery of the Yemen and North African territories to the Abbasid allegiance. He claimed that he had entered Syria in the name of the young king as-Salih for 'under her present government Syria would never find order. She needs a man able to lead her to the conquest of Jerusalem.' He concluded with a request for a diploma of investiture with the lands he had conquered and promised that all his future conquests should be in the name of the caliph of Baghdad. This was something that Nur-ad-Din had never guaranteed, and it is interesting to see how important Saladin, regarded by the Turkish establishment as a usurper, rated the approval of the nominal head of the Muslim world. The respect was, with reason, reciprocated. With such a servant as Saladin, acknowledging only the caliphal authority and making no appeal to the Turkish sultanate, the caliph's prestige was immensely strengthened. Saladin phrased his application diplomatically and chose as ambassador Muhammad-al-Baalbekki, reputedly the first man to make the Sunnite invocation in Cairo. In May an official delegation came to him in Hamah bearing the confirmation of his authority in Egypt and his conquests in Syria, and the diplomas, the honorific robes and the black banners of the Abbasid court which confirmed also his royal title. The same year his name was invoked in the mosques of Egypt and Syria and he had the Cairo mint issue coins with the proud inscription, 'al-Malik al-Nasir Yusuf ibn-Aiyub, ala ghaya,' – 'The king, the bringer of victory, Yusuf son of Aiyub, lift high the banner!'

By the end of May Saladin was back in Damascus. His victories had secured him a breathing space to organise his new territories and ensure control of events in Egypt. The Muslims of the north were licking their wounds, and to give himself time to manoeuvre Saladin agreed a truce with the kingdom of Jerusalem. The mediator was Humphrey II of Toron, the revered elder statesman of the kingdom, respected by Saladin since their friendship of eight years before. Sporadic Christian raiding continued, but nothing serious enough to distract Saladin's reorganisation at home.

New governors had to be appointed and the most important posts went to members of the family. Damascus to Taqi-ad-Din, Homs to Nasir-ad-Din, and Hamah to one of Saladin's uncles; the important command at Baalbek, where Aiyub had once laid the fortunes of the family, was given to Ibn-al-Muqaddam, who had been promised a senior post when he surrendered the citadel of Damascus to Saladin the previous year. Affairs in Egypt needed a strong and loyal hand. Saladin dispatched his secretary al-Fadil with the Egyptian expeditionary force back to Cairo and 'Imad-ad-Din took over his duties at Damascus.

Meanwhile, new trouble was brewing to the north. Saif-ad-Din, furious at the disaster of Hamah, was negotiating again with Aleppo to reopen hostilities. The same ambassador was also instructed to go on to Damascus, after fixing an arrangement with Aleppo, to assure Saladin that Mosul would respect the armistice between the two Syrian capitals. According to one source the ambassador, in his official audience with Saladin, handed over not the document intended for the king but Aleppo's reply to the proposed alliance with Mosul. Saladin certainly heard of the coming attack somehow, in time to call up reserves from Egypt.

To prepare for the coming campaign, Gümüshtigin decided to ensure Christian goodwill by releasing Raynald of Chatillon and Joscelin of Courtenay who had been prisoners in Aleppo for the past fifteen years. He next attended a formal reconciliation with Saif-ad-Din of Mosul. As their armies moved south, Saladin moved up to meet them. The two forces made contact on 21 April, about twenty miles to the north-east of Hamah, while Saladin's troops were watering their horses. His enemy scattered and taken totally unawares Saif-ad-Din had victory in the palm of his hand, but he threw it away. With absurd over-confidence, he rejected his staff's advice for an immediate attack. 'Why should we inconvenience ourselves over the destruction of this upstart? Tomorrow will be soon enough.' Saladin was left to occupy the rising ground of Tall as-Sultan at his leisure. At first the battle on the following day went against him, despite the advantage of terrain. His left wing was being pushed back by the troops of Irbil until a counter-charge led by Saladin himself put a stop to the retreat. Then, at the head of his bodyguard, he went over to the attack in that segment of the front and routed the enemy, unprepared for this reversal. Saif-ad-Din barely got off the field and most of his officers were captured. The camp, as Saladin drily observed, was more like a common tavern. His officers recruited the singing girls to their harems while his soldiers drank themselves stupid on the vast stores of wine. Saladin took only a collection of cage birds. They were sent on to the retreating Saif-ad-Din with the recommendation that in future he confine himself to such amusements and retire from the business of war.

Saladin pushed his advantage. Four days after the battle he was again outside the walls of Aleppo, but this time he had no intention of besieging the place. Instead he aimed to isolate it, and marched north-east to the city of Manbij. Its commander was an old enemy but surrendered the town without a fight on the sole condition that he be given a safe conduct for himself and his treasure to Mosul. When he had left there was still an estimated two millions in bullion and treasure left in the city. Generally Saladin kept little booty for himself, preferring to supplement his soldiers' pay with the proceeds, but on this occasion his fancy seems to have been tickled by the fact that some of the plate bore his name, Yusuf, also the name of the governor's favourite son. It seemed to the conqueror too good a joke to miss. 'Yusuf?' he queried. 'That's me, I will take as my share of the plunder all the pieces that appear to have been reserved for me.'

From Manbij he moved west to Azaz. By 21 June it too was in his hands. Aleppo was now menaced to north and west; and now Saladin moved against the capital itself. It looks as though Gümüshtigin had expected his enemy to complete the encirclement of Aleppo by attacking Harim, twenty-five miles to the west of it, for he himself had taken over the command of the garrison there. In fact this may well have been

Saladin's original intention, changed only when he learnt that Gümüshtigin was not in his capital. He opened negotiations almost at once, and within four days, on 29 July, a treaty was signed whereby Aleppo finally acknowledged Saladin's title of king in his conquests. Saladin had won all he could reasonably have looked for. The heir of Nur-ad-Din had been forced to concede regal honours to his father's lieutenant. This, with the confirmation of those honours which Baghdad had already granted, meant that of the crucial quadrilateral of power only Mosul remained in opposition. It was the next objective, but for the time being it could wait.

Saladin concluded his campaign in Aleppan territory with a characteristically courtly gesture. When the treaty negotiations were finished a young girl came to the court to beg a favour of the new king in Syria. She was the sister of as-Salih and she had come to beg for the castle of Azaz so recently conquered. On the far side of Aleppo from Damascus, it would have been a remote fortress to garrison, and the lands around it had already been retroceded to Aleppo in the treaties. Saladin granted it to his young petitioner, loaded her with presents and escorted her back to the gates of Aleppo with his full staff. He would have been within his rights to have held this citadel, even though the surrounding lands had been returned to the dominion of Aleppo; the fact that he did not do so was not an empty gesture, and the way he honoured the princess swelled his growing reputation for chivalry. By relinquishing his hold on Azaz, and by not pressing a siege of Aleppo where he now had a good chance of final victory, Saladin showed that his objective was not to annihilate his opponents in Islam but to force them to acknowledge his claims.

After his triumph at Aleppo he returned to Damascus in late August. In a twelve-day stay there he appointed his elder brother, Turan-Shah, as the new governor and also celebrated his own marriage to one of the great ladies of the city, Asimat-ad-Din. About the same age as the king himself, she had been one of the wives of Nur-ad-Din. The marriage put the seal on Saladin's two-year military and political campaign to win the inheritance of Nur-ad-Din. On 22 September 1176, to a tumultuous welcome, he made his triumphal entry to Cairo.

Five days before, Kilij Arslan of Konya had won a crushing victory over the Byzantine emperor, Manuel. The emperor had aimed to make the roads of Anatolia safe for Christian armies and if he had won on the field of Myriocephalum he would have been the greatest power in northern Syria and the kingdom of Jerusalem could have contemplated a major offensive. As things turned out, one of the greatest armies Constantinople had ever mustered was destroyed and the military machine of the empire set back a generation. The emperor himself compared the disaster to that of Manzikert 105 years before.

Before we leave the account of these two and a half years, so critical in Saladin's career, there is one strange episode still to be dealt with. Chance had removed some of the most serious obstacles to his rise, his own political sense or military prowess had disposed of others, but how the hostility of the sinister Assassins was also neutralised remains something of a mystery. During the siege of Azaz on 22 May Saladin had barely escaped with his life from a second attempt. He had been resting, not in his own tent but that of one of his staff officers, when his first assailant broke in and struck at his head with a knife. The blow glanced off the cap of mail the king wore under his turban; a second blow to the neck cut through the collar of the thick riding tunic he was wearing but was stopped by the mail shirt underneath. Within seconds the king's personal attendant had courageously grasped the knife by the blade so that it cut his fingers to the bone and then killed the man. But two more attackers followed in a kamikaze-style attempt to complete the mission before the guards could come up. Saladin, shocked to be so vulnerable in the heart of his own camp, and also terrified as he frankly admitted later, rode at top speed for the headquarters compound. The enquiry that followed revealed, unnervingly enough, that the three had been able to enrol in the personal bodyguard of the king without questions asked.

From this time Saladin was to sleep in a specially constructed wooden tower bunk inside his tent. He also determined to rout the Assassins out of their mountain stronghold at Masyaf. He opened the operation with systematic pillaging of the surrounding country and then laid siege to the castle. Sinan himself was away at the time and hurried back when the king's summons for surrender reached him. He demanded an immediate interview with Saladin and then, with only two companions, retired to the top of a hill overlooking the besieging army and awaited developments. Thinking he at last had the old man in his power, Saladin sent troops and messengers to kill or arrest him, but they returned with frightening tales of powerful magic that made their weapons powerless. The king himself now began to fear whether his enemy was something more than mortal, but took the precaution of surrounding the approaches to his tent with chalk dust and cinders to record the steps of any intruder. A few nights later the king awoke to see a shadowy figure glide out of his tent. Some hot scones baked in a shape characteristic of the sect's bread were on his pillow and beside them, pinned to it by a poisoned dagger, was a note with a mystical threat to his life. There was no sign of footsteps outside the tent. Saladin was convinced that Sinan had visited him that night and sent to beg him to pardon his former errors and grant him a safe conduct out of his lands. This was granted only when the siege of Masyaf was raised.

Apart from the magical element in this account, which is based on the version of a biographer of Sinan, it is worth noticing that Nur-ad-Din in his attempts to stamp out the Assassins was the prey to a similar nocturnal visit complete with poisoned dagger and warning note. There were orthodox Muslims who believed in the magical powers of Sinan, and the incredible feats of mind over matter still performed by similar sects today easily explain how people came to fear and avoid their medieval predecessors. Saladin did call off the siege of Masyaf, only days after mounting it, for no identifiable military reason, and he never again suffered the attentions of Sinan.

Maybe he knew when to concede a point. Maybe, in the time-honoured cliché of the officer corps, he 'knew how to handle men' – opponents as well as friends. The career of Ibn al-Muqaddam is a case in point. As Nur-ad-Din's governor in Damascus he had at first held the city against Saladin but then yielded the place to him and became his loyal man until death, even though he was removed from his post in favour of Saladin's nominee. It was to be expected, of course, but clearly the transfer was handled with due concern for the deposed governor's feelings and he accepted the demotion without resentment. In due course he was given the governorship of Baalbek, Saladin's childhood home city, and a few years later we find him leading the Damascus *Hajj* as the proud representative of the liberator of Jerusalem. In fact he died in a skirmish to defend his lord's prestige against the representative of the caliph. The ability to inspire rather than enforce loyalty is a critical quality of leadership. Few men defected from the service of Saladin once they had made their commitment to him.

# Chapter 8

# Triumph in the North

Saladin marched out of Egypt once again as a champion of the *jihad* on 18 November 1177. His spies had told him that the alliance between the Franks and the Byzantines had broken down and also that Count Philip of Flanders, whose arrival in the summer had seemed to threaten the Muslims, had no serious military intentions. As the Egyptian army moved up the coast to Palestine it seemed at first to be aiming for Gaza. The Templars, who garrisoned the place, called up all available reserves only to see the enemy march past on the road to Ascalon. King Baldwin, with 500 knights and the bishop of Bethlehem, was able to get into the fortress before Saladin arrived. The king sent out urgent messages for reinforcements but, leaving a small force to hem in the royal army, Saladin marched confidently on Jerusalem. The road was wide open, the Christians had been divided and decoyed to positions away to the rear of the fast-moving attack. The army was jubilant at the prospect of reconquering the Holy City, and Saladin, pleased at the success of his manoeuvre, relaxed the usually strict discipline. At an uncertain location known to William of Tyre as 'Mons Gisardi' and as the 'Battle of Ramla' by Arab sources, the carefree *razzia* was to be routed.

Young King Baldwin the Leper now roused his kingdom to a heroic effort. A message was smuggled through the Muslim blockade of Ascalon, ordering the Templars at Gaza to join the royal army. When they arrived Baldwin and his knights were able to break out of the encirclement and the combined forces thundered up the road to Ibelin and there turned inland towards Jerusalem. 'Howling like dogs' down the rugged ravines, they took the scattered Egyptian army completely by surprise. Saladin barely escaped with his life; whole detachments were slaughtered where they stood; thousands of others fled in terror without any thought of taking up their battle formations. In headlong flight southwards, they abandoned camp, booty, prisoners and even their weapons. It was a crucial Christian victory. With Jerusalem at his mercy Saladin had held the fate of the kingdom in his hand, but his own over-confidence and the lightning recovery of the Christians had transformed a triumph for the *jihad* into humiliating defeat. The Egyptians were harassed by Bedouin as they struggled back across Sinai, and Saladin, knowing the blow his prestige had suffered, sent messengers ahead on racing camels to Cairo to proclaim his safety and return. From the capital the news was broadcast through the country by pigeon post, and the possibility of rebellion was averted. The Egyptians were back in force in Palestine the next year – but the capture of Jerusalem had been put back a decade.

Baldwin was not strong enough to march on Damascus and so undo all Saladin's progress in Syria, but he did strengthen his own frontiers. Humphrey of Toron, the constable and one of the kingdom's most revered elder statesmen, built a fortress on the Hill of Hunin that commanded the road from Banyas to his castle. The king built a new fortification on the upper Jordan overlooking an important crossing known as Jacob's Ford. It was on sensitive territory. The local peasantry who owed allegiance to Damascus or Jerusalem depending on the side of the river they had their homes used the ford regularly to take their flocks from one grazing to another. Treaty agreements governed the place and the Franks had promised never to fortify it. For this reason Baldwin, despite his great victory, was reluctant to take action which could only be provocative. Urged on by the Templars, however, he did go ahead with the building. The fortress, by militarising a 'friendly' stretch of the frontier, angered Baldwin's own subjects amongst the peasant population as well as those of Damascus. Soon they were appealing to Saladin to force the Christians to abide by their treaty obligations. It was a bad time to ask his help for he was rearranging the administration at Damascus.

His brother Turan-Shah, the governor of Damascus, had been lax in his duties and had also been on suspiciously good terms with as-Salih at Aleppo. Saladin installed his nephew Farrukh-Shah as the new governor, and, much against his will, pacified his brother with the lord-ship of Baalbek – even though for the past three years it had been loyally held by Ibn-al-Muqaddam. With things so unsettled in his high command, Saladin was unwilling to risk a campaign to satisfy peasant petitioners. Instead he offered to buy the king off with 60,000 gold pieces; when this was refused, he upped the offer to 100,000, and when the Christians still refused to dismantle their castle he warned them it would be destroyed and swore an oath to settle the affair as soon as events were propitious.

In the spring of the next year, 1179, the seasonal movement of flocks across Jacob's Ford sparked off the war that was bound to come sooner or later. King Baldwin, based at the new castle, was preparing to round up the flocks and in April Saladin sent Farrukh-Shah with a small force to reconnoitre. In fact they came on the Christians unexpectedly and, attacking promptly, came near to destroying the army and capturing the king. Thanks to a heroic rearguard by Humphrey of Toron, he did escape, but Humphrey himself was mortally wounded and died a few days later at the castle of Hunin. Even his Muslim enemies had respected the grand old man, and his death was a severe blow to Christian morale. Once again Saladin, perhaps caught unprepared by the unexpected success, felt unable to follow up the victory. He laid siege to the castle at Jacob's Ford but withdrew after only a few days to his base at Banyas. From there he sent out detachments of troops to plunder the harvest from Sidon to Beirut while Baldwin moved in force to Toron, across the river from Saladin's headquarters, to deal with the raiders on their return.

Scouts soon brought the Christian leaders news of a plundering party moving slowly south from Sidon under the command of the redoubtable Farrukh-Shah. It was the ideal opportunity to pay off an old score, and the Christians moved up to intercept the isolated column, laden with booty and flushed with success, sure of an easy victory. The armies met in the Valley of the Springs between the Litani river and the upper waters of the Jordan. The king quickly scattered the Muslims while the Templars and a force led by Raymond of Tripoli moved on up the valley, screening the action of the royal troops and reconnoitring the ground for an advance into Muslim territory. Even an attack on Damascus itself must have seemed a possibility. In fact at the head of the valley the Christian advance guard found itself face to face with the main Muslim army commanded by Saladin. Keeping a keen look-out for his raiding parties, which he knew would be vulnerable on their return, he had seen the herds on the opposite side of the Jordan stampeding and had guessed that they had been disturbed by the Christian army on the march. Rapidly mobilising his men he had gone out to the rescue.

Although the Christians had been taken by surprise, the result of the coming battle was by no means a foregone conclusion. The Muslim army was fresh, but so were the Templars and Tripolitans that faced them. Down the valley Baldwin's force had dispersed Farrukh-Shah's men and needed only time to re-form to meet the new threat. Had the Christian advance guard stood firm the whole army might systematically have been brought to bear on Saladin. As it was, the Templars charged haphazard the moment the enemy was sighted. Soon they were being rolled back down the valley on to the disordered, though victorious, troops of Baldwin. In the rout that followed some of the Christian fugitives made their way to safety and the coast while the king and Count Raymond of Tripoli were able to bring part of the army to the crusader castle of Beaufort on the west bank of the Litani. Hundreds stranded on the east bank were massacred or taken prisoner. The dimensions of the disaster were measured by the many noble prisoners taken. Among them was the master of the Temple, who contemptuously refused an offer of his freedom in exchange for one of Saladin's captured emirs, declaring that the Muslim world could not boast a man that was his equal. He died at Damascus the following year. Of the other distinguished prisoners Baldwin of Ibelin was released in exchange for 1,000 Muslim prisoners-of-war and a promise to find a ransom of 150,000 gold pieces.

It had been a great victory yet Saladin did not feel able to push his advantage too far. The royal army had been scattered but a relief force led by Raymond of Sidon, though it had been too late to join the battle, was still in the field. The troops in Beaufort formed the nucleus round which the fugitives could rally; the garrisons at Hunin and Jacob's Ford were still intact and in addition news reached Saladin of the arrival of a large body of knights from Europe led by Henry II of Champagne. But Saladin did decide to fulfil the oath he had taken to destroy the castle at Jacob's Ford. In the last days of August 1179 the place was overrun, the garrison put to the sword and the fortifications levelled to the ground. The chivalrous company from France proved more interested in pilgrimage than sieges and returned to France. Once more Saladin's operations in Palestine lapsed and the only offensive for the rest of the year was a dramatic raid by the Egyptian fleet on the shipping in the harbour at Acre. It was a tribute to the fighting efficiency of Saladin's new model fleet and cost the Christians a good deal in merchandise and vessels, but it had little impact on the campaign.

The year 1180 opened with a highly successful raid into Galilee. But neither side was much interested in continuing hostilities. A drought during the winter and early spring threatened both. King Baldwin's offers of truce were accepted by Saladin, and in May a two-year truce was signed. Hostilities with Tripoli continued for a while – the Egyptian navy made a successful raid on the port of Tortosa but Saladin was repulsed in a foray inland in al-Buqai'ah. Soon after this he came to terms with Raymond and turned his attention northwards.

He had been called on to intervene in a dispute between Nur-ad-Din Muhammad, prince of Hisn Kaifa, and Kilij Arslan the Selchük ruler of Konya. Nur-ad-Din owed his throne at Hisn Kaifa to the patronage of his great namesake. His father had died when he was still young, and the town had been in danger of coming under the domination of Mosul, then ruled by Qutb-ad-Din, brother of the lord of Aleppo. The great Nur-ad-Din had held his brother back and protected the young prince, but Hisn Kaifa still had reason to distrust Mosul and on Nur-ad-Din's death had allied with Saladin. The young Nur-ad-Din had also taken to wife one of the daughters of Kilij Arslan but had subsequently treated her so badly that her father was threatening to march and take reprisals. The approach of Saladin's army from Syria was enough to pacify the angry sultan of Konya, and he even sent an envoy to discuss long-term peace with the new king of Syria. A conference at Samosata on the Euphrates, held we are told in October, settled a two-year truce. This, with the agreement he had already reached with the Christians, gave Saladin time to stabilise his position in Egypt and confirm his hold on Syria.

Arriving in Cairo early in 1181, he spent the rest of that year engrossed in Egyptian affairs, but important developments were soon to draw him north again. During the summer the Frankish lord of al-Karak, Raynald of Chatillon, broke the truce, and in December as-Salih died at Aleppo. The career of Raynald explodes erratically over the next six years, with disastrous effect for the Christian cause, and during that time Saladin learnt to hate him with a personal intensity that he rarely showed towards his enemies. A brief look at the man's antecedents will help to explain why this should have been so.

Raynald came to the Middle East in the train of Louis VII of France, on the ill-fated Second Crusade. The younger son of a minor French noble, he had no prospects at home and decided to stay on in Palestine in the service of King Baldwin III. He was the typical European newcomer. Bigoted in religion, insensitive to diplomacy, land hungry and brutal, he made a promising start as a robber baron in the best Western tradition. He was young, well built, and a brave soldier, and he caught the eye of Constance, princess of Antioch. The marriage of this young adventurer to the greatest heiress in the Frankish East raised a few eyebrows, but Raynald soon proved his soldierly competence by extending the frontier of the principality of Antioch. In a rapid campaign against the Armenian prince, Toros, he reconquered the territory round the port of Alexandretta and handed it over to the Order of the Temple. This was the beginning of a friendship between the prince and the knights that was to have momentous consequences for the Christian states.

It was also a snub for the Byzantine emperor, Manuel, who claimed suzerainty in Antioch. Worse was soon to follow. The emperor, a loyal and valuable friend of the Latin states, had resigned himself to Raynald's marriage and had offered to subsidise him if he would fight for the empire against the Armenians. Raynald considered his side of the bargain fulfilled by the Alexandretta campaign, which had in fact cost him little and had benefited nobody but himself and the Templars, but Manuel now refused to pay the promised subsidy until the Armenians had been thoroughly beaten or the empire had received some tangible advantage. Raynald always found deeply repugnant the notion that treaties he signed could lay obligations on him. Furious at what he saw as Manuel's double-dealing, he promptly teamed up with Toros, recently his enemy, for an invasion of Cyprus. The new allies were temporarily hampered by shortage of funds but Raynald solved this simply enough by torturing, in a particularly bestial manner, the patriarch of Antioch. In a month of rapine and pillage Cyprus was so effectively devastated and the population so terrorised that two years later the Egyptian fleet, traditionally wary in Cypriot waters, was able to plunder there at will.

Four years later, in the late autumn of 1160, Raynald was on a raid in Nur-ad-Din's territory. Returning, loaded with booty, he and his army were overwhelmed in an ambush. Raynald was taken prisoner and held at Aleppo for sixteen years, being released in an exchange of prisoners late in 1175. His first wife had died while he was in prison, yet, now in his fifties, he soon won himself another rich bride, the heiress of the frontier province of Transjordan and the great castle of al-Karak which glowered over the caravan and pilgrim routes from Damascus to Mecca.

From the moment Baldwin and Saladin signed the truce of May 1180 al-Karak was a potential flash-point. To Raynald it seemed outrageous that, thanks to appeasement politics, Muslim merchants should be able to pass unmolested. The fact that the kingdom, torn by political intrigue and harassed by the drought and famines of early 1180, needed the respite was quite beside the point. In the summer of 1181 he led a detachment out of al-Karak south-east to the oasis town of Taima' in Arabia on the Mecca road where, as he learnt from his spies, a major caravan, virtually without escort, was to halt. The Christians took rich plunder and many prisoners. Saladin first demanded compensation from Baldwin, but the king was not able to force Raynald to make restitution. In the autumn a convoy of Christian pilgrims was forced by bad weather to take shelter in the port of Damietta, not realising the strained international situation. They disembarked and were promptly imprisoned to be held as hostages until Raynald should disgorge his plunder. When he still proved adamant, the pilgrims were sold into slavery and Saladin prepared to take reprisals.

The death of the eighteen-year-old as-Salih at Aleppo in December was another reason to move north. There were two obvious candidates for the succession, both grandsons of the great Zengi and both cousins of as-Salih; they were 'Izz-ad-Din, the new ruler of Mosul, and his brother 'Imad-ad-Din of Sinjar. As he lay dying of a mysterious stomach illness – which some ascribed to poison – the talented young ruler had debated the question of his heir with the council; it was divided into two factions. The Turkish party, anxious to secure a strong Zengid succession, naturally urged the case for 'Izz-ad-Din, the strongest member of the family. The Arabs, and no doubt others, were alarmed that Aleppo, so recently the mistress of all Syria, should be subject to her ancient rival. They argued for 'Imad-ad-Din, who was also as-Salih's brother-in-law – 'your father loved him much, treated him with affection and concerned himself with his education'. But as-Salih, more interested in his dynasty's prospects than in sentimentalising the past, argued with the Turks in favour of 'Izz-ad-Din. He pointed out that 'Imad-ad-Din had only the resources of Sinjar and could do little against the might of Saladin: 'If this man be not stopped, there will not remain a single plot of land in the possession of our family.' Leading members went to swear their fealty to 'Izz-ad-Din while the 'Arab' party wrote secretly to his brother.

According to the chronicler Kamal-ad-Din, the most influential minister at Aleppo was Jamal-ad-Din Shadbakht, governor of the citadel. He got wind of the Arabs' dealings and ordered them to take the oath of loyalty to 'Izz-ad-Din; they complied, realising that little was to be expected from Sinjar. Once installed at Aleppo, 'Izz-ad-Din dispensed largesse to his supporters and penalties to his opponents and gave bounty to the population at large; he also guaranteed the customs

of Nur-ad-Din and as-Salih and retained Jamal-ad-Din in the administration. No doubt to strengthen the legitimacy of his take-over, the new
ruler married the widowed mother of as-Salih, and sent her under
escort to Mosul.

He then took possession of all the treasures in the citadel together
with arms and machines of war in the arsenal and sent it all to ar-
Raqqa. He soon moved there himself, making it his headquarters for
the spring. It is obvious that 'Izz-ad-Din's primary interest was the
security of his own state of Mosul and not in mobilising it and Aleppo
in a joint axis against Saladin. He wrote to his brother 'lmad-ad-Din
demanding that he cede Sinjar to him in exchange for Aleppo. The
bargain was struck and 'Imad took up his new command, bringing with
him his treasure and armoury to replace some part of the depleted
reserves of Aleppo. When he heard of the transfer of power, Saladin
was delighted that the great city was now in the hands of a ruler who
'has neither arms nor money' and who had until recently been Saladin's
ally. He was also bitterly incensed that a city, which he claimed by right
of a caliphal diploma, should have been taken by another while
Saladin's own army was actually defending the city of the prophet from
the infidels. In his letter to the caliph complaining of 'Izz-ad-Din's
take-over and arguing against its legitimacy, he wrote: 'If the exalted
commands should ordain that the prince of Mosul be invested with the
government of Aleppo, then it were better to invest him with all Syria
and Egypt as well.'

On 11 May 1182 Saladin marched out of Cairo with an army of 5,000
troops. There were elaborate formal leave-takings between the vizir and
his ministers, and a soothsayer in the crowd called out a verse prophet-
ically interpreted to mean that the vizir would never again return to the
city that for thirteen years had been his capital. He took the route across
Sinai to al-Aqaba and then headed north-east to avoid the Christian
army which had been stationed at Petra to intercept his march. Not only
did he successfully evade battle, he was able to send out pillaging raids
into the district around ash-Shaubak. King Baldwin had been
persuaded to march the main army of the kingdom into Transjordan by
Raynald of Chatillon. No doubt, as a contemporary alleged, his real
motive was to protect as much as possible of his own lands from the
vengeance of Saladin; it was hardly sound strategy to take the main
Christian army so far from the kingdom proper. Saladin's deputy at
Damascus, his nephew Farrukh-Shah, was a commander of proved
ability and, acting under instructions from the high command, seized

the opportunity to raid in Galilee, plundering Daburiya and numerous other places in the neighbourhood of Nazareth. He was also able to recapture the important fort of Habis Jaldak, twenty miles east of Jordan and an irritant long overdue for removal.

Farrukh-Shah's activities fulfilled precisely the warnings that had been given by Raymond of Tripoli, who had urged that the army should remain to protect the heartlands of the kingdom and not be drawn away by the marching of the Egyptian army or the importunities of trouble-maker Raynald. Like his supporters at the time, modern historians have tended to applaud Raymond for a statesmanlike sense of strategy and condemn Raynald. While there is no doubt that the activities of the egregious Raynald forced retaliation out of Saladin where none had been intended, and so brought war on the kingdom at the time it was least able to cope, the strategy of May 1182 was not so easy and straight-forward as it is made to appear. First, to the charge that Raynald was using the forces of the kingdom to protect his own territories, his supporters could quite fairly retort that since Galilee was the domain of Raymond's wife, the count of Tripoli's motives might not be entirely altruistic. Secondly, the customs of the kingdom laid on the monarch the obligation of coming to the aid of any vassal under attack from the Infidel, and at the beginning of the campaign this was certainly Raynald. Thirdly, the lands of Transjordan were no less vital, though only frontier provinces, to the Christian cause as a whole than were the lands of Galilee.

The fact was that Saladin's superior resources and their strategic positions enabled him to strike at will along the frontiers of the kingdom. Although not as yet strong enough to deal the decisive blow, he was able to orchestrate a series of damaging raids in Christian terri-tory – seven in the decade 1177 to 1187. The comparative frequency of these *razzias* into infidel territory helped build the image of Saladin as a champion of the Holy War, they also contributed significantly to the weakening of the Frankish state. Land leases occasionally contained clauses exempting the tenant from rent for a period in which the crops had been laid waste by enemy action, and many a lord found himself forced to sell property to raise the ransoms for kinsfolk or tenants captured in the Muslim raids.

After his successful march up from al-Aqaba, Saladin joined his nephew and the two left Damascus, on 11 July, heading south round Lake Tiberias into the kingdom. They made contact with the Christians, who had called up reinforcements from the garrisons of the castles in the area, at the Hospitallers' castle of Belvoir, also called Kaukab al-Hawa'. A running fight developed in which the Muslim horse archers did their best to lure the Franks into an all-out attack, while the Christians were content to hold their formation and so deny the enemy freedom of action. The fighting was spasmodic it seems, though occasionally very fierce, and when the engagement was broken off the result was inconclusive enough for both sides to claim a victory.

Next month Saladin was again on the warpath; this time against the northern port of Beirut. He had called up his Egyptian fleet by pigeon post but the amphibious attempt failed – the garrison at Beirut held out long enough for King Baldwin to come to its aid, and Saladin withdrew. He had ordered a diversionary raid by his Egyptian troops in southern Palestine, but the Franks had ignored the tactic and thrown the whole of their army against the main enemy in the north. It had been a vigorous campaigning season and from Saladin's point of view a successful one. In five coordinated attacks by various divisions of his forces he had probed the kingdom's frontier from south to north; the Christians had been on the defensive throughout the summer and they had suffered considerable damage from his expeditions.

It was a pattern which had been seen a number of times during the recent fighting. In the next few years there were to be those, even among his friends, who criticised Saladin's apparent slowness in dealing with the Franks – the same thing had been said of Nur-ad-Din. But Saladin's failure to follow up even decisive victories over the Christians was, in part, to be blamed on the fact that he had always to keep an eye on the situation at his back. Since as-Salih's death in December 1181, events had followed the very course which the young king had feared when he tried to ensure the succession of the powerful 'Izz-ad-Din. What remained of the kingdom of Nur-ad-Din was threatening to fall apart at the seams, the power of the Zengid house was being quickly fractured and only Saladin could profit. In the late summer of 1182, as he nursed his disappointment over Beirut, opportunities were opening up in northern Syria which seemed likely to lead to a decisive initiative for him.

The rivalry between 'Izz-ad-Din and his brother 'Imad-ad-Din and their confused negotiations had offered the lesser powers in the area fascinating opportunities for politicking at the expense of their once all-powerful neighbours, Mosul and Aleppo. The lord of Harran, a discontented vassal of 'Imad-ad-Din, drew the rulers of Hisn Kaifa and al-Birah into an alliance against Mosul. Next the allies invited Saladin to cross the Euphrates in the assurance of their support. Their messenger reached him, encamped with his army before the walls of Aleppo. Early in October he crossed the Euphrates and began a triumphant progress through al-Jazirah. Edessa, Saruj and Nisibin quickly submitted and on 10 November he was before Mosul preparing for a prolonged siege. The objective was, and remained, to force 'Izz-ad-Din to admit Saladin's suzerainty and to supply troops on request for the Holy War as Mosul had supplied Nur-ad-Din. Although Saladin persistently demanded a caliphal diploma to this effect, he never asked for the outright lordship of Mosul.

Saladin pointed out that 'Izz-ad-Din was not only financing the Christians to attack him in Syria but was also in alliance with the Selchük ruler of Persian Armenia, one of Baghdad's arch enemies. The caliph was more concerned to take the heat out of a situation that was uncomfortably near his own frontiers. He sent a mediator to settle the terms on which Mosul should collaborate with Saladin. The negotiations broke down over the question of Aleppo, which 'Izz-ad-Din refused to surrender. It was as well that Saladin had to sever his dealings with Mosul since the very fact of the negotiations was troubling his allies a good deal. They had only dared their independent initiative because of the rift that had opened between Aleppo and Mosul – a deal over their heads between Saladin and 'Izz-ad-Din was the last thing they wanted. With diplomacy now at a standstill, Saladin could have been expected to press his offensive but was persuaded by the caliph's representative to abandon the siege. He withdrew to Sinjar, the town that Mosul had won back only months before by trading off Aleppo. After a siege of a fortnight it fell, and Saladin's army, possibly restless after being, as they saw it, cheated of the rich spoils of Mosul, sacked the place with uncharacteristic thoroughness and brutality. The governor was spared and sent with an honourable escort back to Mosul, but the fall of Sinjar had been a severe blow to 'Izz-ad-Din's prestige and he led his forces out on the road to Sinjar in a show of strength. The effect faltered when he sent further offers of a truce to Saladin and when these were turned down because the wanted concessions over Aleppo were still withheld, the Mosul army returned ignominiously to its base.

Throughout his campaign Saladin had kept up diplomatic pressure on Baghdad to grant official recognition to his claim of suzerainty over Mosul. It was consistently refused, but he was granted the diploma for Diyar-Bakr and late in January 1183 marched against it. After a three-week siege it fell and was given as a fief to Nur-ad-Din of Hisn Kaifa. The city held one of the most famous libraries in Islam and Saladin gave his secretary al-Fadil carte blanche to remove the volumes he wished. Even a caravan of seventy camels could take only some of the treasures to Damascus. It is a measure not only of the magnificence of the collection but of the gulf that divided the culture of the West from that of Islam – in twelfth-century Europe the contents of a great library were to be measured in scores rather than hundreds.

At the end of 1182, with Saladin fully committed to his campaign against Mosul and Aleppo, Raynald mounted an audacious expedition southwards towards the heart of Saladin's domains. He took al-Aqaba, which had been in Muslim hands since Saladin captured the place twelve years before. While he himself blockaded the island fortress opposite the port, he launched a fleet of prefabricated ships which had been transported overland from al-Karak. They mounted an expedition down the Sinai peninsula and into the Red Sea; it raided along the African coast and sacked the port of 'Aidhab opposite Jedda. The merchant shipping in the harbour was plundered and an overland caravan from the Nile valley was routed as it approached the town. Next, with considerable élan the Christian pirates carried the attack to the coast of Arabia, raiding the ports which served Mecca and Medina and sinking a pilgrim ship. For a time even Mecca seemed in danger.

But the danger was more apparent than real. Thanks to Saladin's naval reforms Egypt was well prepared. His brother, al-Adil, the governor, promptly dispatched a fleet to deal with the marauders. Al-Aqaba was recaptured and the Christian fleet taken; in military terms the whole expedition, which had occupied less than a month, had been a fiasco. It had also proved that Egypt was quite able to look after itself and that Saladin had complete freedom of movement in his huge empire, sure in the competence of his lieutenants. Nevertheless, Raynald had touched a raw nerve in Saladin's self-esteem. His image of himself as the protector of the Holy Places and the pilgrim routes and his reputation as such in Islam had been tarnished. It is not surprising that his reaction was far stronger than the military danger warranted. Batches of the prisoners were taken for ceremonial execution at the Place of Sacrifice at Mina in Mecca, at Cairo and at Alexandria, where they were escorted by triumphant processions of sufis and other religious enthusiasts who carried out the killings. The picture is as ugly as any Frankish atrocity, but in an age when civilisation and barbarity walked comfortably hand in hand the propaganda value of such public punishment of the Christian sacrilege was of course considerable.

Because the raid had dared to aim at the holiest places of Islam, Saladin's chancellery was able to make immense capital out of it, even though it had failed. He himself was having to campaign against Muslims because they were allied with the Infidel. Every aspect of the episode was exploited in the propaganda of the Holy War. Raynald and his men were compared to the 'companions of the elephant', a group of Abyssinians who, according to the Koran, had attacked Mecca in the days before the Hegira. Political capital was certainly made out of it, but the Red Sea expedition did also provoke a response of genuine horror from the Muslim community. The Spanish traveller Ibn-Jubair, who was journeying in the Middle East at the time, records the impressions the event made, and the *jihad* literature of the thirteenth century abounds with eulogies of Saladin for his part in the protection of the sacred sites of pilgrimage from the impious designs of Raynald.

Hoping perhaps that the swell of public opinion in his favour would reinforce his application, Saladin wrote again, after the capture of Diyar-Bakr, to beg Baghdad's official sanction for his campaign against Mosul. It was, he said, the fact that the attack on Diyar-Bakr had had the authorisation of the head of the Faith that had 'opened the gates of the city to him'. The same would assuredly happen at Mosul, and the obstinacy of this one city was all that now stood between Islam and triumph over the Franks. 'Let the commander of the Faithful but compare the behaviour of his servants [i.e. Saladin and 'Izz-ad-Din] and judge which of them has most faithfully served the cause of Islam.' If, the letter continues, it be asked why Saladin, already so powerful, demands the supreme authority in al-Jazirah, the Lesser Mesopotamia controlled by Mosul, it is because 'this little al-Jazirah is the lever which will set the great al-Jazirah [i.e. the whole of the Islamic Middle East] in motion. It is the point of division and the centre of resistance and once it is set in its place in the chain of allegiance the whole armed might of Islam will be coordinated to engage the forces of Unbelief.' He might have added that the fertile region between the upper waters of the Tigris and Euphrates had been the recruiting ground of the armies of Zengi and had provided vital manpower to Nur-ad-Din. Saladin could not rely exclusively on the manpower of Egypt because its own extended frontiers now demanded a sizeable standing army.

The petition was as unsuccessful as former ones, but the victory at Diyar-Bakr brought the ruler of Mardin and other cities behind Saladin. Having handed over the cities of al-Jazirah to loyal emirs and demonstrated the inability of Mosul to defend even its own interests, let alone those of its allies, he marched on Aleppo, arriving before its walls on 21 May 1183.

As the siege began the garrison made a number of hard-fought sorties, during one of which Saladin's youngest brother, the twenty-two-year-old Taj-al-Mulk Böri, was killed. It was a serious loss for Saladin, who depended heavily on his family in the administration of his domains; but he also loved the boy. In later years, full of remorse, he told Baha'-ad-Din: 'We did not win Aleppo cheaply, for it cost the life of Böri.' If Kamal-ad-Din, the historian of Aleppo, is to be believed, there was also unrest in the army. The poor harvests and arrears in their pay led to grumbling among men and officers which came dangerously near to mutiny. Saladin, it appears, while pointing out that his personal resources were few, promised them rich pickings from Aleppo and its territory once the place was won. The reply he got was curt enough.' Who wants to take Aleppo? If the sultan would but sell the jewels and finery of his wives we should have money enough.' And so, we are told, the sultan did as demanded and paid his troops with the proceeds of the sale.

Kamal-ad-Din, who wrote his history of Aleppo some thirty years after the events described, is our only source for this odd story. Saladin's plea of personal poverty rings true enough. Enemies have accused him of buying popularity, admirers ascribe it to his great-hearted generosity of nature, but no writer on Saladin has ever denied that his distribution of the plunder of war was lavish compared with the practice of other commanders and far in excess of what the military conventions required. The reference to his wives is intriguing because so little is known of Saladin's private life. If we are really to believe that a sale of their personal effects was enough to satisfy an army's demand for back pay he must have been uxorious indeed. But the context suggests that the story is merely a fiction by the Aleppan historian to balance the genuine quandary facing the ruler of the city with a corresponding dilemma in the camp of the enemy.

For 'Imad-ad-Din's troops certainly were demanding their pay – and he had other problems. Although he had been installed at Aleppo on his brother's authority he was little liked by the Turkish party among the emirs who had originally opposed his succession, nor had his brother

greatly helped his prospects by clearing out the armoury and the treasury. Discussing the situation with Tuman, his close adviser who had
come with him from Sinjar, he confessed himself at a loss. Before
making his proposals he asked for a promise that they would be treated
in absolute confidence, for, he went on, 'if the emirs learnt a single word
of our conversation they would start a rising and the affair would turn
against us.' In fact he intended that they should use Aleppo as a
bargaining counter to extricate themselves from what was rapidly
becoming an impossible situation. For the plan to work the town would
have to be surrendered while it still appeared to have some chance of
survival. Secret negotiations were opened with Saladin. He not only
offered 'Imad-ad-Din Sinjar in exchange for Aleppo, but also Nisibin,
Saruj and even ar-Raqqa, where the treasures and armaments of Aleppo
had been housed. For 'Imad-ad-Din, who had only reluctantly surrendered Sinjar at his brother's urgings, the deal was a good one, and on
the morning of 11 June the defenders were dumbfounded to see the
yellow banners of Saladin break out on the battlements.

The Aleppan emirs who had been opposed to Saladin ever since his
arrival in Syria now feared they would lose their fiefs; the population at
large feared they would lose their lives. The *rais* (or mayor), with a
group of city elders, went up to the citadel to protest against the
surrender, but 'Imad-ad-Din, wisely not coming out to meet them,
returned the scornful message: 'The thing is settled.' The capitulation
was in fact immensely valuable to Saladin. Aleppo was virtually impregnable and Saladin was no master of siege warfare. Had 'Imad-ad-Din
been as determined as the citizens, Saladin might have had to be content
with the kind of deal he eventually struck with Mosul, where the ruler
recognised his suzerainty but retained his own position in the city. As it
was, 'the thing was settled'.

The garrison and citizenry hurriedly made up a joint deputation
which met Saladin during the ceremony of surrender at the Green
Hippodrome. They were astonished and delighted at his reaction. The
officers and commanders of the defeated garrison received robes of
honour for the boldness of the defence and the city was spared a sack.
Secure now in the good graces of their new master, the population
poured their contempt on the outgoing governor. Before he left, a
fuller's bowl was presented to him with the words 'Royalty was not
meant for you; this is the only trade you are fit for.' (Stale urine was one
of the standard bleaches of the medieval fuller.)

Of Aleppo's dependencies only Harim still held out. Its governor tried for help from Frankish Antioch, but this time the traditional manoeuvre disgusted public opinion. The governor was deposed and the city was formally made over to Saladin on 22 June. He was poised for the last great decade of his career.

Exercising uncontested authority from Egypt to Syria, including the territories of Damascus and Aleppo and areas of what is now southern Turkey, recognised as lord in Arabia and patron of the Holy Cities of Mecca and Medina; supported by the caliph in Baghdad, now that his authority was unchallenged by the once mighty city state of Mosul, and his friendship cultivated by the Selchük sultans of Konya in Anatolia, Saladin directly ruled territories of imperial dimensions and exerted influence and authority more extensive than those enjoyed by any other Muslim ruler west of Iran in 200 years.

Saladin had owed his rise in large part to loyal Syrian troopers, noted even then for their violence and termed his 'rough companions' by Imad-ad Din; he was himself capable of ruthlessness when occasion demanded it, and though noted for his magnanimity to his enemies, was rigid in his observance of the dividing line between those of the true faith of Islam and Unbelievers. A famous anecdote relates how he restrained two of his young sons, barely in their teens, from participating in a slaughter or prisoners. But this should not be understood as an instance of altruistic humanitarianism on the part of Saladin, or a wish to check a burgeoning blood lust. It was right that warriors should kill the Infidel – but only when, with mature understanding, they knew the distinction between them and the people of the Faith.

Saladin was a hero indeed, but a hero of the *Dar al Islam*, the region of the religion. As such his face was always set hard against the *Dar al Harb*, the region of war. To fight the good fight it was necessary for him to subdue other rulers to his will. The service of the Faith required resources and obedience of imperial dimensions. It was the logic of his life that made of Saladin a dynast.

# Chapter 9

# Dynast and Hero

Muslims and Christians rated the submission of Aleppo very highly. Some fervent *jihad* enthusiasts might deplore this continuing war between the Muslims, but many more were jubilant that Islam was once again being united. Events had shown that the Zengid princes were too envious of the power of the Kurdish 'usurper' to help him against the Christians. And just as Nur-ad-Din from Aleppo had concentrated on winning Damascus and then Egypt before risking the final blow against the kingdom of Jerusalem, so Saladin had refused to commit himself against it with a hostile Aleppo on his frontier. Baha'-ad-Din tells us that Saladin looked on Aleppo as the basis and key to his power while from William of Tyre we learn that the news fell in the Christian camp like a bombshell. 'It ran through the land of the Christians who were much afraid, for this was the thing they had been dreading. They well knew that if Saladin could conquer that city then their country could be swept and besieged in every part.' Another Frank said quite simply that the Christians were now in a permanent state of siege.

Saladin was the greatest power in Islam; but his newly won empire brought with it deep political complexities. His own early career had shown how difficult it could be for the lord of Syria to maintain his grip on Egypt, even when it was held by a loyal lieutenant. Now Cairo dominated the North African coast as far west as Tripoli, thanks to raiding campaigns by the ambitious Sharaf ad-Din. He had set up this far-flung presence of Aiyubid power almost single-handed, and moreover, as a general in the forces of Saladin's nephew Taqi-ad-Din, owed his first allegiance to a member of the family whose own ambitions made it necessary to watch his loyalty constantly. Taqi-ad-Din had been posted in Syria since 1175 (an inscription shows him as governor of the town of Hamah from 1179) and the government of Egypt had been entrusted to Saladin's brilliant younger brother al-Adil. Another brother, Tughtigin, had been given the provinces of Arabia the year before the Aleppo campaign, and from the peace that reigned in that part of the empire we can assume that his loyalty was never in doubt. Turan-Shah, the dynamic and colourful conqueror of the Yemen, after a chequered political career including governorships of Damascus, Baalbek and finally Alexandria, had died in semi-disgrace, too addicted to his pleasures to be a useful member of the family team, in 1180. A far more serious loss was the death of Saladin's nephew Farrukh-Shah, who had proved such a capable soldier and commander at Damascus, in September 1182. His cousin, Nasir-ad-Din, was governor of Homs. He also was the son of Shirkuh, the conqueror of Egypt, and his loyalty too could not be completely relied upon.

Saladin now ruled an empire that far exceeded the state of Nur-ad-Din. His colleagues in empire were a numerous family, some of whom, like Taqi-ad-Din and Turan-Shah, had shared in the founding of his greatness, and all of whom, given the separatist nature of twelfth-century Islamic politics, could be supposed to have their individual ambitions. Where Nur-ad-Din had been free of importunate relations and had been able to use subordinates like Aiyub and Shirkuh who depended on him for their advancement, Saladin needed all his considerable political intuition to harness the abilities of a competitive family, many older than he, and check their rivalry. The empire was to fall apart soon after his death, just as the domain of Nur-ad-Din had done. To maintain it in being during his life required force of character, constant attention and time-consuming work.

The first decision was the appointment of a new governor of Aleppo. For six weeks Saladin was busy reorganising the administration, and perhaps satisfying himself about the loyalty of the place. He had little to fear. Despite their fierce traditional loyalty to the Zengid house, the people of Aleppo had been shabbily treated. Only two years back, 'Izz-ad-Din of Mosul had traded the proud former capital of Syria with his brother, and now that brother had shamefully betrayed it to the man whom the Aleppans had long regarded as the arch enemy of their city and their dynasty. Saladin's clemency, following so fast on the mean, inglorious expedients of the Zengid princes, dissolved the threat of any immediate opposition. The long-term integration of the great city into the Aiyubid realm would need the guiding hand of a loyal and experienced man. The nearest of Saladin's relations was Taqi-ad-Din at Hamah. His talents as a soldier were  proven but his political abilities and loyalty in a sensitive post were not. Back in 1175 he had held the governorship of Damascus, but had had to be removed twelve months later. For the time being things in Aleppo were peaceful enough for Saladin to install as temporary governor his third son, the ten-year-old az-Zahir, with an experienced adviser. We are told that he was his father's favourite son and, naturally enough, that he was virtuous and wise beyond his years. However, at the end of the year he was to find himself replaced by his renowned uncle al-Adil who for the past nine years had been directing the Egyptian administration with cool efficiency. Just when Saladin decided on the switch we do not know, but there is some reason to suppose that it was during the summer of 1183.

By 24 August he was back in Damascus. He had announced his intention of another campaign against the Franks in a well-publicised dispatch to the caliph. Having assembled a large army he left the city on 17 September and moved south in easy stages to reach the eastern bank of the Jordan, below the Lake of Tiberias, on the 28th. On the morning of the next day he crossed over into the kingdom. His leisurely march to the frontier ford, about fifty-five miles in eleven days, had given time for all the expected detachments to join the main army: it had also given the Christians ample time to muster. The regent, Guy of Lusignan, called all the forces of the kingdom to his standard at Saffuriyah in the hills about Galilee. Well placed for access to the port of Acre and the coastal plain, and with large and reliable supplies of water, the position also enabled the defending army to block equally rapidly an enemy advance from across the Jordan north or south of the lake.

The chief men of the kingdom were with the regent: among them the brothers Balian of Ibelin and Baldwin of Ramlah, Count Raymond of Tripoli, soon to contest the leadership of the kingdom with Guy, and Raynald. Hurrying up from the south were further reinforcements, drawn from the garrisons of Raynald's castles, al-Karak and ash-Shaubak (Montreal), and led by his stepson, the young Humphrey IV of Toron. Despite its great size, the army's function was purely defensive, to remain in the field in force so as to cramp any major manoeuvres by the enemy, not to seek out a decisive engagement.

On 29 September Saladin swept into the town of Baisan, which had been deserted by its population on the news of his coming. The soldiery was left free to pillage and burnt everything they could not carry off. It was an inspiriting start to what looked like being a profitable *razzia*. The next day the army pushed on south-west a few miles to the head of the

valley of Jezreel which stretched inland from Haifa to modern Yizre'el.
Saladin pitched camp overlooking 'Ain Jalut, a pool known to the
Christians as the Spring of Goliath. He had also sent on ahead a flying
column led by 'Izz-ad-Din Jurdik, formerly one of the most loyal
of Nur-ad-Din's mamluks. He successfully ambushed Humphrey of
Toron's forces on the slopes of Mount Gilboa barely twenty miles short
of its destination, and destroyed it. The news reached the main army on
30 September and raised its pitch of euphoria a notch higher. In forty-
eight hours they had sacked a Christian town and destroyed a significant
enemy force.

But the Christians were now heading south to contest the vital
watering place of 'Ain Jalut with Saladin. 'Because he meant to pit his
forces against them in the field', Saladin drew up his army in formal
order of battle and sent a vanguard of 500 on to harass the enemy. In
the words of his biographer these were soon 'eyeball to eyeball' with the
Christian van, commanded by the regent's brother, Amalric. There was
a fierce clash, but the main Christian force soon came up and the
Muslims had to draw off.

Now began one of those battles on the march which had been a characteristic of crusading warfare from the earliest years. 'The Franks kept
their ranks closed, their infantry protecting their knights, they neither
charged nor stopped, but continued their march to the spring and there
they dressed their tents.' Saladin, using traditional Turkish tactics, sent
his horse archers down on the compact column time and again in a vain
endeavour to make it break ranks. But a Christian army which kept
discipline and was not outrageously outnumbered was almost impregnable, even on the march. The superior physique of the Franks and their
heavy armour gave them the advantage. It is largely for this reason that
many of Saladin's campaigns seem ineffectual – so much of the time was
spent trying to lure the Franks to break their formation. On this occasion the armies confronted one another for five days. Then Saladin
withdrew to Jabal Tabur (Mount Tabor) some ten miles away hoping to
tempt the Christians from their position to attack him. In the meanwhile
his marauders had sacked many villages round about the battle zone and
had attacked a monastery on Jabul Tabur itself. Although hard pressed
and for a time desperate for supplies, the Christians had held firm, and
now, instead of pursuing Saladin to Jabal Tabur, they withdrew back
towards their base at Saffuriyah. Saladin, his army bloated with plunder
and flushed with triumph, broke off the action and was back in
Damascus by 14 October.

If we are tempted to ask just what had been achieved and indeed what had been intended, few of his subjects had such doubts. In a dashing *razzia* their army had plundered at will, taken the fighting to the enemy, and forced on him the humiliating role of inaction while all around him his peasants and townships were pillaged. Saladin received a hero's welcome on his return to Damascus. The Christian camp, by contrast, was bitterly divided. The common soldiery, plagued by the insolent arrows of the enemy, had wanted to fight – the view urged in the councils of the leadership by the fire-eating Raynald. The seemingly timid advice that the array must be maintained intact, which the regent had followed, had come from Raymond of Tripoli and the Ibelin brothers. Their enemies now charged that they had been motivated not by wise strategy but by an envious determination to deny Guy any chance of glory. The fact that the army was still in being and could stop any major invasion was not the kind of military achievement that the average man could understand or would be interested in. There must have been many Christians who cast envious eyes at the triumphs being celebrated in Damascus. Among his own people Saladin's reputation, tarnished a little perhaps by his campaign against Aleppo, was once more bright.

A week later he was once more on the road south. This time the objective was al-Karak. Al-Adil had been summoned up from Egypt and Saladin was scheduled to rendezvous with him under its walls. Baha'-ad-Din tells us that while waiting for news of his brother's progress Saladin 'set out several times on the road for al-Karak'. This is just one of the pointers that leads to the suspicion that the famous siege of November 1183 was not the simple military operation it appears to have been.

The siege, which coincided with the marriage between the young Humphrey IV of Toron and Isabella of Jerusalem is a centrepiece for the chivalric tapestry later woven round the crusading wars. The marriage had been sponsored by King Baldwin in the faint hope that it would heal the rift between the house of Ibelin, Isabella's step-parents, and the allies of Raynald, Humphrey's stepfather. The politics of the kingdom had been fragmented into two fierce factions when, in 1180, Sibylla, the sister of the leprous King Baldwin, had married Guy de Lusignan, specially brought over from Europe for the purpose by his brother, Amalric, the constable of the kingdom. With the king a leper the succession was a vital question, and this marriage seemed to threaten the baronage with an untried, upstart young French nobleman as their future monarch. The Ibelins represented the baronial party, while Raynald, himself very aware of his European allegiances, was whole-heartedly behind de Lusignan. Baldwin, bravely trying to keep harmony between the strong men of a realm, which needed unity above all things, had arranged the betrothal of Humphrey and Isabella although the princess was at the time only eight. Now, three years later, it was thought possible to celebrate the marriage. Raynald was determined that, little as he welcomed the political implications supposed to lie behind the union, if it was to be celebrated at all it should be in his castle with all the pomp he could muster. As well as the wedding guests, enter-tainers and jugglers thronged to the castle from all parts of the Christian states, and by the middle of November the party was in full swing. Meanwhile, from the south, the forces of al-Adil were at last on the move from Egypt.

He joined Saladin and Taqi-ad-Din outside al-Karak on 20 November. Saladin was able to force an entrance into the town below the castle with a rushed assault but was beaten back at the entrance to the fortress. He now set up his siege engines and began a heavy and relentless bombardment. Taqi-ad-Din was with the Damascus army and took a hand in directing the operations. It looked like a major attempt to take a castle which had caused the Muslims so much trouble for so long. Within the walls the festivities defiantly went on. One contemporary account informs us that the bridegroom's mother even prepared dishes from the wedding feast and had them sent out to the chivalrous Saladin. In return he courteously enquired where the young couple's marriage chamber was and ordered his artillery men not to fire at that section of the wall. However, if he left the bride and groom some relative peace, Saladin continued the bombardment on the main circuit of the walls, which was as fierce as ever. In desperation the garrison got a message to Jerusalem and beacon fires soon brought the reply that reinforcements were on the march. It was enough to decide Saladin to withdraw. The Christian army pressed on and the king was carried in triumph into the castle. Saladin was back in Damascus on 11 December, and at first glance it would seem as though he had achieved little.

Most historians have regarded this expedition against al-Karak and the one that followed in 1184 as failed attempts to take the place by storm and have supposed that al-Adil came up from Egypt solely to bring reinforcements. A cynical modern biographer of Saladin, noting the speed with which he fell back on news of an approaching Christian relief force, suggests that the campaigns were mere charades designed to bolster Saladin's reputation as an untiring warrior in the *jihad*. Both interpretations seem a little improbable. It may well be that Saladin did not plan for a protracted siege. Karak was one of the strongest of the many very formidable castles the Crusaders built; when it did fall in 1188 it was only after a stubborn year-long siege. Saladin was perfectly aware of the military problem posed by this strongpoint. Had its capture been the first objective in 1183 and '84 he would have prepared his position against the inevitable attempt by the enemy to relieve the place. We deduce that the reduction of the fortress was not the point of his campaign. Equally, the object can hardly have been to win prestige – there is little of that to be had from failure. The clue to what lay behind Saladin's planning is found implied in Baha'-ad-Din's account of the 1183 campaign. Baha tells us that 'a number of merchants and others travelled with al-Adil', and ends with the observation that Karak 'caused great damage to the Muslims for . . . it obliged the caravans to travel with an armed escort'. After the armies had made their junction at Karak they promptly separated again. Al-Adil marched on northwards, where he was to take up the post of governor in Aleppo, while Taqi-ad-Din, a better soldier, headed southwards to take over command in Egypt. According to Baha'-ad-Din Saladin had grown apprehensive of the Christians marching against that country. In the autumn of 1183 then Saladin's concern was not with the capture of a great Christian fortress but to ensure the smooth transfer of commands in two of the most important provinces and to protect the passage of a rich convoy. Had al-Karak fallen he would no doubt have been as much astonished as delighted, for the campaign had been intended to draw the forces of the kingdom to a position where he could hold them, and he knew that a feint against Karak would be the surest way of doing this.

A similar pattern can be discerned behind the siege of Karak in August/September 1184. This time it was Taqi-ad-Din who brought up the army from Egypt and this time the precious goods under convoy were the household and treasures of al-Adil on their way to join him in Aleppo. The armies of Saladin and his nephew made their junction on 30 July, and a fortnight later a fierce bombardment of Karak began. A month after, they were back to a triumphant reception in Damascus. Saladin had an additional cause for self-congratulation, for this brief campaign was the first in which his army had included contingents from the sensitive areas to the north which he was contesting with Mosul.

Despite his disappointment there in the winter of 1182 Saladin was still determined to force his suzerainty on the city. In February 1184 a deputation reached Damascus looking for terms of compromise. It was headed by Baha'-ad-Din, at that time one of the senior advisers of Mosul, and with him was the prestigious Badr-ad-Din, who bore the honorific title of Shaikh of Shaikhs at the caliphal court. Saladin, with his characteristic respect for age and wisdom, visited the venerable ambassador from Baghdad almost daily, but he refused to back down from his claims on Mosul. As Baha'-ad-Din was later to learn, part of these discussions were concerned with him. Saladin, impressed with the leader of the Mosul deputation, persuaded the shaikh to offer Baha'-ad-Din a tempting opportunity to enter his service. But he was met with a refusal. The ambassador feared, reasonably enough, that, with the negotiations clearly heading for an impasse, to accept the job would provoke charges of double-dealing against him. Possibly, in fact, Saladin was hoping that he could undermine the authority and prestige of 'Izz-ad-Din at Mosul if he could persuade one of his chief advisers to quit his service. But the fact that the offer was to be repeated and eventually accepted proves that such an ulterior motive was not his only one.

While Baha'-ad-Din was at Damascus the entourage of az-Zahir arrived from Aleppo. After six months in office the boy and his adviser had been displaced by al-Adil, who reached the city in the middle of December. Considering the boy's age the replacement was hardly surprising, yet he seems to have resented it. Baha'-ad-Din, watching with the professional diplomat's eye, reported back to Mosul that: 'the boy submitted to his father in all things and concealed his discontent, but it did not escape the eye of Saladin.' The next month al-Adil was at Damascus to celebrate the Feast of Sacrifice with his brother, and no doubt to report.

With the festival over, Saladin sent out messengers to recruit allies for a campaign planned for later that summer against the Christians. Among other things Saladin was anxious to demonstrate the reality of his influence in al-Jazirah. The first among the princes of the area to join the standard was Nur-ad-Din of Hisn Kaifa, who was received by al-Adil with high honour when he marched into Aleppo on the last day of May. A week later they went to Damascus together and Saladin, who had been ill, hastened out to meet them on the road as another gesture of honour to this very welcome ally. He had good reason to be pleased when his

A dramatic monument to Saladin was erected in Damascus in the twentieth century. Non-Muslims often suppose that there is a Koranic injunction against the depiction of the human form and personalities in art. In fact this is not so.

This famous image of Saladin, dating from about 1180, is attributed to an artist of the Fatimid school.

Built between 685 and 691, the Dome of the Rock, sometimes called the Mosque of Omar, is the earliest great architectural monument of Islam. Not in fact a mosque but a shrine, it was built to shelter the Rock, sacred to the memory of Muhammad. It is located on the Temple Mount, where w the Temple of Solomon, and it was here that the Christian Knights Templar made their headquarte When Saladin recaptured Jerusalem for Islam in 1189 the building had to be ritually cleansed. Som 18 meters in diameter, the dome is a wooden structure, clad originally in lead, later in gold leaf, an resting on a drum supported by 16 columns and piers, surrounded by an octagonal arcade.

The interior of the Dome of the Rock showing the Rock itself, honoured by Muslims as the place from which the Prophet Muhammad made his mystical ascent to paradise. The circle of piers and columns supporting the actual dome is surrounded by an octagonal arcade of 24 piers and columns. The structure owes much to Roman and Byzantine architecture. Over the centuries it was adorned with mosaic and faience tiles and marble.

The Citadel at Jerusalem, showing fortifications from the time of the Crusades. The picture shows both Frankish foundations and Turkish upper works.

This nineteenth-century print of Jerusalem depicts the Holy City within its walls much as it must have looked to Saladin preparing to lay siege to the place in 1189. The Dome of the Rock can clearly be seen in the centre of the picture with, to its left, the Al-Aqsa mosque.

The interior of the great mosque at Damascus, the Mosque of the Umayyads. Begun (AD 705) under the Umayyad caliph Abu al Abbas al Walid, it was built on the site of the former Christian basilica of St John the Baptist. Eighth-century mosaics on the walls depicted a scene of houses set among gardens and streams that may have been intended as a vision of paradise but may in fact have been based on views of Damascus.

A view of the Mosque of the Umayyads at Damascus, showing the colonnaded courtyard with the city laid out beyond. At the time of Saladin, Damascus, thought by some to be the world's oldest continually inhabited city, was set among gardens and orchards, rivers and streams 'as if by a halo' according to one contemporary.

A nineteenth-century view of the ruined classical temples at Baalbek overlooking the Beka'a valley. It would have been a familiar sight on the landscape to the young Saladin on rides from the family home in Damascus.

A watercolour view of Tyre, seen from its isthmus, by the nineteenth-century topographical artist David Roberts. Accessible from the mainland only along this narrow neck of land, the city was secure against anything but a closely coordinated land-sea operation.

The ruins of the crusader castle of Belvoir, known to the Muslims as Kaukab. It fell to Saladin's forces in 1188.

The most famous of all crusader castles, Krak des Chevaliers. A rebuild on the site of a former Muslim stronghold known as the 'Castle of the Kurds', it was the greatest stronghold of the Knights of St John of Jerusalem who held it from 1141 to the 1270s.

About twenty-five miles to the south of the Dead Sea, the crusaders' castle of Montreal, known to the Muslim forces as ash-Shaubak, was ideally sited to plunder caravans en route from Aqaba to Damascus . It finally fell to Saladin in 1188.

The site of Saladin's great victory of the Christian forces at 'The Horns of Hattin' overlooking the Lake Tiberias (the Sea of Galilee) in 1187. The picture well captures the dramatic nature of the terrain.

army was joined by detachments from Mardin and Sinjar. It was an impressive force that the Egyptians found awaiting them at the rendezvous outside al-Karak. An artillery train of fourteen mangonels put up a fierce bombardment – a contemporary letter, quoted by the historian Abu-Shamah, boasted that no defender dare show his head for fear of the Muslim archers. Saladin had men sapping the foot of the walls under the protection of covered approach ways. Abu-Shamah's anonymous correspondent thought that victory was close, but news came that the Christian army was on the march. Saladin interrupted the siege and marched to intercept them, again apparently hoping to force a full engagement. But again it was denied him, and the Franks, maintaining their compact column on the march, forced their way through to relieve the beleaguered fortress. Denied the rather improbable bonus of a quick capitulation from al-Karak, Saladin took advantage of the fact that the Franks were once more concentrated at the castle and sent out raiding columns as the main army headed back for Damascus, to ravage from Nablus northwards into Galilee.

On 15 September Saladin returned in triumph to Damascus. Greeted by his own people as a hero, he was careful to honour the ruler of Hisn Kaifa publicly, even investing him with a robe of honour which the caliph had sent for the victorious Saladin himself. For the rest of the year Saladin was busy with the administration of his large empire, and it appears that he also had to pacify complaints from Cairo. With the bulk of the Egyptian army away in the north the country felt vulnerable to surprise Christian raids. These protests were to become more plaintive the following year when Saladin took the Egyptian forces with him still further from their home in a campaign against Mosul.

Though his admirers may have been unhappy at yet another conflict with a Muslim city, Saladin knew there was little to fear from the Christians. The tragic life of Baldwin IV was nearing its end and he had designated his eight-year-old nephew Baldwin as his successor. Thus at the very time Saladin, with Aleppo subdued and the lesser princes of al-Jazirah his willing allies, was welding Muslim Syria into the most convincing unity it had known since Nur-ad-Din's death, the Franks were faced with a long regency. Better still, Guy of Lusignan had been explicitly excluded from the regency which had been given to his rival, Raymond of Tripoli, so that some bitter and damaging politics lay ahead for the kingdom. For the moment its most pressing problem was a threat of famine. The winter rains had failed and the peasantry seemed faced with starvation; the plundering expeditions by Saladin's troops of the previous year had not helped matters, while the Christians were desperately short of men if the enemy should decide on a major invasion. Emissaries had been sent to Europe to beg reinforcements, but without success. When the new regent met his council to decide what was to be done they agreed, with little debate, to his proposal that a truce should be sought with Saladin.

Not only did Saladin readily grant the truce, willingly according to one Western source, he also ordered supplies into the disaster areas. In fact, according to the Frankish source known as Ernoul, 'the Saracens brought in so much provender that the Christians had all they needed; had there been no truce they would have died of famine. For this the count of Tripoli was much blessed and honoured by the peasants, for the truce that he had made with the Saracens.' For the French historian Grousset the factors in the situation proved that Saladin, 'satisfied with the constitution of his Syrio-Egyptian empire, was prepared to tolerate the Frankish presence in coastal Palestine, despite his *jihad* protestations.' It must be conceded that, strictly within the context of the Holy War, the situation in early 1185 was good for an attack on the Christians. But Saladin had commitments to his allies in the Islamic world and news was already coming in that 'Izz-ad-Din at Mosul, with the help of the Persian Selchük, Pahlavan, was mounting an attack on his ally the lord of Irbil. Determined to settle the perennial disturbances that threatened on his northern frontiers, Saladin was delighted that his southern border was secured by the four-year truce the Franks had begged of him.

He crossed the Euphrates at al-Birah to be joined there by Gökböri, governor of Harran, and envoys from Irbil and other parts of al-Jazirah. Despite warnings from Konya he continued his march, judging rightly that the sultan would not send troops against him. He reached Harran in mid-May and there followed a brief episode which has remained a puzzle. Gökböri, who had long been one of the most ardent advocates of Saladin's intervention in the area, was almost immediately arrested 'for something he had done and for certain words attributed to him by his ambassador which angered Saladin, though certainly he had not thoroughly investigated the matter'. It seems that Gökböri had promised 50,000 dinars to the expedition which were not available when Saladin called on them; more seriously we get a hint that the governor of Harran had been accused of having dealings with Mosul itself. Perhaps these are the 'words attributed to him'. The fact that Baha'-ad-Din, still in the service of Mosul at the time, comments that Saladin could not have investigated the matter properly suggests that he had inside information and knew that the governor had in fact made no approach to Mosul. It seems that Saladin soon discovered that the accusations were slanderous. Gökböri was stripped of all his titles, yet within a matter of days, he had been released and had given back the governorship of Harran with the assurance that Edessa too would be returned to him in due course. His complete restoration to favour was symbolised when Saladin magnanimously clad him with a robe of honour.

A month later the army was once again outside the walls of Mosul. And once again they promised to be more than a match for Saladin's siege craft. More seriously, signs of sickness began to spread; yet while 'Izz-ad-Din, whose allies were now too concerned with their own affairs to come to his aid, begged for a compromise, Saladin was adamant. It was believed that he was toying with plans to divert the course of the Tigris and so rob the city of its water supply. But developments to the north diverted him from a full blockade of Mosul, and a few weeks after setting the siege he led the bulk of his army out on the road to Akhlat on the coast of Lake Van. The Selchük prince of the place had died, and his successor, called Baktimore, learnt with dismay that Pahlavan, the lord of Azerbaijan, was planning to march against him. Baktimore sent a desperate plea for help to Saladin.

Saladin responded promptly, and on the march north he was accompanied by his cousin Nasir-ad-Din, lord of Homs, and 'Isa-al-Hakkari, a senior member of the Egyptian administration on the campaign with Egypt's army. Since Pahlavan alone of 'Izz-ad-Din's allies had actually sent troops to the aid of Mosul a point scored at his expense would emphasise the wide reach of Saladin's influence. Perhaps, too, there was an element of nostalgia behind the decision. Akhlat lay on the edge of the Kurdish homelands from which Saladin's family had come. Finally, there was trouble brewing up on this distant northern frontier which could, and in fact soon did, impinge on the security of northern Syria in general and Aleppo in particular. At about the time of Baktimore's appeal, turbulent warfare had broken out between a new wave of Turkomans moving in from central Asia and the Kurdish population of the Upper Jazirah. The Turkomans won an outright victory and massacred their opponents. From that point on through to the winter of 1186 they ravaged the Christian and Muslim lands from Georgia to

Cappadocia virtually unopposed: by 1187 they would be threatening even the northern frontiers of Antioch and Aleppo.

If he had won control of it, the fortress city of Akhlat would have provided a valuable outpost from which to keep a check on these threatening developments. A further factor must have reinforced Saladin's decision to intervene and this was the somewhat surprising arrival of an embassy from Constantinople. The prospect of having an ally on the northern boundary of his inveterate and nagging enemy Kilij Arslan at Konya was worth an immediate gesture in response. The situation in Akhlat gave him a chance to show his capacity for operations remote from his own base in support of a prospective ally as well as offering immediate advantages.

The diplomatic minuet between Saladin and the Byzantines which was alternately to enrage and fascinate the Muslim and Christian Middle East for another five years revolved around certain common interests. The Emperor Andronicos knew the Muslim world at first hand. When as a young man he had been exiled from the Byzantine court, he had been befriended both by the caliph at Baghdad and by Nur-ad-Din at Damascus. Andronicos also badly needed allies. His accession was regarded by some as mere usurpation, others were infuriated by the cruelty of his régime: he had many enemies and some of the most influential were in exile. At the time of his approach to Saladin, King William II of Sicily was advancing into the Greek provinces on behalf of one of them. And there were two other more long-term threats. The sultanate of Konya, which had already overrun vast tracts of Byzantine territory, and the island of Cyprus, theoretically a Byzantine dependency, was in revolt and so possibly an ally of the Franks in Palestine. Both these states were also potential or actual enemies to Saladin.

An alliance between Saladin and the Byzantines made political sense, but it was obvious that Saladin, lord of Syria and Egypt, would expect to be the senior partner. Obvious, that is, to all but Andronicos, who could not break loose from the time-honoured conventions of Byzantine diplomacy, which had recognised no equal since defeating Zoroastrian Persia in 628. Saladin was asked to do homage to the emperor, and the division of any conquered territories was weighted in favour of Constantinople. Andronicos even supposed that he was strong enough to insist on the return of Jerusalem to the empire. But in fact he was not strong enough to retain his own throne. When Saladin's ambassadors arrived at the capital with their reply to the proposed alliance, it was to find that the emperor had been deposed by mob action and replaced by a new emperor, Isaac II Angelus. The first movement of the minuet was over.

By this time, September 1185, Saladin had learnt that Akhlat had eluded him. Baktimore had been able to come to terms with Pahlavan and married one of his daughters. Saladin returned to Mosul. In November 'Izz-ad-Din, hoping to appeal to his renowned chivalry, sent his wife and two princesses to intercede with him, but without success. The outlook for Mosul was not good. There was no hope of relief from the outside, and Saladin's army seemed ready to press the siege throughout the winter months. But at this point Saladin's fragile health broke down in the sultry humidity of the winter rainy season. With him in command the army would fight beyond the demands of convention, without him it would do nothing, and on 25 December Saladin fell back to Harran. Despite the critical nature of his condition he refused to ride in a litter and stayed in the saddle for all the army to see he was still in command.

During the next few weeks, his life in the balance, Saladin tried to ensure a peaceful succession by forcing his emirs to swear loyalty to his sons. But ambitious men were stirring. Nasir-ad-Din of Homs, who apparently felt that he had been promised the governorship of Mosul when it fell, obviously thought he had a strong claim, and secured promises of support from groups in Aleppo and in Damascus, being assured that the capital would be held for him if Saladin died. There was also trouble in Egypt where Taqi-ad-Din, proud of his military reputation, was beginning to chafe at his position as tutor and second string to Saladin's eldest son, al-Afdal. During his illness Saladin had urgent discussions on the situation with al-Adil, who had hurried up from Aleppo with his own physician.

During January 1186 Saladin's health began to mend, and in February he was able to receive another deputation from Mosul headed by Baha'-ad-Din. He tells us that Mosul had seen Saladin's illness 'as an opportunity not to be missed for we knew how readily the prince lent his ear to an appeal and how tender-hearted he was'. But Saladin, disturbed by the unrest that was brewing in the empire, was as eager for a settlement as was 'Izz-ad-Din, and on 3 March their ambassadors signed a treaty. 'Izz-ad-Din remained lord of the city of Mosul, but the city finally acknowledged the overlordship of Damascus, and the lands across the Tigris to the south of Mosul were put in the charge of emirs appointed by Saladin.

Two days later news arrived in Harran that Nasir-ad-Din had died from an excess of wine. 'Like father, like son' would cover the facts, though some were later to suggest that Saladin himself had had a hand in the death. There is no evidence to support the rumour, nor is it probable. His cousin's death would certainly have suited Saladin's book a few weeks earlier. Assured of the security of his own provinces he could have driven a harder bargain with Mosul. As it was he hastened to confirm the twelve-year-old heir of Nasir-ad-Din, Shirkuh II, as ruler of Homs, and early in April was back at Damascus.

Saladin now had the goodwill of Baghdad, and the three other cities of the quadrilateral of power under his direct authority. The Franks were divided amongst themselves by bitter political wrangling and the truce with them had, in any case, three more years to run. The new Byzantine emperor, Isaac II Angelus, had been entertained once at Saladin's court while an exile and now confirmed the 'treaty arrangements that Saladin had proposed in response to the initiative of Andronicus. Saladin was free to put the finishing touches to the reorganisation of his empire.

The situation in Egypt was disturbing, and during June al-Adil came down from Aleppo for a number of conferences with his brother. Also at the capital were Saladin's two young sons, the fourteen-year-old al-'Aziz and the thirteen-year-old az-Zahir, still languishing after his brief period of glory as nominal ruler of Aleppo three years before. The result was a general post which reveals a good deal about Saladin the dynast. His sons were approaching manhood. Nur-ad-Din's son and heir had been only eighteen when he died, but even by that time he had wielded sufficient influence at Aleppo to sway the choice of his successor. Men expected the sons of princes to be ready for responsibility at an early age. Saladin was anxious to establish his sons firmly in the administration of the empire, to assure their loyalty and the continuance of his dynasty. But he also realised the strain that advancing them too fast would impose on the loyalty of his gifted and energetic brother al-Adil and the hotheaded but equally talented Taqi-ad-Din.

In the summer of 1186, Taqi-ad-Din seemed to be the most pressing problem. Saladin decided to recall him from Cairo and at the same time summoned his eldest son al-Afdal. He was now sixteen and had spent all his life in Egypt; he was well established and he was ambitious – when his father lay dying seven years later, he calmly took the seat of honour in the banqueting hall. Saladin, who had already detected signs of his son's ambition, was clearly not willing to leave him at Cairo to preside over the change of administration that was to follow the recall of Taqi-ad-Din. Instead, the younger al-Aziz was sent to Cairo with al-Adil as his *atabeg*.

There was mounting criticism in Cairo of Saladin's policies and growing exasperation at the long-drawn-out struggle with Mosul. Even al-Fadil, for years Saladin's most loyal minister in Cairo, bitterly complained that the wars against Mosul were draining the wealth of Egypt and taking thousands of her troops to remote theatres of war. Far from sympathising with his sovereign when he was convalescing from the near-fatal illness of early 1186, he had lectured him for back-sliding from the cause of *jihad*, 'God has given you a warning. Take a vow that if you recover from this illness, you will never again fight against Muslims and that you will devote your energies to war on the enemies of Allah.' One Arabic source seems to hint that even he had dabbled for a time in opposition politics; other critics of Saladin had been descanting pointedly on the evils of wars between Muslims for some time.

As a result of the discontent in the upper reaches of the administration the atmosphere at the court of Damascus was heavy with suspicion. The intrigues of Nasir-ad-Din had involved important figures both there and at Aleppo. When he accepted the post at Cairo, al-Adil, although Saladin's brother and most respected adviser, took the remarkable step of clearing his position with the two young princes as a precaution, after a summer of rumour-mongering, against the whisperings of ambitious rivals. He found the boys sitting together and took the place between them. To al-'Aziz he said: 'Your father, my lord, has commanded me to enter your service and to go with you to Egypt. I know there are many wicked people and some of them will come to you and will abuse me and counsel you not to trust me. If you mean to listen to them tell me now so that I may not go with you.' Despite the boy's assurance al-Adil next turned to his brother. 'I am quite well aware that your brother might listen to men who devise mischief and that, if he did, I could not rely on any but you.' Az-Zahir's answer was calm and re-assuring, 'Bless you! All will go well.'

In August az-Zahir was nominated the ruler of Aleppo by his father while his elder brother, al-Afdal, arrived at Damascus. Messengers were soon on their way to Egypt to demand the return also of Taqi-ad-Din. Years before, in the council which received the embassy commanding Saladin's return to the capital of his suzerain Nur-ad-Din, he had been the one to urge that the family should defy their rightful lord and dare him to come and assert his claim. Now he was equally outraged when his own uncle commanded his return. He vowed that he would join his general Sharaf-ad-Din campaigning in the maghrib and raise rebellion. But he too was urged by his advisers not to defy the orders of Damascus, and in November there was a reconciliation between uncle and nephew. As a consolation Taqi-ad-Din received the appanage of Hamah, where he had already served as governor and where he could hope to find neither the resources nor the obscurity to raise further trouble. The year ended with two marriages designed to heal some of the ruptures among the ruling family. At Aleppo az-Zahir married a daughter of al-Adil to whom he had been betrothed for some time, while at Damascus the Aiyubid heir, al-Afdal, took a wife from among the daughters of the dead Nasir-ad-Din.

The rumblings of discontent beneath the surface of the great empire quietened. By contrast, Christian politics shattered in rivalry, intrigue and treason. In August the boy king Baldwin V died, attended by the regent Raymond of Tripoli and the seneschal Joscelin, who, at Raymond's insistence, had held the custody of the king's person. Raymond, while accepting the regency, had refused the guardianship of the weakly child for fear that he would be accused when the king died. The will of Baldwin IV had provided that in the event of the boy's death Raymond should be regent until the emperor, the pope and the kings of England and France should decide between the claims of the two princesses of the royal house, Sibylla (wife to the unpopular Guy de Lusignan) and Isabella. But the partisans of Sibylla and Guy, among them the seneschal and Raynald, outmanoeuvred Raymond. They held Jerusalem and the royal regalia and forced through the coronation of Queen Sibylla and King Guy.

While most of his supporters accepted the coup, Raymond retired to Tiberias, demanding that Guy restore to him his city of Beirut. There he made a separate truce with Saladin to cover his own county and his wife's principality of Galilee. A few months later he was reported to be negotiating for Muslim aid in a bid for the crown itself, and according to Muslim chroniclers he definitely received troops. Neither his enemies' sharp practice nor the provocation he had received could justify such outright treason – Christian ranks were more bitterly divided than ever. It was as well for them that the truce with Saladin still had two years to run.

Then came stunning news from the south. Raynald had overrun yet another rich caravan, slaughtered the convoy and interned the merchants with their treasure at al-Karak. Saladin at once dispatched an envoy to demand the return of the hostages and restitution of the treasure. He poured reproaches on the truce-breaker and threatened him with fearsome vengeance, but Raynald, secure behind the walls of al-Karak, contemptuously refused an audience. The envoys went on to put their case to King Guy. Knowing full well what could now be in prospect for the kingdom, he was conciliatory and sent orders to Raynald to make reparation. But his messenger returned from al-Karak with nothing to report save a neatly apposite misquote from the jeering Jews who had surrounded Christ at the crucifixion. 'They trusted in Muhammad that he should deliver them; let him deliver them!'

Western historians have, in general, cast Raynald of Chatillon as the evil genius who presided over, even guaranteed, the collapse of the kingdom of Jerusalem. Some have suggested that Saladin might have been content to contain the Christian threat; to renew the truce indefinitely; and to wait for European apathy and the dwindling resources and morale of the one-time Crusaders to submerge the infidel settlements in the overwhelming facts of Muslim population and culture. Yet it is doubtful whether, increasingly cornered by his own ostentatious *jihad* propaganda and no doubt driven on by his own genuine religious piety, Saladin could or would have left the Christians in peace much longer. As it was, Raynald made all such speculation irrelevant. Nor is it entirely clear that his view of things was mistaken. However keen the Franks of Outremer may have been to see themselves in the role of a European aristocracy merely set in a foreign landscape, they were still the warriors of religion. They faced an Islamic world up in arms against their intrusion and their raison d'être was not the administration of landed estates but the protection of the Holy City and the War against the Infidel. Perhaps diplomacy and appeasement would have saved them from sudden disaster, but it must, in the end, have meant the losing of their identity in the polyglot world of Middle Eastern politics and society. The flaring, blood-red militancy of Raynald suited better with the origins of the state and the nature of a European-derived martial class than pliant and subtle politicking.

And there was some military sense behind his handling of his command in Transjordan. Al-Karak and ash-Shaubak were a standing menace to the lines of communication between Syria and Egypt. No caravan could risk running the gauntlet without a really powerful convoying escort. In 1183 and 1184 Saladin had had to mount large diversionary attacks to secure a safe passage for merchants and courtiers. Bloody-minded though he may have been, Raynald occupied more of Saladin's time and resources than any other single Christian prince. He could reasonably argue that if the Muslims could pillage Christian lands at will, and so weaken their war effort as well as reaping plunder and ransoms, there was little point in castles which commanded the richest trade routes in Syria and one of the great arteries of Muslim pilgrimage if they were not to be used. Up till that time even the worst provocation had not stirred Saladin to crushing retaliation.

But now his suzerainty over Mosul, confirmed by his name stamped on its coinage and invoked every Friday at the bidding prayer, gave him authority to command its fighting men to his banners. He was lord of all the territories once ruled by Nur-ad-Din and, in addition, under him the cause of Islam was now backed by the resources of Egypt. Perhaps because the knock-out blow had been so long in coming, the Franks may not have fully appreciated the fate that lay ahead for them.

Now, in the spring of 1187, the tocsin of *jihad* was reverberating from Cairo to Mosul. It was not just one more flurry of *razzias* that was in preparation but a determined attempt to win at last the Holy City of Islam. The vast forces assembled and the well-thought-out strategy with which they were deployed were going to probe the resources and military adaptability of the Christians to the full. And to his vow to recapture Jerusalem Saladin had now added an oath to finish once and for all the career of the infidel oath-breaker, Raynald.

# Chapter 10

# Oh! Sweet Victory

At the beginning of 1187, 'Saladin wrote to all the provinces to call them to arms in the Holy War'; troops were called up from Egypt and the Syrian cities, and the lords of Mosul and the other cities of al-Jazirah. Among them was Gökböri of Edessa and Harran; the ill-feeling between him and Saladin, whatever may have been its cause, was obviously long forgotten: Gökböri had received both his lordships back. During the middle of April the army left Damascus, marching due south for Ra's al-Ma'. Here they were joined by numerous Syrian contingents and al-Afdal was left to continue the muster. His instructions were to dispatch the incoming detachments on harrying raids in Christian territories and particularly to probe the situation in Galilee where Count Raymond of Tripoli, lord of the principality through his wife Eschiva, was still on terms of alliance with Saladin.

It seems obvious that Saladin was developing a major strategical plan aimed at the destruction of the Christian army and the conquest of Jerusalem. Because the crucial victory, when it came in July, depended to some extent on Christian errors, some of Saladin's modern critics have proposed that his success was due as much to good luck as good judgement. They suggest that the massive forces were intended for nothing more than a large-scale *razzia*. The developments of the spring and summer give the lie to such theorising.

The coming campaign posed two related strategic problems. Saladin could not hope to take the cities and fortresses on which the kingdom of Jerusalem rested unless he first destroyed the army in the field. But long experience had taught that the Franks, if well led and well disciplined, were virtually indestructible unless taken by surprise or at some other disadvantage. From this it followed that the second problem was to manoeuvre them into a situation in which they were forced into mistakes. It will become quite clear that Saladin fully understood the issues involved. The sheer size of the military forces that were building up in the Hauran would not guarantee success, they would have to be handled with cunning and the psychology of war exploited to the full.

Here Saladin held an important card. His dealings with Count Raymond had already considerably weakened the Christian cause with mutual recrimination and suspicions. Now King Guy had gone so far as to summon the army of the kingdom to meet him at Nazareth with a view to forcing Raymond's submission before the Muslim attacks really began. Guy was his declared enemy; Saladin his only friend but the ambiguity of Raymond's position was heightened when, at the end of April, he received an envoy from al-Afdal. He was not prepared for what was to come. As one ally to another, al-Afdal blandly requested permission to send a force of 7,000 horsemen through Galilee. The purpose and destination do not seem to have been discussed; all that was asked for was a safe conduct for what amounted to a small army.

Raymond's dilemma was acute. Well-informed sources in the Muslim camp believed that the objective of al-Afdal's expedition was the hinterland of Acre itself, and Raymond can hardly have failed to make a similar deduction. Many Christians had already classed him as a traitor, if he collaborated in such a project his reputation would be blackened indelibly. Yet he could not afford to abandon the Saladin connection completely until Guy's threat on his southern frontier had lifted. He proposed a compromise. The 7,000 could go through on condition they harmed neither town nor peasants and that they crossed the Jordan after dawn and returned by the same ford before nightfall.

The fact that al-Afdal was content with these terms confirms the suspicion that Saladin's objective was diplomatic rather than military. The Acre rumour is reported by Ibn-al-Athir, who was not with the northern army at the time, and it seems that Saladin was wishing to probe his ally's reliability and test how far he would commit himself. However, al-Afdal made full use of the opportunity for his staff to survey and reconnoitre the theatre of the coming campaign. The expedition was led by Gökböri, commander of the contingents from al-Jazirah, and the commanders of the Aleppan and Damascus troops. Thanks to Raymond's embarrassed cooperation the Islamic forces were able to ride over the country between Tiberias and Saffuriyah – the traditional assembly point for the Frankish army when faced with invasion in the north of the kingdom.

Unexpectedly it also gave them the chance to liquidate a force of

Hospitaller and Templar knights. To avoid a breach of the truce by his own people, Raymond had dispatched messengers throughout the principality to warn of the march by the Saracens. What he did not know was that King Guy had finally agreed to moderates' advice to seek a settlement with him and that an embassy was already in the principality on its way up to Tiberias. It was led by Balian of Ibelin, and with him was Roger des Moulins, grand master of the Hospitallers, and Gerard de Ridefort, grand master of the Templars. He was not the man to let infidels ride unmolested through Christian territory. On hearing the news on the evening of 30 April he at once ordered all the Templars in the neighbourhood to come to his standard. With other knights who joined the colours they made up a force of close on 150. The next day they rode out in search of the enemy, Roger protesting but shamed into the absurd adventure by the taunts of his fellow grand master. The Muslim horsemen were watering their horses near to Saffuriyah, when to their astonishment they found themselves under attack from a mere handful of Christian knights. Joyfully they prepared themselves for this bonus battle which quickly became a massacre. Only three of the knights survived, among them Grand Master Gerard. The blond head of Roger des Moulins was among those borne back in triumph on the lances of the Saracen troopers.

The main army greeted the news with jubilation. When he heard it Saladin was on the road south to deal another blow at the Christians. News had come through that Raynald was going to attack pilgrims (moving up the Mecca road) and then return to bar the Egyptian army from joining up with the Syrians. The situation was almost a carbon copy of 1183 and 1184. Once again a caravan escorting prestigious travellers – this time Saladin's sister and her son – was obliged to run the mailed gauntlet of Raynald, poised between the two halves of the Muslim empire. Once again there were important manoeuvres pending. Then it had been an exchange of posts by high officials, now it was a military campaign which could not be allowed to go off at half cock. The Egyptian contingent was vital; for the moment it was more important to neutralise Raynald at the least possible cost than crush him. But this time the Muslim forces were very much larger. It was enough for Saladin to march south without even laying siege to al-Karak to persuade Raynald to leave the caravan alone. Once it was out of the area Saladin marched, systematically ravaging Raynald's territories.

At the end of May he moved back northwards and in June set up his standard at al-'Ashtara, some twenty miles nearer the Christian frontier than Ra's al-Ma', where the main muster had now been completed. The enemy too was closing ranks. Shocked by the disaster at Saffuriyah, Raymond had come to terms with the king and was now with the army. It was the biggest in living memory, some said the biggest that the Franks had ever put in the field. But that gathering round Saladin's standard was bigger and, because of late arrivals, growing. In the third week of June he held a general review and gave his officers a detailed briefing. The duties of the coming campaign were explained and duties allotted; the words of command were run through a final time to ensure as far as possible against misunderstandings in the field, among a force drawn from widely scattered regions and different traditions of service. Each emir was given a specific post and ordered strictly to stick to it and the three senior commands were appointed. Taqi-ad-Din on the right wing, Gökböri on the left, and Saladin himself in command of the centre. The review finished, he next paid out the bounties which he had had to promise to various commanders to persuade them to come on the campaign.

At last the army was ready and, on Friday, 26 June, Saladin moved out of al-'Ashtara towards the ford of Senabra, just south of Lake Tiberias. He pitched camp at al-Uqhuwanah. 'The vast sea of his army surrounded the lake. The ship-like tents rode at anchor and the battalions flooded in, wave upon wave. A second sky of dust spread out in which swords and iron-tipped lances rose like stars.' Here they rested for five days while the scouts brought back the news that the Franks were indeed mustering at their usual base of Saffuriyah, where only a few weeks before the Muslim high command had taken the opportunity of checking the lie of the land at first hand. In 1183 the Franks had not been lured into battle on unfavourable terrain, even by Saladin's capture of Baisan – clearly a bigger inducement would have to be found. The objective was Tiberias.

On 1 July the army crossed the Jordan. The main force was sent on a few miles to the north-west with orders to camp at Kafr Sabt and from there to monitor the Franks' movements. 'If they tried to reach Tiberias, the Muslims were to set out immediately to attack them. Saladin went to Tiberias with his personal guard and his most faithful troops.' The town soon fell but the Countess Eschiva and the garrison left behind by Raymond withdrew into the citadel. From there she got a message to the royal army begging the king to relieve the siege that Saladin was laying to the citadel. The day was Thursday, the date 2 July.

The campaign was barely forty-eight hours old and the bird seemed ready to come to the lure.

Tiberias lies about fifteen miles due east of Saffuriyah, though the most level road, curving to the north, stretched the distance to some twenty miles – the limit of a day's march. This road lay across an arid upland plain and then descended to the lake about a mile to the north of the town. An alternative route bent to the south-east, leading to the southernmost tip of the lake and thence northwards up its coast. Again the distance was about twenty miles, and this road, though not so good, was well watered. But with Saladin's main force straddled across the south-east route at Kafr Sabt, it was not even an option to the Christians. If they were to relieve Tiberias they would have to face a long day's march under enemy action across waterless uplands in the heat of a Syrian mid-summer. By the capture of Tiberias, by the placing of his forces, and by blocking up the few wells and springs along the northern road, Saladin had done all in his power to force on the Christians that all-important mistake. Now he could only wait on the decision of the high command at Saffuriyah.

The council of war, which was to decide the fate of the Christians in the Holy City, began early in the evening of 2 July. The arguments against the relief of Tiberias ran roughly as follows. Saladin could not destroy the army where it was at Saffuriyah but stood a good chance of doing so on the march. Thus inaction would keep the army in being, and since the Muslim army usually broke up of its own accord at the end of the campaigning season the loss of Tiberias could be seen as only a short-term matter. If, flushed with his success there, Saladin should decide to attack, then it would be his troops and not the Christians who would be fighting under the handicaps of heat and thirst with no safe base to fall back on. Up on the exposed plateau the army would be inviting destruction. If it were lost then so would be the whole kingdom. Better to lose Tiberias. The majority of the commanders urged prudence, and they were headed by Raymond, although Tiberias lay in his wife's domain and it was she who, as commander, had begged for support. Raymond pointed out that even if the garrison were taken prisoner they could easily be ransomed in due course.

But the arguments on the other side were equally compelling, and it was these that Saladin must have been depending upon. He knew that the two fire-eaters, Gerard de Ridefort and Raynald, were with the army and both had been humiliated by his activities of recent months. When the council broke up just before midnight on the 2nd, it was with the king's agreement to follow the Raymond line and stay at Saffuriyah. But Gerard and Raynald stayed behind in the king's tent to persuade him to reverse that decision. They had some cogent points to put. They reminded Guy that three years before he had been in command of another great army which had refused battle to Saladin at the Springs of Goliath and that subsequently he had been charged with cowardice and deprived of his position as regent. Then he had followed similar cautious advice from Raymond, and it had been Raymond who had replaced him as regent. Furthermore, they argued, Raymond had been treacherously allied with the enemy until only weeks before and the result of that alliance had been the slaughter of more than a hundred knights. If the king, commanding the biggest army yet put in the field, refused the chance of destroying the enemy on the advice of a traitor then, said Gerard, the continuing loyalty of the Order of the Temple could not be guaranteed. One can only admire the skill with which Saladin had combined military and diplomatic manoeuvres during the foregoing months to open still further the divisions within the enemy councils so that the crucial error of judgement was virtually forced.

But there was another point which must surely have influenced Guy's decision to attempt the relief of Tiberias. The party of Raymond had argued that as the campaigning season came to an end the Muslim army would melt away. Now while it was true that the troops and emirs of al-Jazirah would certainly return to their distant bases, the Aleppan and Damascene troops and much of the Egyptian force would stay. Saladin would have ample forces to hold Tiberias over the winter. Guy must have asked himself what exactly the army was for if it could not prevent one of the kingdom's major cities falling to the enemy. If Tiberias could fall, which would be the next town to go and how long could the integrity of the state survive such encroachments? At dawn on Friday the 3rd, the army emerged from the security of Saffuriyah to begin its fateful last march. Saladin's jubilant reaction, reported by Baha'-ad-Din, fully supports the assumption that the whole 1187 campaign had been carefully calculated to the final grand objective, the recapture of Jerusalem. He told his secretary that this development 'confirmed that his decision, based on his earlier judgement, had been accurate', and continued,' "If they are defeated, killed and captured, Tiberias and all Palestine will have no one left to defend them and impede our conquest." '

Once it had been decided to march at all, it was crucial that the Christians reach the shores of Lake Tiberias in a single day's march. The second blow to Christian hopes came when Saladin succeeded in forcing the army to a halt in the evening of the 3rd. The morning had begun blazing hot and dry, and within hours of leaving the trees and gardens of Saffuriyah the Franks 'were suffering greatly from thirst'. A thick dust cloud choked the parched throats and caked on the sweaty skins of the labouring troops. Soon the Saracen army moving up from Kafr Sabt made contact and their horse archers poured an almost unbroken stream of arrows into the enemy. Their men and horses gasping for water, and under constant attacks on flanks and rear, the Christians' progress was slowed to a crawl. A running battle like this was one of the classic manoeuvres of crusading warfare – the Christian tactic was to maintain a steady march for its objective; the Muslim aim was of course to force the enemy to a standstill or break his column. Ahead of Guy and his troops Saladin and the army of Tiberias barred the way to the lake and made ready to check any attempt by the vanguard to charge. But it was the constant attacks in their rear that eventually forced the Christians to halt. The army was in danger of losing touch with the rearguard and Guy made camp near Lubya a mile or two from a low peaked hill known locally as the Horns of Hattin. The Franks had covered barely ten miles.

Surrounded by the misery of their wounded and dying they spent a fearful and demoralising night punctuated by jubilant shouts of the chant – 'God is great; there is no God but God' – from every quarter of the enemy camp. Ibn-al-Athir tells us that the Muslims 'had lost their first fear of the Franks. They could smell the victory in the air and the more they saw of the unexpectedly low morale of the Franks the more aggressive and daring they became.' While all this was going on Saladin ordered up reserves of arrows and checked troop placements. By dawn the Christians were completely surrounded, so tightly 'that not an ant could have got out.' The battle opened with a charge led by Saladin. Although weakened and demoralised by thirst, the knights put up a furious resistance and Saladin ordered the archers to begin firing. The Christian infantry abandoned all formation and attempted a wild break-through towards the waters of Lake Tiberias which lay shimmering in the distance. A prairie fire, started by a volunteer in the Muslim army, added its scorching smoke to their miseries. Most were cut down or taken prisoner. In a desperate attempt to break out Raymond, acting apparently on the orders of the king to open a way through the Muslim

ranks for the rest of the army, led a charge against the wing commanded
by Taqi-ad-Din. But Saladin's nephew was not willing to risk the break-
up of his formation in a mêlée with the heavily armed enemy, and
opened his ranks to let the knights thunder through ineffectually.
Looking back up the hill Raymond could see that the remnant of the
army was in a hopeless plight, he also realised that he could not break
back through the reformed ranks of Taqi-ad-Din's force. He and his
men rode away to Tripoli.

Hoping perhaps that the Muslim ranks would open to any determined
attack, other groups of Frankish knights mounted a series of charges
which almost dislodged the Muslims from their positions in spite of
their numbers. But they were steadily driven back leaving their dead
behind them. 'The Muslims wheeled around them like a circle about its
diameter'; inexorably that diameter was contracting. Guy and a party of
a few hundred made their way up the hill to the Horns of Hattin and
there they pitched the king's red tent for a last gallant stand.

It is apparent from the asides in their chronicles that Ibn-al-Athir,
Baha'-ad-Din and 'Imad-ad-Din were mightily impressed by the
Frankish knights. Now Guy, Gerard and Raynald, and the knights with
them, showed the superb fighting qualities that had so often saved the
kingdom from disaster and which had always forced Saladin to treat the
Christian army with respect. The final stages of the battle are described
for us in the words of his son al-Afdal, fighting in his first major
engagement, as reported by Ibn al-Athir:

> I was at my father Saladin's side during the battle, the first that I
> saw with my own eyes. The Frankish king had retreated to the hill
> with his band and from there he led a furious charge against the
> Muslims facing him, forcing them back upon my father. I saw that
> he was alarmed and distraught, and he tugged at his beard as he
> went forward crying: 'Give the Devil the lie!' The Muslims turned
> to the counter-attack and drove the Franks back up the hill. When
> I saw the Franks retreating before the Muslim I cried out for joy:
> 'We have defeated them!' But they returned to the charge with
> undiminished ardour and drove our army back toward my father.
> His response was the same as before, and the Franks retired back to
> the hill. Again I cried: 'We have beaten them!' but my father turned
> to me and said: 'Hold your peace; we shall not have beaten them
> until that tent falls!' As he spoke the tent fell, and the Sultan

dismounted and prostrated himself in thanks to God, weeping for joy.

The fact that these last charges were aimed at Saladin's position indicates that this was a tactical bid to win a last-moment victory and not a suicide last stand. In a council of war immediately before the battle a knight called John, who had served as a mercenary in Turkish armies, had advised that the best way to victory against these motley forces was to attack the commander-in-chief. If his section could be routed the whole battle was as good as won. The idea of a Christian mercenary in service with the Turks, which may sound oddly in our ears, would not have surprised Frank or Muslim. It is just one more instance of how the high-flown passions behind the rhetoric of crusade and *jihad* were often served by men with purely professional interests in warfare. In fact Sir John's sound advice nearly saved the day for Guy and his friends. A forlorn hope it certainly was, but from the intent and far from confident way in which Saladin followed the closing stages of the battle we can sense how well he knew the dour determination of his enemy and doubted the drive of his own troops.

By late afternoon, when the last grand gesture was made, it is possible that fatigue had finally finished the fighting spirit of the Christians. When their tent was at last overrun the king and his knights were found sitting and lying on the ground, totally exhausted. Their resolve had been finally broken by the loss of the True Cross. Taken into the battle as a standard by the bishop of Acre, it fell to the troops of Taqi-ad-Din and the bishop was killed.

'Stumbling like drunken men', the king and his companions were led before Saladin in fetters. To understand what was to happen it is important to remember the feud between Saladin and Raynald and also the fact that Guy was a recent arrival from Europe. The two were ordered to sit together and then Saladin began to berate Raynald as an oath-breaker. He replied coolly enough through the interpreter: 'This is how kings have always behaved; I have only followed the path of custom.' The other prisoners were not so calm. The king, who after hours of exhausting battle had lost his kingdom and the most prized relic of Christendom, was shaking, it appeared with fear, more probably from delayed shock. He appealed for a drink and Saladin affably ordered snow-cooled water to be brought. Guy passed the cup on to Raynald when he had drunk his fill. Immediately Saladin intervened. 'Tell the count,' he said, 'that you gave him that drink without permission from me. He has not received food or drink at my hand and so he cannot claim the protection of my house.' With this he left the pavilion to supervise the return of the army to its camp stations and the pitching of his own tent, and also 'to let Raynald roast at the fire of his own fear'.

Returning in the evening he entered the tent housing the prisoners and at once summoned Raynald to stand before him; then and there Saladin felled him with a blow which caught him on the shoulder. A guard struck off the head and the corpse was dragged out by the heels. Guy, already exhausted physically and emotionally, assumed this was the beginning of a general killing. His European background made it impossible for him to accept that the lord of the infidels could be a man of his word. Saladin tried to set his mind at rest after this macabre episode of rough justice. 'Twice have I sworn to kill that man when I had him in my power; once when he tried to attack Mecca and Medina and again when he broke the truce to capture the caravan.' Guy and his other noble companions were spared, and were in due course released – even the grand master of the Temple.

But the lesser knights of the order were not so fortunate. Their devotion and rigorous military training made them the most feared of the Christian troops and, with uncharacteristic coldbloodedness, Saladin ordered the slaughter of the hundred or so Templars and Hospitallers among the prisoners. Seated on a dais before the whole army he watched as the band of scholars, sufis and ascetics who had flocked enthusiastically to the army when the *jihad* was proclaimed and who had begged to be allowed to kill one of the knights, carried out the ceremonial killing. The day after the victory at Hattin the Countess Eschiva formally surrendered the citadel of Tiberias and was sent under Saladin's safe conduct to Tripoli.

It was the first of many capitulations. Hattin had cracked the defences of the kingdom wide open and castellans and city governors throughout the country knew this to be so. Saladin moved fast, to pick the fruits of victory while the Christian morale was at its lowest ebb. Acre, commanded by Joscelin of Courtenay, seneschal of the kingdom, was the first objective. On 10 July the place capitulated on condition that the lives of the citizens were spared; the majority of the Christian merchants marched out with their household possessions under the safe conduct but they left behind warehouses crammed with stocks of silks and metals, jewels and arms. As the streams of refugees marched through the city gates Saladin celebrated public prayers in the mosque:

the first Friday prayers to be held in the city since the infidel Franks first invaded Islam. Saladin, who loved to begin his campaigns and if possible fight his battles on the Muslim's Holy Day, found his victory the sweeter for being on a Friday, but the rest of the surrenders that summer could not always be timed so conveniently – they happened too fast. His commanders systematically took the submissions of the towns and castles of Galilee. Nazareth, Saffuriyah itself, Haifa, Caesarea fell without a fight, Nablus played a two-day masquerade of resistance, and the castle at Toron held out for a fortnight before yielding on 26 July to a force led by Saladin. Meanwhile, the Egyptian army under al-Adil had taken Jaffa by storm and sent its people into slavery to be sold in the markets of Aleppo. Beirut, Sidon, Jubail and many other places followed, so that by the end of August in the whole kingdom the Christians held only Tyre, Ascalon, Gaza and Jerusalem, apart from a few castles. To the south al-Karak and ash-Shaubak were still held for the Cross, yet after a bitter long siege they too eventually fell. It seemed that, short of a miracle or massive help from Europe, the collapse of the Christian adventure in Palestine was only a matter of time, and a fairly short time at that. Two events and two men combined to falsify this prediction.

It was exactly forty years since the last European intervention had ended in the disastrous Second Crusade, and though there had been appeals for help fairly regularly since that time nothing had come of them. In August 1187 Saladin would have needed a sophisticated intelligence network in Europe, combined with the skills of prophecy, to foresee the advent of the Third Crusade and the military genius of Richard of England. Nor could he have predicted the arrival of Conrad of Montferrat at the port of Tyre in mid-July.

A closer look at the crowded days which followed Hattin shows him building on the victory systematically and thoroughly. At the Field of Blood nearly seventy years before, the victory had been wasted; Il-Ghazi had been content to feast his triumph at Aleppo and send boastful dispatches to the caliph and others. By contrast Saladin was hard at work the next day. The battle was fought on a Saturday. Sunday was occupied with Countess Eschiva's surrender of the citadel at Tiberias. Next, officers and squadrons had to be detailed off to begin the quicksilver conquests already sketched. Yet on Wednesday Saladin and the bulk of his army were pitching camp before the walls of Acre, a good two days' march from Tiberias. The speed with which Seneschal de Courtenay conceded the town must have surprised Saladin; it certainly angered the townspeople who rioted in protest. Nevertheless, within two days the place was handed over and the Muslim troops were soon avidly dividing the spoils. The commanders had received bounties which lured them to the war before the campaign at al-Ashtara, but the common soldiery too expected war to be profitable. The field of Hattin had yielded little, but the bursting warehouses of Acre were a different matter – little serious fighting could be expected from the army for some days. However, Saladin still had work to do: he opened negotiations for the surrender of Tyre.

The ancient city stood on an island joined to the mainland by a narrow sandy spit which was crossed at the landward side by a massive wall. Even the weakest defence could hold it against assault from the shore. It had fallen to the Franks in 1124 only after six months of blockade by sea and land. Saladin knew he had to win the place as soon as was convenient, he also had no time for a long-drawn-out siege. Both for personal and political reasons Jerusalem must be higher on the agenda, but after the success at Acre, he felt confident that Tyre would capitulate quickly. His confidence was well founded. Negotiations moved rapidly and the commander took delivery of the yellow banners of Saladin which were to be flown on the city walls at the handing-over ceremony. Yet when, a few days later, Saladin and his official party arrived for that ceremony they found the gates closed against them. The near-miracle needed to save the town had happened in the person of Conrad of Montferrat.

He had arrived from Constantinople, a fugitive from justice and quite ignorant of Saladin's victory. He sailed into Acre harbour on 14 July and was a little puzzled that the ship's arrival was not greeted in the usual way. Soon he learnt that the place had just fallen to the Muslims and that Tyre was the nearest port still in Christian hands, Conrad made good his escape from Acre and headed north. In Tyre he agreed to take over the defence of the place on condition he was accepted as absolute lord there. The citizens and refugees crowded in the town agreed, the former commander left that night, and the town's walls were soon manned.

Saladin made no attempt to force the assault, nor to lay a siege, There was little reason he should. There were still important places, above all Jerusalem, to be taken. Tyre, strong as its defences were, would eventually be reduced when the army and Egyptian fleet could be jointly mobilised. Among the prisoners at Hattin had been Conrad's father, the aged marquis of Montferrat. Saladin paraded him before the walls of the town and threatened to kill him if it was not surrendered. Conrad refused to trade a Christian city for a single knight, even though it be his father. Nonplussed by such unfilial piety, Saladin spared the old man's life and moved on.

Elsewhere his hostages proved more useful. Jubail surrendered on the orders of its lord, who was then released. At Gaza the Templar garrison, obliged by the rules of the order to obey the grand master in all things, handed the citadel over to Saladin when he brought Gerard de Ridefort before the walls to order the capitulation. Ascalon, however, refused even when Gerard and the king himself first ordered and then begged the commander to give in. A fortnight of brave defence cost Saladin the lives of two of his emirs, and involved al-Adil and the Egyptian army. But Ascalon too was forced into surrender. Despite their resistance the people and garrison were granted honourable terms and allowed to leave the town in peace. It had been the same all over the conquered land. Saladin's clemency did much to win him the chivalrous reputation that soon surrounded his name in the West. It also encouraged the rapid collapse of the Christian establishment. With virtually the whole kingdom in his hands after two months of campaigning, the time had come to redeem the great pledge of the *jihad*. The army turned its joyous face to Jerusalem.

An intriguing sidelight on the fall of Jerusalem is the connection Saladin established early in the siege with the Orthodox Christians in the city. It seems they were preparing to open one of the gates for his troops but were forestalled by events. It was natural for Saladin's secret service to enlist the Orthodox whose hatred of the Latin authorities made them a natural fifth column. His dealings with the Emperor Isaac were on an altogether different plane. The two had been friendly since 1185 when it had been agreed that Saladin would transfer Church government in Palestine to Constantinople. Accordingly, soon after the fall of Jerusalem he handed over control of Christian affairs to the Byzantine patriarch, though not before he had sent a triumphant embassy to announce his victory at the imperial capital. It carried rich gifts, among them an elephant, jars of precious balsam, a thousand Turkish horses and rare spices. The emperor housed the envoys in one of the magnificent palaces at the centre of the city. When they returned they brought with them, as reciprocal presentations, part of the vast armoury Isaac had captured from the Sicilian invasion army some months before, as well as robes of honour for Saladin and his sons together with a crown.

It was typical of the shrewd diplomacy of Byzantium to mix the practical with the flattering, and also entirely typical to fit the present to the recipient. While in the Byzantine world the crown was the classic symbol of kingship, among the princes of Islam the most coveted distinction was a robe of honour from the hands of the caliph. It was usually accompanied by some honorific title or administrative appointment, and it was precisely such an honorific that Isaac hoped now to confer. His predecessor had demanded Saladin's homage, without success; rather more subtly, Isaac hoped now to bribe him into submission with a kingdom. 'I send you this [crown],' he wrote, 'because in my opinion you are and shall be rightfully a king, with my assistance and God willing.' No doubt Yusuf ibn-Aiyub Salah-ad-Din, al-Malik al-Nasir, king of Syria, ruler of Egypt, lord of Damascus and Aleppo and suzerain of Mosul, was amused by the pretension of the emperor of Greece and parts of Anatolia. But they remained good friends and at a full court held outside Acre on 6 January 1188 attended by his sons, nobles and officials of his court, and the ambassadors of the Greeks, Saladin reaffirmed the treaty.

He must have looked on this glittering assembly as some compensation for two disastrous months that had led up to it. After the triumph of Jerusalem, Saladin had confidently sent his army north to Tyre to finish off a resistance that was becoming irritating. In July he had not been ready to devote the time needed to take the city; now in November he was to find that the situation had changed radically. The city teemed with the refugees – merchants and nobles – Saladin had sent there from the fortresses and towns he had taken during the summer. This clemency had certainly encouraged many of the surrenders during those months. Perhaps Saladin had also assumed that when the time was ripe he could persuade the refugees, conveniently now concentrated in a single port, to embark en masse for the West. He was to be disillusioned. Conrad of Montferrat proved to be 'a devil incarnate in his ability to govern and defend a town and a man of extraordinary courage', and during the three months in which Saladin had been rounding off his conquests Conrad had been building up the already impressive defences of Tyre, and firing the demoralised population to resistance. He knew that without help from Europe he would have to surrender eventually, but luck and initiative had brought him the lordship of a rich town and he was not going to be dislodged easily. In fact he was confident of European intervention – he believed that the loss of Jerusalem would stir his generation as deeply as Edessa had their forebears. The archbishop

of Tyre was already in the West preaching the cause and in the meantime Conrad would hold out.

When, in mid-November, Saladin joined his army at Tyre, his heart
must have sunk. His crushing superiority in manpower was now virtually useless. Even if the wall and the new ditch that stretched in front of
it from the sea were overrun, his troops would have to fight step by step
up the narrow causeway and could easily be held by a fraction of their
numbers. Galleys were at station either side of the isthmus, armed with
ballistas and archers, so that the army 'was under constant attack not
only from the citizens in front but also from their flanks.' On his side
Saladin brought up no fewer than seventeen ballistas to play on the wall
and the town day and night, and divided his troops into companies to
keep up a twenty-four-hour action.

The other commanders with the army included Saladin's sons al-
Afdal and az-Zahir, his brother al-Adil with the Egyptian contingent,
and his nephew Taqi-ad-Din. But the key to the situation was a
squadron of ten Egyptian galleys which had been called up from Acre.
When, late in December, the Franks put these out of action by a boldly
pressed surprise attack, the whole operation came to a halt. For Saladin
to have held the army together as long as this was something of an
achievement. Before Hattin, Raymond had advised inaction precisely
because experience had taught that Muslim armies broke up of their own
accord with the advance of winter. Saladin's victories in the Muslim
world were too fresh in his commanders' memories for them to risk
outright insubordination, but now, with the possibility of a winter-long
campaign ahead of him, Saladin had to call a war council if only in the
interests of 'participation'. The feeling of the meeting was clearly against
him, though the decision rested with him.

Against continuing the siege it was argued that losses had been heavy,
that the troops were exhausted and they were discontented with the
long-drawn-out campaign and with the shortage of supplies. 'Let us go
away and rest during the cold winter and take up the fight again in the
spring.' Behind this specious reasoning, according to Ibn-al-Athir, the
emirs concealed the fear that if they stayed on station Saladin would
force them to contribute funds to the war effort. The war chest was
indeed empty. With the bounties paid at the beginning of the campaign
and booty from six months' successful war, which had gone straight into
their coffers, the emirs had made good profits. It was no part of their
plan to use them to finance a Holy War which only extended the power
and influence of the greatest man in Syria. Now Saladin had nothing to

offer but a hard cold winter siege with no promise of victory or money. He must have sensed that to leave the business unfinished would be a mistake, but his commanders were obviously unwilling to continue. He hesitated. Seeing his uncertainty, the opposition emirs, again according to Ibn-al-Athir, deliberately sabotaged the war effort – ignoring or mis-interpreting orders and eventually refusing to fight, arguing that there was too much discontent in the ranks. 'So', says the historian quite simply, 'Saladin was forced to go.' Pro-Zengid in sympathy, Ibn-al-Athir stresses the failure to take Tyre and blames Saladin exclusively. But he is honest enough to record the kind of obstruction that sometimes faced him when success began to flag. No doubt the fickle enthusiasm of his troops and officers explains in part why he avoided long-drawn-out sieges and major battles except on his own terms. 1187 had been a year of sweet victory and tremendous achievements. The kingdom of Jerusalem had been rubbed off the map and the third of Islam's Holy Cities was back in the Faith. But during the remaining years of his life Saladin and his armies would have to put the months of easy triumph behind them and struggle to hold what had been won. Those Byzantine ambassadors attending the brilliant court of Acre in January 1188 brought news that gave a disturbing glimpse of the clouds that lay in the future.

It seemed Europe was mobilising. But Saladin had also to face hostility from Baghdad. Successor to the heretical Fatimid rulers in Cairo, his name was even mentioned in Friday prayers in the great mosque of Mecca: enemies had whispered he intended to displace Caliph al-Nasir. In February 1188 the great *Hajj* from Damascus, led by Ibn al-Muqaddam in honour of Saladin as thanksgiving to Allah for the liberation of Jerusalem, came to blows with the *Hajj* from Baghdad outside Mecca, over a matter of precedence. Al-Nasir complained bitterly. He already resented Saladin's use of the honorific al-Nasir, which he claimed as his exclusive right; he even challenged the Kurd's claim to be the conqueror of Jerusalem, on the grounds that it had been taken in the name of the caliph, and so by the caliph himself. Saladin reacted with indignation, telling the envoy to his face that Jerusalem had fallen to his own army under his own banners – his official written response was more emollient. As he prepared to lead the fight against the Infidel once again, Islam's champion deferred to the leader of the Faithful.

# Chapter 11

# The Threat from the North

The Greek envoys had warned Saladin that crusading propaganda in Europe seemed likely to produce a high response. In fact the pope had taken up the cause, and in the very month that Saladin heard the depressing news the kings of France and England were pledging themselves to the Cross. In March the Emperor Frederick I Barbarossa followed suit and sent letters to Kilij Arslan in Konya and to Saladin to warn them of his intentions. Although he was nearly seventy his tall figure was little bowed and his immense charisma and authority were undimmed; he demanded that Saladin return the whole of Palestine to the Christians and challenged him to combat in November 1189. Saladin set about preparing his northern frontiers against the coming invasion. The problem of Tyre took second place.

Because, when it finally came, the Third Crusade was largely a French and English affair, and because some of the contingents came by sea to Tyre, historians, forgetting the long shadow cast by the German threat, have censoriously blamed Saladin for failing to force the capture of the town as a matter of urgency. Yet until April 1189, when a Pisan fleet made landfall there, this important commercial port had no military record at all. In any case, Saladin had only the historical precedents to guide him and neither the First nor the Second Crusade had come by sea. Even in 1147, when the whole of the seaboard was in Christian hands, Louis of France had chosen the land route through the Balkans and Anatolia, just as Barbarossa was now proposing. Two contingents had come by sea to the Second Crusade but they naturally made for Acre. Saladin had made it his immediate business after Hattin to take that great military port. In fact no one but the historians seems to have rated Tyre very highly in military terms. Henry II of England planned to travel overland, and wrote to the emperor in Germany, to the king of Hungary and to the emperor in Constantinople asking for a safe passage.

He also wrote to the archbishop of Antioch to assure him that he would be marching to the city. When the major forces did eventually arrive at the Crusade they ignored Tyre. Both Philip of France and Richard of England were to sail direct to their siege lines outside Acre. Saladin did well to leave the question of Tyre – the more so perhaps, we might think, because the army that did keep the Christian cause truly alight was not commanded by Conrad of Montferrat at all but by King Guy, to whom Conrad consistently refused access to Tyre or reinforcements from the troops with him there.

In the spring of 1188 all this was in the future. Saladin had to prepare against the long-term possibility of invasion from a German army that would be coming overland from the north through the territories around Antioch. In the summer of 1188 he backed up a vigorous military campaign both there and in the kingdom, while continuing negotiations with the Byzantine empire.

The fortifications of Acre needed repair, and while Saladin held his winter court there he called in the architect, the emir Karakush, who had designed the defensive works at Cairo during the 1170s. With the work well in hand Saladin left for Damascus in the spring, and then, in the early summer, he headed north. The march lay past Baalbek, up the wide valley between Mount Lebanon and the Anti-Lebanon which led to the valley of al-Buqai‘ah, running down to the coast. The fortresses of ‘Akkar and al-Arqah, which dominated the valley, fell with little opposition. He may have hoped to conquer Tripoli, but the town received help from William II of Sicily and Conrad from Tyre, and Saladin's chief objectives at this time were the fortresses inland and the north, which could be expected to give aid and succour to the Germans when they eventually arrived. The army, reinforced by contingents from al-Jazirah under the command of ‘Imad-ad-Din of Sinjar, soon had an impressive line of Christian capitulations to its credit.

The fortress of Krak des Chevaliers was by-passed, and at Tortosa, where the town was overrun, the Templar garrison managed to hold out in a strongly fortified tower; the great Hospitaller castle at al-Marqab was left in the rear with a masking force posted to contain the garrison, but the ports of Jabala and Latakia were quickly taken, and on 29 July the supposedly impregnable and truly intimidating castle of Sahyun fell. Pushing deeper into the territories of Antioch, Saladin took the important castles of Burzey, Sarminiqa and Bakas Shoqr. Ibn-al-Athir, who was with the army, was considerably impressed by the immense strength of the castles and by the sultan's vigour and courage. At Burzey his personal guard led one of the assaults and 'Saladin armed at all points went in amongst them to spur them on.' At the end of August he continued northwards to secure the strategic points of Darbsaq and Baghras, which controlled the pass through the hills to the north of Antioch known as the Syrian Gates. In two months Bohemond of Antioch had been reduced to his capital and its port of St Symeon; he had made no attempt to relieve the outlying castles, despite their appeals, and even when Saladin attacked Baghras he stood idly by.

Yet a determined sortie could well have saved the place. Before the siege was laid, Saladin had conferred with his emirs, and a strong party was opposed to attacking the town, arguing that it was so close to Antioch that the army could easily come under attack from the city. But Saladin continued with his plans even though the army was 'inspired by fear of the inhabitants of Antioch who they believed could easily overrun the army with the support of the neighbouring population'. As the siege dragged out the troops became convinced the place would hold out and so increase their danger from the city. Despite their earlier successes, Saladin's troops were still frightened by the Franks. Saladin himself was prepared to attack Bohemond's capital, but the troops from al-Jazirah were anxious to get back to their homes to rest and renew their equipment. When Bohemond offered an eight-month truce it was eagerly agreed to.

The whole army returned to Damascus with the sultan, but there he discharged the troops from Sinjar and Mosul and the other cities of the east. His advisers urged him to release his own troops for the winter, but he refused while Kaukab, Safad, al-Karak and other such fortresses were still in the hands of the Franks. 'It is absolutely essential that we rid ourselves of these irritants in the midst of Muslim territory, for there can be no guarantee that their inhabitants will not attack us.' This was no mere rhetoric, as the chronicler confirms that the inhabitants of the towns within striking distance of a castle like al-Karak were frightened of the Franks living there and dreaded the possibility of attack from them. Accordingly in mid-November, after barely a month's rest in Damascus, Saladin led his own men to the siege of the Templar castle of Safad, a few miles to the north of Lake Tiberias. Despite driving rain which reduced the field of battle to a quagmire, he held his men to the siege for a month, and in early December the garrison surrendered. The foul weather continued, but Saladin had more work to do and pushed on to the greater and more inaccessible fortress of Kaukab. A month later this too had fallen, and these triumphs were soon followed by exciting news from the south. The army of al-Adil had received the surrender of al-Karak. The siege had lasted more than a year, and the defenders had sold their women to the Bedouin in exchange for supplies. Later the same year ash-Shaubak fell too.

But Saladin was listening for news from the north. Crusaders had traditionally depended on the goodwill of Constantinople, and Saladin hoped to persuade Isaac to deny a passage to Frederick Barbarossa. Early in 1188 a new embassy had been dispatched with more rich presents and, according to Latin chroniclers, large supplies of poisoned wine and grain to be used on the German troops. The evidence for this early episode in the history of chemical warfare is prejudiced – the Latins were understandably keen to blacken the reputation of Isaac, so shamelessly willing to deal with the Infidel. In exchange for the Orthodox control of the Church in Palestine, he had offered his protection to Islam in Constantinople. At his invitation Saladin sent a minbar (pulpit) for the Muslim community in Constantinople. But the ship carrying it was captured by a Genoese squadron and the pulpit taken back to Tyre. Conrad sent letters to Europe reporting the capture as proof positive of the double-dealing of the emperor.

At first Saladin hoped for great things from the alliance. It is clear from the Muslim historians that all Islam was terrified by the news of the German advance. Barbarossa had put in the field the best-trained and best-equipped army yet known to the Crusades. They set out from Ratisbon in May 1189 and crossed the Danube in June; Isaac was quite powerless to stop their progress through the Balkans. Yet at the same time he was entertaining an embassy from Saladin with every mark of distinction. When a German envoy, led by the bishop of Munster, reached the capital in July to announce the emperor's intended time of arrival, Isaac had them thrown into prison and gave their insignia to Saladin's ambassadors, no doubt as an earnest of his good faith. Soon after this they returned to Saladin, finding him in his camp in Marj Uyun at the siege of Shaqif Arnun (Beaufort). They were able to tell him of developments in the Balkans, and also brought an invitation from Isaac for Saladin to send a second minbar along with *imams*, and a muezzin to the imperial capital. Later that year there was an event to shock the imagination of the Western Christian world when the name of the caliph of Baghdad was invoked in a Sunni ceremony held in Constantinople in the presence of Muslim inhabitants and visiting merchants, with the connivance of the Emperor Isaac. It was an achievement of which Saladin could reasonably be proud, but he was beginning to realise he could hope for nothing more practical from Isaac.

In the March of 1190 his supposed ally provided the transport which carried Frederick's army across the Dardanelles. The Greek alliance had provided little positive advantage. Even the once formidable sultan of Konya, who had troubled both Saladin and Isaac, was powerless against the Germans, and in May Frederick entered Kilij Arslan's capital. Saladin, now involved with the Frankish forces outside Acre, sent a detachment of troops north to guard the passes through the hills north of Antioch. At the beginning of June Frederick came through the last range of the Taurus mountains and led his troops down into the Cilician plain with the sea glittering in the distance beyond the port of Seleucia (modern Silifke). The best approach to the town meant a river crossing, and it was here that the emperor met his death, 'drowned at a place where the water was not even up to his waist'. Perhaps the tough old man took a chill, either after bathing or from the shock of cold water on sweltering armour. (See page 146.)

Saladin and all Islam saw the hand of God in this miraculous deliverance. Such terror had been inspired by the approach of the Germans that in the district near Mosul administered by Ibn-al-Athir's brother the price of corn was affected. One of Saladin's emirs had a village in the district; the bailiff of the estate wrote at harvest time asking instructions for the sale of the crops. The emir, with the army in Syria, ordered his agents not to sell a single grain but only a few days later gave permission for the sale to go ahead. When he returned to Mosul he was asked to explain his change of mind to his friends. 'Well,' he replied, 'when we got news of the German king's advance, we were convinced that he would drive us out of Syria and so I took precautions to ensure a good reserve of provisions on my estates back here. But when God destroyed the Germans there was no need for food reserves.'

For the death of Frederick did effectively destroy his army. There were Germans too who saw the hand of God in the great emperor's death, and some of the leaders turned back, though barely a hundred miles from the Christian states they had come to help. Others left the army to go by sea from Seleucia to Tyre, and Duke Frederick of Swabia, who took over after his father's death, found himself with a weakened and demoralised force. Because he too was ill, the remnant of the Germans, whose numbers had in any case been reduced by guerrilla attacks in Turkey and by disease, pushed on without him and lost still more men in a running battle with Saladin's men guarding the northern passes. When they reached Antioch in August the magnificent fighting machine which had set out from Ratisbon fifteen months before was now an irrelevant, indisciplined rump. In June, when the German emperor lay dying in Asia Minor, the kings of France and England had not even set out for the Holy Land, and they did not arrive there until some ten months later. In those months Saladin should have been able to demolish the beach-head positions round Tyre and Acre. We must now attempt to see why, even with the German threat lifted, he could not.

The story begins back in July 1188, when Saladin released King Guy and the knights with him after they had sworn to leave Palestine and never take arms against him again. Arriving at Tripoli, Guy of course found no difficulty in getting a prelate to release him from this oath – given, so it was claimed, under duress and to an infidel. In addition Saladin had allowed defeated garrisons safe conducts to Tyre and other places still in Christian hands; so that while the kingdom of Jerusalem had lost its lands, it had once more its leaders and a growing number of soldiers. In the eyes of Saladin's Muslim critics such clemency was suicidal. But Saladin had not necessarily miscalculated. The political infighting around Guy's kingship had only been thinly papered over for the Hattin campaign. With Guy back in the arena the controversy became still more acrid. In the autumn of 1188 he marched down to Tyre and demanded the place be handed over to him. But Conrad, from being a mere adventurer, was now regarded by many as the saviour of the kingdom; Guy, on the other hand, was remembered as the man who lost Hattin. Obviously playing for the highest stakes, Conrad refused to hand over Tyre, claiming to be acting as trustee for the European monarchs who would settle the dispute on their arrival.

Guy had to retire to Tripoli for the winter, but in April 1189 he was back, determined to force Conrad to surrender. It looked as though the Christians were settling down to a full-scale civil war. It is hardly surprising that Saladin was not much worried about Tyre, now being blockaded for him by the Christians themselves. In a letter to his brother in the Yemen he wrote: 'Only Tyre remains to them; if it were not on the coast and so can be revictualled from the sea, it would have been taken long ago. But, thanks to the Grace of God, Tyre is no longer a fortress which protects its inhabitants but rather a prison that hems them in; they are prisoners enjoying provisional liberty, dead men whom life has not quite abandoned.'

But in April 1189 there was another development which should perhaps have worried the sultan. The Pisan fleet which arrived outside Tyre in that year to help Conrad fell out with him and went over to Guy. Sea power gave the king an important new advantage. But at this moment Saladin encamped with his army at Marj Uyun was engrossed with the attempt to take Beaufort, commanded by Raynald of Sidon. He was one of the few Christians with a genuine enthusiasm for Islamic culture, he was fluent in the language, and it was even rumoured had passages from the Koran read to him at meals. He now used all his guile to persuade Saladin that if encouraged he might actually become a Muslim. He also claimed to be fearful that if he handed over the castle too easily his wife and family, at Tyre with Conrad, might be in danger. He asked to be allowed until August to prepare the ground for the surrender. Fascinated with his enemy's high culture and adroit intellectualism, the sultan spent long hours in debate with him while Raynald's agents openly bought provisions in the markets set up for Saladin's army. When August came and Raynald still failed to deliver the castle Saladin eventually lost patience and sent him to prison in Damascus. Beaufort was not taken until the following summer, but by that time events had swept on in a dramatic and unexpected way.

In August 1189 Guy, realising that Tyre was virtually impregnable, lifted the siege, and with the Pisans sailing down the coast in convoy marched down to Acre. It was a reckless gamble by a man desperately needing success to retain any political credibility. Saladin immediately saw the opportunity offered and marched out in pursuit, intending to destroy the small Christian army on the march. But the Christians were to be spared once again. 'When Saladin consulted his emirs, about whether they should take the enemy by the heels and attack them on the march, or meet them face to face by taking a different route from theirs, the emirs said: "There is no need for us to follow them, for their road is difficult and narrow and we could not easily take them as we want. It is better to proceed by the broader road and attack them from the rear as they approach Acre, where we will disperse them."' Saladin was totally unconvinced. 'If the Franks reach their destination and get a firm hold of the territory, it will not be easy for us to dislodge them.' But, as on other occasions, his dependence on his allies, made it possible for them to override him. Nevertheless, he did order skirmishers to keep in touch with the Christian march and harass stragglers. Their success suggested to at least one dispassionate observer that had Saladin's full strategy been adopted it would have been successful. As it was, Guy made good his rash expedition, and, on 27 August 1189, began to pitch his tents around the walls of Acre.

It must be said that the failure of the German campaign pleased others besides the Muslims. The Byzantine emperor, Isaac Angelus, was more than content to see the collapse of the Western initiative, even though it meant a reverse for Christian arms. Since Gregory VII before the First Crusade, popes had envisaged the union of Orthodox Constantinople with Rome by force of arms. The leaders of the Christian churches in Asia both feared and hated their Latin opposite numbers in the Crusader states. In a letter that reported the death of Barbarossa, the head (*catholicos*) of the Armenian Church dubbed himself Saladin's mameluke and prayed that God would 'bless our master' who had reunited the Faithful (and here of course he was referring to the Muslim Faithful). This was surely beyond the requirements of diplomatic sycophancy. Incidentally, it is the *catholicos* who seems to suggest that the emperor took a chill after bathing; but a near contemporary illustration most graphically depicts a rider, without armour, thrown by a stumbling horse – the Latin reads '*in flumine defunctus*', i.e. 'dead in the river'. An angel lifts the soul, innocent of sin as a babe, to the hand of God.

In the forthcoming struggle between Saladin and Richard of England the Christian East seems in general to have sided with its oriental masters against its Western co-religionists. After the fall of Jerusalem, Saladin had been urged by his more extreme advisers to demolish many of the Christian shrines, including the Church of the Holy Sepulchre, as monuments to idolatry. While Muslims revere Jesus Christ (Isa) as a true prophet in the line leading up to Muhammad, they deny his crucifixion and divinity. Other advisers argued that the proposed destruction, while in conformity with Islam, would enrage the idolaters, i.e. the Christian population in Muslim territories. The shrines in question are, of course, as sacred to the Eastern churches as they are to Western Christendom. In fact, at the request of Emperor Isaac, guardianship of the Holy Places was assigned to the Orthodox authorities and the celebrations of the Latin rite in those places largely superseded.

If the rump kingdom of Jerusalem, with the help of its European crusader allies, could recover the city, this settlement would be overturned. Meanwhile, it lessened the danger that the governor of Jerusalem and other cities might face subversion from the indigenous Christian populations.

# Chapter 12

# Acre, the City for which the World Contended

The modern town of Akka stands on a hook-like promontory jutting south into the Bay of Haifa. In the middle ages the harbour, the safest on the Syrian coast, was embraced by the curve of this peninsula and was further protected by a mole running eastwards from its tip. The mole was guarded at its landward end by the strongly fortified Tower of Flies. The result was a large military harbour, virtually inaccessible to seaborne attack. The landward defences were still more formidable, consisting of two massive walls which ran due north and due east to meet in a right-angle heavily fortified by the Cursed Tower. Acre had been one of the wealthiest cities of the Christian kingdom and a favoured royal residence. Now it was the chief arsenal for Saladin's Palestine provinces and its great defences had been restored to war readiness by Karakush, the architect, who had also been appointed the commander of the city. Considerations of strategy and prestige ensured that the coming battle would be hard. It did not seem likely to be very protracted.

Guy had his small army pitch camp in a wide arc from north to south with Acre at the focus. For a complete landward blockade he had to cover the ground from the River Belus in the south to the coast north-wards at more than a bowshot range from the city walls. He did not have enough men. If he was to take the city he had also to blockade it from the sea, but in the autumn of 1189 the Muslims were able to sail in and out almost at will. Just how the Christians were able to hold this perilous situation for two years, in the face of Saladin's massive army, is the critical question of the later years of his career. Regrettably there is no one conclusive answer. The starting point of any analysis must be Saladin himself. Whatever was achieved for Islam in Palestine in the 1180s was the doing of this one man. There was nothing automatic or overriding about the drive to recover Jerusalem. When Nur-ad-Din united Aleppo and Damascus way back in 1154 the Christians had believed, with reason, that their hour had come. Yet twenty years passed and the great champion of Islam died without having made any serious move to recover the Holy Places. The lesser lords of Syria who were eventually forced into alliance with Saladin had little real motivation to join the *jihad* but fear of him and hope of plunder. Once Jerusalem fell it became another province in his massive empire, and the enthusiasm for battle with the infidel became still weaker. Only the will of Saladin kept the Muslims at war while it was only his skill and personal inspiration on the field of battle that saved them from defeat. Apart from his brother al-Adil, none of his commanders was capable of the sustained effort and imagination that the slogging war against the Franks demanded. Even the dashing Taqi-ad-Din had called up Saladin to conclude the siege of Toron – a standard enough operation – while throughout the Acre campaign only his personal presence could bring success.

But Saladin, now in his early fifties, was beginning to weaken under the strain of a lifetime of work and war. His health had never been strong and a recurrent stomach complaint laid him up more and more frequently, causing lapses in the fighting at often critical moments. For the army in general had little interest in continuing the war. Most of the great cities of the kingdom were now in Muslim hands and the opportunities of plunder correspondingly reduced. Nor did the coming campaign offer much in the way of exciting action. Since its nomadic days the Turkish army had relied on speed and mobility – the static warfare of the siege was not its métier. After Hattin, Saladin had systematically bought towns and fortresses with the lives of the garrisons. Strong Christian forces remained in the field, but the price was worth paying to save his troops the kind of action where they were at their weakest. Once King Guy had begun to establish himself around Acre in the last days of August just such a campaign began to seem unavoidable.

At first, however, things must have seemed promising. For the first month there were almost daily skirmishes and battles between garrison and Franks, Franks and the main Muslim relieving force. The weather was kind and an almost tournament atmosphere developed. Knights and emirs and the soldiery of both sides got to know each other so well that the battle might be halted for an hour or two while they exchanged news and views or even brought up the musicians from the rear for a session. When the entertainment was over the fighting was resumed by common consent. On one occasion a mock battle was even arranged between two lads from the city and two from the besieging army. One of the Muslim boys threw his Christian opposite number to the ground and claimed him as prisoner; a Christian knight solemnly offered the victor a ransom of two dinars, which was gratefully received, and the prisoner duly released.

A note of reality was struck in mid-September when Taqi-ad-Din, commanding the northern wing near the coast, succeeded in forcing a way through the Christian lines. Inevitably Saladin was closely involved. His concern with the details of the operation was 'like that of a mother, threatened with the loss of one of her children', for three days he ate virtually nothing. But the outcome was a triumphant entry with his entourage into the city. While the sultan went the rounds of the defences his courtiers enthusiastically shied stones down at the ranks of the besieging army. 'Great had been the fear of the Franks and they would have fled if they could; but our leaders considered the opening of the road as an unexpected success and did not finish off the job although had they seized the moment they would have exterminated the enemy who were completely demoralised. Given this respite they were able to re-establish their position and close the road.' Ominously for the future, they began to fortify their camp with trenches and revetments. It was the first experiment in a system of defences that would soon make the Franks impregnable.

There were to be many times in the future when Saladin was robbed of a decisive advantage by the unwillingness of his men and their commanders to push home an unexpected victory; but on this occasion he himself may have been hesitant to commit his whole force, as his army was not yet up to strength. Reinforcements were expected from Egypt and three sizeable detachments of the main army were still in the north, blockading the garrisons of Antioch, Tripoli and Tyre. The troops at Acre ranged from the relatively untrained bands of Diyar-Bakr, 'men completely ignorant of military matters', as Baha'-ad-Din called them, to veterans who had fought under Shirkuh at the conquest of Egypt twenty years before. They were encamped in a semi-circle round Acre, matching the arc of the Frankish besieging army. But it was more than a camp; it was a standing line of battle carefully planned by Saladin to reduce, as far as possible, the weaknesses of the material that made it up. It was a general principle with him to order his line of march meticulously to be ready for action at any time, and this camp was arranged on the same lines.

The northern anchor point of the two-mile crescent was made up of veterans under the command of Taqi-ad-Din, one of the best soldiers in the army. A firm link between this wing and the forces of the centre was made by further divisions of trustworthy troops, next came the contingents from Nablus, Diyar-Bakr and Mosul, a right of centre bloc consisting of soldiers of less sure loyalty or ability. The centre itself consisted of divisions under al-Afdal and az-Zahir, with their father nominally in overall command. On Saladin's immediate left the cohorts of warlike Kurds under their commander al-Mashtub and further along the line the forces of Sinjar, of Harran and Edessa under Gökböri, and on the extreme left wing the ever reliable old guard of Shirkuh. Saladin's HQ was on a low hill a mile or so in the rear. The morning of 4 October found him galloping down to the army to prepare for what looked like a major offensive being mounted by the enemy.

Since Taqi-ad-Din's mid-September victory the Franks had been reinforced by a force from Tyre under Count Conrad, though the quarrel with Guy was only patched up. He would fight with the king's army but only if he were treated as his equal. Also with the royal army were the count of Thuringia, with a contingent of Germans, and a force of Templars. It was the biggest concentration the Christians could hope for in the foreseeable future, and the last chance they could expect for a decisive engagement with the Muslims. Both Baha'-ad-Din and Ibn-al-Athir stress that the Christian attack was quite unexpected. That morning 'the Muslims were about their usual duties, some coming down to offer battle, others doing chores about the camp or going to fetch the provisions for their group for the day.' From the vantage point of his HQ Saladin had been able to see the signs of unusual preparation in the enemy camp, but there was not time to do more than give the signal for a general muster to action stations as soon as possible. Now the point of that carefully planned camp could be seen. 'Because the sultan had disposed his troops even in camp, according to their order of battle, they did not have to change their positions when they heard the signal for action.'

The first attack was a charge by the Templars against Taqi-ad-Din. He decided on the time-honoured tactic of the feigned retreat, perhaps to give the rest of the line more time to come to bear by drawing the attack off-centre. Saladin had left the immediate command of the centre to Isa, the governor of Jerusalem, while he 'rode up and down the battalions, urging them on to the battle and calling on their zeal for the true religion.' Without his tireless inspiration throughout the battle it is probable that the surprise achieved by the Christians would have brought them a notable victory. As it was the need to be everywhere at once in the opening stages, anxiously keeping an eye on the success with which his emirs were bringing their forces to bear even as he rallied the morale of the troopers, led Saladin into a serious and surprising mistake. Both our two chief authorities for the battle agree that it was by his order that a few contingents were detached from the centre to go to the help of Taqi-ad-Din. Perhaps the sultan assumed the right was as disorganised as some other parts of the line and was in real retreat. He did not have the chance to recover his misjudgement. The enemy high command at once sized the situation up and a phalanx of foot and horse was soon doubling 'as one man' towards the weakened centre. Surrounded by foot soldiers the knights' horses were almost proof against the Muslim bowmen, and then at the last moment they opened up and the cavalry crashed through in perfect order to scatter the ill-fated men from Diyar-Bakr. The rout continued up to the shores of Lake Tiberias – some of the Turks did not stop their flight until they reached the streets of Damascus itself. As for the citizens of Tiberias, they fled their city immediately, on what sounded like the news of a massive Christian victory.

Returning from their invigorating chase over the hills of Galilee, the knights made for the hill on which Saladin's tent was standing, killing a few camp-followers and chamberlains as they went. 'It was only by God's grace that they did not cut down Saladin's tent for if they had, the whole Muslim army would have realised how far they had got and that the centre of their own army had fled before the enemy, and this would have led to a general flight.' As it was, a little tired from their exertions, they looked about to find with some surprise that they were divided from their own people by a fierce battle. On the right, Taqi-ad-Din still held firm and forced the Christian troops launched into the gap into the centre to turn aside and deal with this opposition first. On the left the Muslim ranks were almost unbroken and some detachments were moving up to cut off the retreat of the Christians returning from the rout. Even the centre was reforming, inevitably as we have now learnt to expect, under persuasion and threats of the ubiquitous Saladin. And it was with a group of horse drawn from this demoralised section of the army that the sultan tipped the scales decisively against the Franks. Under his leadership they were once more a fighting force and were straining to get at the small, isolated body coming down from the hill.

Saladin, who had marshalled them in a fold in the ground, held them back until the knights had passed and then unleashed the charge. The rest of the Christian army saw their supposedly victorious brothers stampeded into a panic flight and rushed pell mell back to their lines.

The moment could be turned into a crashing victory and Saladin prepared to gather his men for the *coup de grâce*. The whole engagement had shown him at his brilliant best as a commander in the field. The careful planning at the outset of the campaign had ensured the army was virtually on a war footing at a moment's notice, and it was his tireless energy at the moment of battle that had raised the whole line into action. The mistake of the weakened centre, if it was in fact his and not that of Isa of Jerusalem, had been magnificently recovered, and the final charge, made possible only because he, yet again, had restored the shattered morale of the centre, had revealed his incisive tactical sense. Now, even after exhausting hours of battle, he grasped the nub of the reversed tactical situation and was girding for the conclusive encounter – only to find his army would not follow. An alarm was spreading all along the line that the camp had been pillaged and men and officers were peeling off in all directions to check the safety of their possessions and hard-earned booty from earlier campaigns.

The rout of the central divisions and the pell-mell cross-country pursuit by the Franks had been seen from the tents behind the battle lines where the servants and camp-followers had deduced the total defeat of the Muslim army. Supposing their masters dead or in flight, they looted the rich camp furniture and stored plunder, and, taking the pack horses, made their best speed eastwards. When the battleweary warriors got back to their tents it was to find that they had 'escaped the danger of death only to fall into other misfortunes. The rich found themselves paupers and the bravest man hesitated.' Himself overgenerous when dividing the spoils of war between his emirs, Saladin now found himself obliged to leave a won battle to organise a treasure hunt for their lost possessions. There was nothing else to be done if he expected still to have an army the next day. Messengers and armed posses were dispatched across the hills to bring back the miscreants and a proclamation read through the camp that everything was to be brought before the specially convened court of redistribution.

To add insult to injury, it was Saladin who had to preside over the court. Yet he did it with 'a firm and generous heart, a smiling demeanour and with the rectitude of judgement he had shown in trust in God and that energy he had in the defence of religion'. Somewhat unnecessarily the chronicler adds that the whole business was for Saladin 'a great fatigue'. It is a measure of the man's strength of will that he was able to remain completely unruffled while he dealt with a matter supremely indifferent to him but vitally important to the loot-hungry captains who manned his armies. It is evidence of his shrewdness as an adjudicator that we hear of no disputed claims afterwards. Despite the disruption all this had caused, Saladin called a council of war within the week and urged a new attack in force before the Franks could recover their position completely. But 'they reached the conclusion that it would be best to withdraw the army a few miles further back and allow the men to rest'.

It must be confessed that the emirs may have had other good reasons on their side. The stench from the thousands of decaying corpses, either on the battlefield or dumped in the River Belus, chief supply of fresh water to the Christians, was threatening to become a major health hazard. Saladin, exhausted by the almost ceaseless exertions of the past week, had again relapsed with his old illness; while the soldiery at large, having been in the field for an unbroken fifty days, was entitled to a respite. Even so it was this week more than any other which made possible the Third Crusade. The Franks used it to strengthen their defences. Their camp became transformed into a strongly fortified town with numerous sally ports and posterns, which made it easy for them in the future to launch sorties where and when they wished. 'Every day the spies informed Saladin of the Franks' activities and the seriousness of the situation. But he, sunk in illness, was in no state to act.' His advisers could now see, as the walls and trenches continued to grow round the Frankish perimeter, what the hesitation of a few days previously was going to cost the Muslims, and some urged Saladin to send the army back under a different commander to put a stop to these activities. Perhaps if al-Adil had been there to take charge Saladin would have considered the proposal but he knew the rest of his staff commanders too well. 'If I am not there with them they will achieve nothing whatsoever and might well do more harm than good.'

It was only a few days after this that he received definite confirmation that the German Crusade which he had long been dreading and preparing for had been on the march since May. The royal chancellery was set hard at work and on 23 October an embassy left the camp at Acre on the road north to rally support for the *jihad*. It was led by the secretary Baha'-ad-Din, who carried letters for the rulers of Sinjar, Mosul and Irbil – to send yet more troops – and for the caliph, to lend his support to Saladin's appeals. Hoping to shame the Islamic leaders into action he bitterly compared the Muslims – 'lacking in zeal, not one of them responding to the call' – with the zeal of the Christians – 'for Him they worship, and in defence of their faith'. 'In defence of their religion they consider it a small thing to spend even their life, and they have kept their infidel brothers supplied with arms and champions in war.' Muslims with Saladin's army were genuinely astonished by the degree of European support that was arriving. A prisoner told Ibn-al-Athir that although he was his widowed mother's only son she had sold their house to equip him for the Crusade. There were many similar tales to fire the indignation of Saladin's courtiers when they considered the general indifference of Islam, for the fact was that the only territories to send troops to the Holy War were those whose rulers were Saladin's subordinates or clients. The caliph sent merely good wishes, a consignment of arms and incendiary chemicals used in the making of Greek fire, and authority to raise taxes up to 20,000 dinars from some of the western provinces nominally under Baghdad's authority.

In November al-Adil arrived with the reinforcements from Egypt; these replaced the contingents from the eastern cities, most of which were returning home for the winter. At the end of October fifty galleys had broken through into the harbour, while in December a large Egyptian fleet under the personal command of the renowned admiral Lulu brought supplies and men. But these were the only successes Saladin could boast for months ahead. Torrential rains reduced the plain about Acre to a sea of mud. However, if this stopped all Muslim attacks it did not prevent the Christians from completing their trench and walls of circumvallation, so that by the end of November Acre was almost completely blockaded by land. Moreover, the Christians too were getting new recruits, men who had become impatient of the political saraband which was keeping the kings of England and France in Europe, and with the slow progress of the Germans. In the early winter months, Danes, Frisians, Flemings, Frenchmen, Germans and Hungarians were among those to make landfall on the broad beaches in the bay below Acre. Then, in March, Conrad was able to sail up the coast to Tyre and return with more men without any effective opposition from the Muslim ships.

Apart from desultory fighting at the Christian fortifications, more than six months passed without Saladin's men making any attempt to dislodge their enemies. During the spring of 1190 the contingents from Harran, Aleppo and the other eastern cities began to return to the camp, but many of these were immediately sent northwards to watch the passes where the Germans were expected. For their part the Christians did not make another attempt to force a full-scale battle; they were content to keep within their massive defences and keep up the pressure on the garrison. At the end of April they were ready for a major assault. Conrad had come back from Tyre with a load of specially seasoned timber and other materials with which the army carpenters built three siege towers, each about ninety feet tall and with five separate floors crowded with troops. They overtopped the walls so that the bowmen could keep the defenders under heavy fire while the fosse at the foot of the walls was being filled up. If this could be done, and the siege towers rolled up to the walls, the future of the city would be black. An operation on this scale would be able to put enough troops on the walls to force a massive bridgehead.

Saladin ordered heavy attacks on the Christian defence works, and for eight days battle raged without a break. The Frankish attack on the walls was slowed down but by no means halted. From contemporary accounts it is clear that the siege towers were exceptionally well designed and well protected. Not even constant bombardment with Greek fire destroyed them, and the garrison commander, Karakush, was almost frantic with fear that the town was lost. At last he was persuaded to listen to the proposals of a Damascene inventor and scientist who, apparently, had come to settle in Acre after its capture. He asked and got temporary command of the garrison's ballistas and directed the fire. The first salvo was of the standard naphtha canisters which had so far produced no results, and when they again failed the defenders saw their enemies dancing in derision on the top of the towers. But then followed the patent compound, and almost at once the towers burst into a sheet of flame. Perhaps this anonymous twelfth-century chemist had discovered an explosive compound which detonated spontaneously on mixing, and, lacking the technology of fused, compartmented shells, was obliged to discharge the constituents separately. Whatever it was, his invention was a total success. The first tower was destroyed with all hands; by the time the artillery had trained round to the other towers their soldiers had fled back to the lines and watched the destruction of the doomed military hardware. It was the end of the attack and the city was saved. The inventor was granted an audience with Saladin, who asked him to name his reward.

To the sultan's astonishment, no doubt, the reply came: 'I want no reward but the love of God.' It must have been a refreshing change to meet a man truly devoted to the ideals which Saladin had so often proclaimed.

During the rest of the season the relieving army was involved in only two battles, though both were hard. A fortnight after the destruction of the siege towers by the garrison the Franks came under a heavy attack from Saladin's army. But after an eight-day battle Saladin had not made a dent in the great defence works. His army was not at full strength – the siege of Beaufort still tied down a large number of men, and others had been sent north in preparation for the coming of the Germans. But nothing suggests that even at full strength the army had either the imagination or the determination to solve the problem of trench warfare posed by the Frankish position. Perhaps at this stage Saladin's objective was to contain the threat at Acre until the northern danger had been dealt with. In June a large Egyptian fleet fought its way into Acre harbour with supplies, but the situation in the Christian camp was also improving. In July it was reinforced by a large French force commanded by Henry of Champagne. Later that month, however, the northern divisions of the Muslim army won a crushing victory over a body of thousands of Frankish foot who attacked against the advice of their officers. Thousands were killed, among them, to the astonishment of the Muslims, a number of women who were not recognised until their corpses were being stripped of their valuable chain mail. It was the last major encounter that summer.

The city's defenders can hardly have been satisfied with the slackening off in the army's efforts, especially as their hold on the sea route was weakening. In June an Egyptian fleet had pushed into the harbour by sheer numerical superiority, but the average small squadron had to expect a rough passage. In September, Saladin had watched tensely with his army as three ships battled furiously against a Christian flotilla. At the last moment the wind changed in their favour, and to wild cheering from the garrison, echoed by shouts from the distant army, they made their way to safety. The supplies they brought were vital, since the Christians were still receiving new recruits. In October the remnants of the German army reached the camp. As we have seen, the mere rumour of their coming had been enough to divert important divisions from Saladin's army; their arrival under the command of Frederick of Swabia, the dead emperor's son, raised the spirits of the besiegers. New machinery, including a massive battering ram, was deployed in the heaviest attack mounted on the city to date. A few days later Baldwin, archbishop of Canterbury, marched into the camp at the head of a well-equipped force of Englishmen.

Like other new arrivals before him, Baldwin was shocked by what he found. The free and easy social fraternisation between Muslim and Christian when they were not actually fighting was barely credible to the European mind. To a churchman the morals in the Christian camp were outrageous. The army in which 'there was neither chastity, sobriety, faith nor charity' was 'given up to shameful practices' which, if we are to believe the Arab historians, is hardly to be wondered at. For a few months previously 'there had arrived by ship 300 lovely Frankish women, young and beautiful, assembled from beyond the sea and offering their bodies for sin.' Archbishop Baldwin was not alone in being shocked that crusaders should behave like this. 'Imad-ad-Din the chronicler was piously appalled by this further example of Frankish depravity. As to the girls themselves, they were clearly fascinated by the set-up. They announced that they too were serving the Cross by being served by its soldiers and 'could make no finer sacrifice to win the favour of God than to dedicate as a holy offering what they kept between their thighs'. But what really worried 'Imad-ad-Din was that 'a few foolish mamluks and wretches' from his own side 'slipped away under the fierce goad of lust and followed the people of error'. These diversions apart, conditions in the Christian camp were slowly deteriorating. As with any medieval European siege army, the overriding and largely unrecognised danger was the total lack of hygiene and the resultant endemic camp fever. In October it killed Queen Sibylla, perhaps the most important single person in the Christian camp. King Guy owed his throne to his marriage with her, and when Conrad of Tyre won the struggle for the hand of her half-sister, Isabella, who was now the heiress of the royal family, the old political divisions were widened.

The marriage of Conrad and Isabella took place at Tyre in late November, and, to the anger of many Christians, Conrad had taken a number of ships to escort him up the coast. Because Guy refused to relinquish any of his kingly rights Conrad stayed sulking at Tyre while his co-religionists faced an atrocious winter of famine and disease. Wheat fetched 100 gold pieces the sack, and eggs were selling at six dinars each; knights slaughtered their costly war horses; the foot soldiery scavenged in the middens for the rotting entrails or fed off the grass; and even the gentry were reduced to thieving. In February, when morale was at its lowest ebb, Saladin got a relieving force into the city. It was to be his last success. As the spring came and the weather eased, supply ships managed to get through, and then, in April, King Philip II of France arrived with six ships. Richard of England too was at last in Eastern waters, and Saladin's hopes of wearing down the Christians had slipped away. The only way to victory now was straight defeat on the field of battle or the overwhelming of the Christian defence works which had stood unbreached for eighteen months. The prospects of such victories were slight indeed.

When Philip and Richard at last arrived, the siege entered its final phase. Philip reached the siege lines on 20 April and for a time the Christian attacks had new heart and determination. His engineers built new siege machinery and managed to drive a zig-zag rampart out from the camp to within an easy bow-shot of the walls. The dangerous and laborious work of filling in the fosse pressed inexorably forward. Earth, debris, the bodies of dead horses and even men were thrown in – some of the dying bequeathed their corpses to this pious purpose. Yet the upsurge in morale seems to have died slowly away, and the optimists among the defenders looked back on the happy omen of the 'white falcon'. Soon after his arrival, Philip had been riding down the battle lines, his favourite falcon on his fist, when the bird unexpectedly flew off over the walls of the city. It was a magnificent white bird, bigger than the species common in the Middle East, and the jubilant citizens sent it as a present to Saladin. There could hardly have been a more brilliant augury. It faded in the light of the bonfires which greeted the arrival of Richard of England seven weeks later.

Considering how little interest the Muslims generally showed in the European background of their enemies, Saladin was well informed on the relative standing of the two monarchs whose arrival was to decide the fate of Acre. He knew that the king of France, who was to assume the supreme command, was 'one of their mightiest princes'; he also knew the king of England ranked lower, but that 'his wealth, reputation and valour were greater'. The Angevin empire Richard had inherited from his father, Henry II, comprised half of France as well as England, so that though he was technically the feudal subordinate of Philip of France the realities were as Saladin's agents reported them. Richard's fame as a soldier had gone before him. 'He was a man of great courage and spirit,' commented Baha'-ad-Din, 'and showed a burning passion for war' – and the conquest of the Byzantine island of Cyprus made a deep impression on Saladin, whose alliance with the emperor had, at one time, been intended to prevent just such a union of interests between Christian states in Cyprus and Palestine.

On the night of 8 June trumpets brayed through the Christian camp at Acre and fires blazed along the beaches to welcome the king. The crackling flames lit up scenes of wild jubilation, and they also illuminated for the anxious lookouts in Saladin's army the huge supplies of weaponry and stores being unloaded from the twenty-five ships of the English fleet. For weeks past, Frankish officers enjoying safe-conduct passes into the Muslim camp had been bragging about the brilliance and drive of the king of England and how they 'were only waiting for his arrival to put into effect their plan to besiege the city with more vigour'. Richard's coming, we are told, 'put fear into the hearts of the Muslims'. They had reason.

Richard had struck his first blow in the Holy War even before he came in sight of Acre. Sailing down the Palestine coast on Friday, 7 July, he had sighted a galley heading past Beirut *en route* for Acre. A patrol gig sent out to investigate reported back that the ship claimed to be French. The ruse had worked before, but not this time. Richard ordered up a warship in pursuit. In addition to armaments and stores, the ship had 650 veteran troops on board, heading to reinforce the garrison at Acre, and they fought fiercely. The Christian forces fell back until the king sent the word along that if this prize escaped any Christian not killed in the action would die on the gallows. A team of swimmers dived under the enemy ship and lashed the rudder round. But still the Turkish galley thrashed on and its troops continued to repel all boarding parties. Eventually Richard resigned himself to the loss of the cargo and gave orders to prepare to ram. But the Turkish captain had come to the same conclusion, and even as the enemy galley came in for the kill he scuttled his ship rather than let her strategic cargo fall into enemy hands. Of almost eight hundred soldiers and sailors on board only thirty-five survived the systematic slaughter that followed – they comprised emirs who were good ransom prospects and a team of military engineers.

That night Richard anchored off Tyre, and the next day made his grand entry to the camp at Acre. Within hours he went sick with camp fever, but from his bed he was soon directing the construction and placing of yet more siege engines. Little more than a month later Acre was once more a Christian city. The Muslims believed that the loss of the supplies in the ship sunk by Richard was to blame. But the siege, under Richard's direction, had become overpowering. The bombardment was ceaseless, and a new ballista built to the king's specification was lobbing its missiles into the very heart of the city – the stone could kill twelve men. The defenders had to service their artillery, man the walls, clear the fosse, and man the ships in the harbour with reduced forces and on twenty-four-hour stand-by, while the enemy fought in shifts and so could maintain an offensive for days on end.

Late in June reinforcements joined Saladin but, as was soon to be obvious, he needed more than numerical strength. The walls and trenches that the Franks had begun nearly two years before were now perfected and were effectively impregnable to Muslim attack. To relieve Acre Saladin's soldiers had to overrun these walls, and it was at last obvious that this they would never do. The credibility of the sultan's army as a relieving army collapsed conclusively on Wednesday, 3 July. The day before had been hard fought. The Franks' attack had been announced from the city by the agreed drum-roll signals, and for the rest of the day Saladin was at the front. He galloped back and forth among the battalions, urging his men on with the battle cry 'For Islam!' his eyes swimming with tears and turning again and again to the bitter fighting on the distant city's walls. He ate nothing all day and drank only the medicine which his doctor had prescribed. The next day he led the attack once more, but was called away to hear the latest dispatch brought in by swimmer from the city. Its contents were shattering.

If nothing concrete was done to relieve the pressure that day, wrote al-Mashtub and Karaqush, they, the commanders, would offer the Franks the city in return for their lives and those of the garrison the following day. This, after a day's fighting, twenty-four hours without food, and a sleepless night, hit Saladin so hard that his officers at first thought he would die. The news was the more bitter as al-Mashtub the Kurd and the Cairo emir Karakush were two of his oldest friends and best trusted officers. At this point he must surely have known that Acre would be lost. Yet his valiant spirit recovered, and after an hour of prayer he prepared to rally the troops for yet another assault on the grim fortifications round the enemy camp. 'But on that day the army did not support him, for the enemy infantry stood like an unbreakable wall with weapons, ballistas and arrows behind their bastions.' The news that the army would no longer follow even Saladin was enough for al-Mashtub: before nightfall he had begun truce talks with the enemy.

Acre was saved for a few more days when the Franks refused to guarantee the lives of the garrison in the event of a capitulation. That night three emirs took a small boat out of the harbour and slipped past the end of the Christian siege lines to reach Saladin's camp before dawn. Two had the good sense to disappear while the third was, on Saladin's orders, thrown into prison. The next day the army refused Saladin's order for a frontal assault. Shortly afterwards three emissaries arrived from Richard of England. They had come to propose further peace negotiations – they also visited the camp market to buy snow and fruit. Their report on the low state of the army's morale can only have strengthened Richard's determination to yield nothing.

The city held out for another week, and the army still made some effective diversions. For the whole of one day a group of Kurdish emirs, among them the brother of al-Mashtub, made attack after attack on the enemy trenches, and at the height of the battle they were joined by 'Izz-ad-Din Jurdik, once one of Nur-ad-Din's staunchest mamluks but now devoted to Saladin. Nevertheless, despite such acts of herosim, and despite the arrival of yet more reinforcements, few of Saladin's commanders really believed the city could now be saved. The search was on for peace terms to save the lives of the garrison. The Franks carried on negotiations with the city and the army simultaneously. The negotiators at Saladin's camp were offered the city, its armoury and stores and the return of the True Cross. But they insisted, probably on King Richard's instructions, that all former Christian cities be returned as well as all Frankish prisoners. Conrad of Tyre acted as mediator in dealings with the city. The terms finally agreed by al-Mashtub and Karakush were sensational. They yielded the town and its contents, and in addition all the ships in its harbour, 600 prisoners, including 100 nobles listed by name by the enemy, the True Cross, and a ransom of 200,000 dinars. Conrad received a fee of 4,000 gold pieces for his part in the transaction.

When, on Friday, 12 July, a swimmer got news of the terms to Saladin he was nonplussed. His own offers had proposed nothing of substance. To him the 'True Cross' was merely the gaudy fetish of a pagan culture, while the military arsenal in Acre, valuable though it was, could not be saved once Richard was in the city. The fleet, on the other hand, could possibly have been fought to safety, and would in any case have taken a heavy toll of the Christian shipping. As to the ransom, such a sum would beggar his already overtaxed war chest. But it quickly became apparent that his view of the terms held only academic interest. Even before he began to draft his refusal of the terms the Christians' banners were seen breaking out on the walls of the city and on the minaret of the great mosque.

The shock of losing the great city seems to have overbalanced Saladin's military judgement. He persuaded himself that even at this stage the Christians might be lured from their entrenchments into an open battle, if the inducement was big enough. The main army was ordered to fall back while the sultan, with a small force, remained in an open and clearly vulnerable position. But the Christians had no need to rise to this bait, while Saladin's advisers pointed out that unless he confirmed the surrender the garrison would certainly be lost. He agreed. He arranged to pay the 200,000-dinar ransom in three instalments. On 11 August he delivered the first payment and a group of the stipulated prisoners. But King Richard was less interested in money at this point than military advantage. The defenders of Acre, who had won the respect of the Christians with their skill and courage, were, in his eyes, too numerous to be guarded and too professional to be returned to the enemy. On 20 August he had them systematically slaughtered on the plains outside the city, in full view of Saladin's army. It was a barbarity which far outdid the ceremonial killing of the Templars at Saladin's orders years before, and it added a new dimension to the terrible name of Richard the Lionheart.

In military terms Richard could argue that he was eliminating a fighting force which otherwise would have to be held, at his expense, with the permanent possibility of escape back into friendly territory. Saladin's Christian prisoners could be and often were sent off to the slave markets. Indeed, the fact that the war was fought on his territory gave Saladin a permanent and priceless advantage, for Richard was bound to go home at some point. The massacre also meant that Saladin's men were ever after loath to garrison any city threatened by a siege from Richard.

Henceforward Saladin would often retaliate in kind by slaughtering his prisoners. Neither monarch regarded the other as a 'war criminal', the concept had yet to be born. Kings lived above the plane of ordinary beings. All Christians were equal in the sight of God; all Muslims in the sight of Allah – but on this earth the rule of man more usually prevailed. The courtesies of courtly life between the camps would recover; though Saladin never agreed to a meeting with the king.

# Chapter 13

# Saracens and Crusaders

Richard's wars in Palestine lasted another year. For posterity this is the high romantic period of the Crusades. Arab and Christian sources alike are full of anecdotes about the dealings between the two great champions. A genuine and close friendship grew up between Richard and Saladin's brother al-Adil Saif-ad-Din, known to the Christians as Saphedin; but there was fraternisation among the lesser emirs and knights also. Just as the king girded al-Adil's twelve-year-old son with the belt of knighthood and banqueted with his father on Frankish and Arab cuisine, so the Frankish nobility had grown into eastern ways. Respect could sometimes soften contempt on both sides.

The original armies from Europe had been officered by an ambitious and ruffianly nobility and the troops had been recruited from the riff-raff of a society where brutality was commonplace. A German writer in these early days observed that 'most of the knights are brigands', and others accused the nobility of taking the Cross with all solemnity but abandoning their vows once the Saladin tithe had been levied on their tenants. A recruiting drive in Wales for the Third Crusade was considered a great success when the region's most hardened thieves and murderers opted for freedom with the army in Palestine rather than imprisonment at home. Later Pope Gregory X had to instruct the Frankish clergy not to defend crusaders who had committed 'theft, homicide or rape simply because they had crusading indulgences'.

The more sophisticated European visitors were ashamed of the Frankish society that generations of such recruits had produced in the Holy Land. The German Dominican Burkhard wrote: 'Our own people, the Latins, are worse than all the other people of the land. . . . And thus is the place of our redemption brought into contempt.' With Germany one of the least numerous of the European nations in Palestine, Burchard would have a natural antipathy for its predominantly Latin population. Yet he was by no means the only traveller to complain at the shameless way the Christians overseas exploited their fellow Catholics, on pilgrimage from Europe. Westerners were willing to believe any tale about the Franks across the water. In Jerusalem. it was said, there was not a man, whether rich or poor, who thought twice about exposing his daughter, his sister or even his wife to the lust of the pilgrims for money.

Yet even this did not evoke such outrage as the fraternisation between Christian and Muslim. The ideological conflict, so important to Europeans, was kept artificially alive in the kingdom and principalities by the appointment of Europeans to all the senior posts in the church. Throughout the century, William Archbishop of Tyre was the only native-born churchman to reach the bench of bishops. No doubt it was necessary to keep the Faith overseas pure and fervent with regular injections of untainted blood; left to themselves men showed a disturbing willingness to live in peace and to accept their differences. At Damascus itself there was a holy image that healed Jews, Christians and Muslims equally; while Muslim and Christian together venerated the spring where the Virgin Mary had washed the clothes of the infant Christ and the palm that had bent its boughs to give her food. Where even the saints and the shrines could be held in common, the cause of sectarian solidarity needed constant nurturing.

The luxury of eastern life seemed as wicked as the all too frequent tolerance of the foreign religion. Knights and nobles who could boast the lineage of the greatest families of Europe were to be seen wearing the outlandish burnous and turban, and riding into battle with their armour covered by a long surcoat and their helmet by a flapping kefieh. Gentlemen of middling rank and the *nouveaux riche* Italian merchants covered their houses in mosaic and marble; carpets lay on the floors and rich damask hangings graced the walls. Inlaid furniture, meals served on gold and silver, elegant cutlery and the new-fangled convention of eating meat with a fork, regularly laundered bed linen and fresh water brought on tap through the great aqueducts built by the Romans, contributed to make a way of life that the hardy European found alien and suspected as effeminate.

Visitors were also shocked by the way that commerce seemed to govern everything. The wealth of the kingdom largely depended on the trade passing from the Muslim hinterland to the ports of the coast. Muslims had to be allowed free access and given the protection of the law. The Italians – Genoese, Venetians, Pisans, Amalfitans – and French merchants from Marseille, had their business in every city of importance, with special districts in Antioch, Tripoli, Beirut, Tyre and Caesarea in which they were subject to their own customs and administered their own laws. Their ships transported the pilgrims and the armies of the kingdom – at a price. They had little interest in religion; it was said that a man of Venice would rather help a Muslim than a Genoese. Venetians, Pisans and Genoese were with the Sicilian fleet at Alexandria in 1174, but Saladin noted they fought half-heartedly.

One of Saladin's long-term objectives had been to lure the Italian trade from the Syrian to the Egyptian coast. For the fact was that, despite their abominable religious beliefs, the Christians had brought a heavy increase in the trade of the Palestinian coastal cities and had also provided a prompt and efficient merchandising operation to get the goods to the new markets in Europe. Trade brought Christian and Muslim together as nothing else could; Saladin had little difficulty in negotiating treaties with Genoa and Venice and once commented to an adviser that there was 'not one of them [the Italians] which does not supply our land with its materials of war . . . and treaties of peaceful intercourse have been negotiated with them all'. Even the Knights Templar, who by the latter part of the twelfth century had developed their immense assets and endowments to become rich and powerful bankers, operated regular accounts for Arab clients.

It was all a far cry from the bloodthirsty days of the First Crusade. The chaplain of King Baldwin I (d. 1127) had commented in the very early days: 'We have become true Easterners. The Roman and the Frank are transformed into the Galilean or Palestinian, the native of Rheims or Chartres into a citizen of Tyre or Antioch.' The rhetoric of religion, important to the fanatics and statesmen of both sides, made little impression on merchants or local politicians who criss-crossed the lines of ideology in their single-minded pursuit of wealth and power.

In the minority, and representative of a more backward civilisation, the Franks moved more easily to assimilation. There were many who could speak Arabic and a few, like Raynald of Sidon, who even took an intelligent interest in Arabic literature. Muslim chroniclers, on the other hand, display little interest in the history of the Crusader states and no interest at all in their countries of origin; though they do show considerable concern with the histories of the high civilisations of the Near and Far East and, in the thirteenth century, even analysed the origins and motives of the Mongols. For the Christian newcomers, their prevailing mood came to be one of contempt: 'The Franks (May

Allah Render them Helpless!) possess none of the virtues of men, except courage.'

Some Muslim comments on Christian customs and religion were as obtuse and ignorant as European invective against Islam. The belief in the Trinity was branded polytheism and the adulation of the True Cross, when it was taken into battle, seemed the rankest idolatry. 'They set it up and then bow the knee to it and prostrate themselves. . . . It is coated in red gold, and encrusted with pearls and precious stones. At times of danger, or during great festivals the priests present it to the people who . . . pray to it as if it were a god, bowing their faces in the dust and singing hymns of praise to it. There are numerous others like it which they set up in their houses to do honour to.'

Even the sophisticated Usamah, prince of Shaizar, whose memoirs provide a full and fascinating insight into life in twelfth-century Palestine, was sometimes nonplussed by the strange doings of the Franks. He spent many years at the court of Damascus, during the middle years of the century when it was frequently in alliance with Jerusalem, and he travelled a good deal, both as tourist and diplomat, in the Christian states. He made a number of friends, but he never really understood them. When he came to recount the cases 'regarding the Franks', he disclaimed all responsibility for the tall stories that were to follow, piously commenting, 'Mysterious are the works of the Creator, the author of all things!' Usamah had friends among the Templars who were the custodians of the Aqsa mosque; they reserved one of the porches for Muslim worshippers who were regularly to be seen at the appointed times of prayer bowing in the direction of Mecca, that is southwards. One day Usamah was brutally interrupted in his devotions when a Frankish pilgrim, horrified by his first sight of an infidel practising his abominable creed, rushed up to him and swung him roughly round to face the East, crying out: 'This is the way thou shouldst pray.' Although he was pulled off by a group of highly embarrassed knights, he returned to the attack as soon as their backs were turned, determined, apparently, that at least one Muslim should learn the right way to pray. This time he was thrown out of the church and the Templars attempted to mollify their friend by explaining that the offender had but recently come from Europe. For his part Usamah was not only shocked by the experience but also, it would seem, a little frightened 'at the conduct of this devil of a man, at the change in the colour of his face and his trembling'.

Such fanaticism was a little out of place in cosmopolitan Jerusalem, but the average Muslim would at least recognise the Christian's religious fervour. But when it came to the sexual mores of the Franks a Muslim was completely at a loss for words. Women not only walked openly in the streets with their husbands, but if they happened to meet a friend, the husband stood patiently by while they had their chat. If the conversation dragged on, the Frank thought nothing of leaving his wife with the man while he went about his business.

Frankish behaviour was still more unconventional in the public baths. They thought it absurdly prudish to wear a towel round the waist as the modest conventions of the East required. One day a boisterous young gentleman whipped off the towel being worn by one of the attendants. Stopping in his tracks he stared in astonishment, for the man's pubic hair had been shaved. The narrator continues: 'He shouted for me, "Salim!" As I drew near he stretched out his hand over the place and said, "An excellent idea. By the truth of my religion do the same for me." Accordingly he had himself shaved after the Saracen fashion.' What then followed might cause a few raised eyebrows even in a uni-sex sauna. Ordering his servant to bring his lady to the hot room the knight there and then had his wife's skirts pulled up and personally supervised the bath attendant as he shaved off her pubic hair.

Eccentricities like this must have afforded hours of entertainment round the dinner tables of Usamah and his friends. But on one occasion his ears were affronted by words 'that would never come from the lips of a sensible man'. He got on to such good terms with a Frankish pilgrim that the two called one another 'brother'. When the time came for the European to return home he took Usamah aside and solemnly urged him: '"Send thy son with me to our country, where he can see true knights and learn wisdom and chivalry. When he returns to you he will be a wise man." Such were his words, yet even if my son were to be taken captive, he could not suffer a worse misfortune than to live in the land of the Franks. However, I replied as follows: "By thy life, this has been exactly my idea. But the fact is, his grandmother, my mother, is so fond of him that she exacted an oath from me that I would return him to her." Thereupon he asked: "Is thy mother still alive?" "Yes," I replied. "Well," said he, "disobey her not." '

The obtuseness of this well-meaning Christian was positively enlightened compared with the attitudes of many churchmen to the hostile faith. The similarities between Christianity and Islam convinced some writers that Muhammad began his career as a Christian heretic, while others believed he was subject to fits of demonic possession. In view of the religion's fierce antipathy to all images, whether of the godhead or of the prophet, it is barely credible that one of the commonest Christian charges against Islam was that of idolatry. The legend grew up that the crusaders had found a silver idol of Muhammad in the Temple at Jerusalem, and in 1200 we find the Frenchman Jacques Vitry asserting that: 'as often as the followers of Muhammad possess the temple of Solomon they set up his statue there'. Yet more accurate information was to be found. Burkhard, the German who had served on a mission from Frederick Barbarossa to Saladin, reported the tolerance he had seen shown to the Christians of Egypt and contradicted many of the prevailing European myths about Islam. Although polygamy was permitted to Muslims, he found that most had only one wife. Like other unprejudiced observers he was greatly impressed by the Muslim's strict observance of the hours of prayer, and reported that they believed in one God who had created heaven and earth, as did the Christians, and that they even revered Jesus Christ as one of the prophets. Whereas these similarities indicated to some Europeans that Muhammad was but a renegade Christian, to Burchard they seemed signs of hope, and to a local Frankish bishop they seemed to be proof that God was leading the Infidel to himself in his mysterious divine plan for the universe.

On their side, the Muslims had equally mixed notions of their enemies and some equally admiring views. Saladin, who had to maintain the whole Muslim war effort from his own territories, spoke admiringly of his Christian enemies who came from all parts of Europe to fight for their Faith. Whereas they drew volunteers from Scotland, England, Italy, Germany and from all over France, he could win the support of the armies of Mosul only when he had conquered its prince and forced him into submission. If courage was the only manly quality which some of the Muslims conceded to their enemies, no one denied that they had it to the full. Watching the heroic march of the Christian army to Arsuf, one of Saladin's staff wrote: 'One cannot help admiring the patience displayed by these people, who bore the most wearing fatigue without having any part in the management of affairs or deriving any personal advantage.'

These dogged fighting qualities and the faltering enthusiasm for the war among his own emirs made the period of King Richard's campaigns in Palestine one of constant tension for Saladin. In August 1191 the glorious triumph at Jerusalem was four years in the past, and since that moment he had been fighting to defend his conquests. The longterm situation was swinging in his favour. During the siege of Acre Guy and Conrad had continued their rivalry for the kingship. Even after the loss of the city, Saladin could have stabilised the frontiers if Richard of England had returned with the French king after the Christian victory. As it was, during the next thirteen months Saladin was almost constantly in the field, and when at last a treaty was settled with Richard he had less than six months to live.

The halo of chivalry which surrounds the rival champions is not merely the invention of posterity. Saladin and his emirs, bred in the tradition of the Muslim gentleman, delighted to entertain the Franks with all the luxury of eastern courtliness, and had come to respect the courage and brilliance of the European fighting man, while their enemies were enthralled by the burgeoning European cult of knighthood, and intensely admired the dashing style of Turkish warfare. The air of glamour and excitement gripped the leaders. Saladin and his brother al-Adil were obviously fascinated by their great antagonist, while Richard was in his element where chivalry and military problems were so richly compounded.

But in the weeks immediately after Acre the air of mutual admiration was poisoned for 'Saladin was terribly wroth at Richard's massacre of the prisoners at Acre'. Frankish stragglers brought into the camp were unceremoniously killed after interrogation, and many horribly mutilated. It is doubtful whether Saladin would have been obeyed had he tried to intervene. The slaughtered garrison had had family and friends in the army, and these troops had fought bitterly all that cruel August day to save their comrades. Then they had been beaten back by the Franks; now a few defenceless prisoners were the anguished victims of their pent-up fury. Saladin did not doubt the justice of the deaths: vengeance was part of the code all men lived by, but wanton cruelty was not in his nature. Years before he had refused his young sons permission to kill a prisoner in cold blood because it was not right they should learn the habit of killing men before they learnt the ways of justice. Even in the fervid weeks after Acre he managed to save some of the victims from mutilation.

The news the prisoners brought in was disquieting. Since marching out of Acre on 22 August Richard's army had made only slow progress on its way south along the coast road, but this it emerged was because the king was keeping in touch with the fleet and its supplies. This was not a rash gamble like the march of Guy to Acre but a measured opening to a long-term strategy with ambitious objectives. The target was Jerusalem. Richard planned to march down the coast to Jaffa and, with this port as a base, to strike inland at the Holy City. But Jaffa was more than sixty miles away along a difficult road with eight river crossings and the march was in the height of the Mediterranean summer. It was shadowed by a massive Muslim force in the nearby hills.

For two weeks the Christians marched doggedly southwards, the sea on their right and the Muslims on their left. They made barely five miles a day. Richard had divided his force into three divisions parallel to the sea. In the centre was the cavalry, to protect the horses from the Turkish arrows, the baggage and the standard. This was a wagon carrying 'a tower as high as a minaret from which floated the banner of the people'. Since the capture of the True Cross the Christians had been searching for a new rallying symbol. At Acre Guy had been preceded into battle by an illuminated copy of the Gospels under a canopy carried by four knights. Perhaps this had been changed because it was unfortunately reminiscent of the Muslim custom of carrying the Koran into battle. Either side of the Christian centre were two columns of foot, the one on the right being protected by the sea, the one on the left carrying the weight of the Muslim attacks. Periodically the two changed stations so that each had a chance to rest from the fighting. Under their regulation mail shirts the troops wore heavy felt jerkins so that the hail of arrows caused little damage. The brunt of the battle fell on the rearguard, which had to march backwards, fighting as best it could. The Christian crossbows inflicted terrible wounds on the Muslims, but there were not enough of them.

For the most part the Christians had to trudge on in the dusty heat, powerless to strike back at the Muslim archers and light cavalry. Men died of heat stroke, of fatigue, of chance arrows in the face. Yet day after scorching day they kept formation, to the angry admiration of Saladin and his staff. As we have noted what impressed them about 'the patience displayed by these people' was that they 'bore the most wearing fatigue without having any participation in the direction of the campaign or deriving any personal advantage.' It was a rueful comparison with the position of Saladin, who had to consult his emirs over every decision. Too often, as we have seen, they overrode him and robbed him of victory.

On 30 August the Christians reached Caesarea. Now their ordeal intensified. Saladin had already reconnoitred the terrain and settled on the approaches to the port of Arsuf for a massive assault; here the coastal plain widened to give additional manoeuvrability to his horsemen. On 7 September the running action reached the dimensions of a major battle. Over the blaring trumpets and rolling kettledrums, over the sound of rattles, gongs and cymbals, rang out the strident battle cries of Turks, Arabs, Bedouin and blacks. Saladin was at the centre of the action. With arrows flying round his head and accompanied by pages leading two reserve horses he rode slowly up the line between the two armies, urging his men on to break the enemy formation. Under the wild fury of the assault the Christians at last began to falter. Knights who had swallowed their pride and kept their station throughout the march now begged Richard to authorise a charge. Still he held them back, waiting until Saladin's skirmishers and cavalry were too far committed to withdraw; nevertheless the knights began to break through the wall of infantry all along the line. 'The knights gathered together in the middle of the infantry; they grasped their lances, shouted their war cries like one man and rushed in a great charge, some on our left, some on our right and some on our centre.' The charge was only moments before he had intended it but Richard gathered and led it with a vast momentum that shattered the Muslim ranks and sent men flying for their lives. Saladin stayed firm by his standard with only some supporters; once again he had to rally his force to prevent a rout.

The Christian success at Arsuf was not a crushing victory. It enabled Richard and his army to make their way safely into Arsuf, certainly, but Saladin's army re-formed at near full strength. What the action had done was to undermine fatally the whole tactical assumption on which Saladin's campaign was based – that the way to defeat the Franks was to lure them into a battle of movement and break their formation. The triumph at Hattin had flowed from careful manoeuvre, brilliantly calculated and executed to drive the enemy into a position of multiple disadvantage; Arsuf demonstrated that without such preparation the defeat of a Christian army – well armed, well disciplined, and professionally led – was beyond the resources at Saladin's disposal. The blow to Saladin's reputation had been far heavier than the military consequences. Seeing now the real possibility that Jerusalem itself might be lost, he fell back to Ramlah to block Richard's road from Jaffa.

But at the moment Richard had no intention of moving to the next stage of his campaign until Jaffa had been properly secured. In any case his army was not in a fit state to fight. After the hazards of the last few weeks his men relaxed into the luxury and night life of Jaffa as completely as they had at Acre. Not a few made their way back up the coast road that they had helped to clear, to renew the acquaintance of those 'lovely Frankish women' we have already heard about. A few of these had sailed down to Jaffa, but obviously it was considered a little provincial in comparison with Acre. There was little fighting. While Richard was strengthening his base at Jaffa, Saladin was at Ascalon. Barely credible though it may sound, he was supervising the systematic destruction of the defences and large areas of the city itself.

The reverses at Acre and Arsuf had totally demoralised the Muslims. Now Saladin feared that Richard, if he could make a firm foothold in Ascalon as he had done in Jaffa, would be poised for an attack on Egypt. The nightmare that the whole of his life's work might be over-turned did not seem beyond possibility. The night before the decision to raze Ascalon he slept fitfully and discussed the pros and cons of the case with his son al-Afdal into the small hours. 'I take God to witness,' he said, 'that I would rather lose all my children than cast down a single stone from the walls.' The recapture of Ascalon, that once great Egyptian outpost in Palestine, had been one of the proudest moments of the 1187 campaign. To destroy it was a bitter admission of weakness. Yet Saladin recognised that after his army's past performance he could not rely on any garrison to hold it. Once the decision had been made, this stern man did not shirk the seeing it through. Accustomed all his life to supervise his subordinates in everything he regarded as a top military priority, he was now to be seen going up and down the streets of this prized city helping personally in the recruiting of the workmen, and assigning portions of the ramparts to groups of labourers or towers to an emir and his troops. Fearing Richard would reach the city before the job was completed the sultan forced himself to urge on the demolition squads just as he had exhorted his troops in the heat of the battle.

The destruction of Ascalon was a full military vindication for Richard's barbarous massacre of the Acre garrison. Saladin himself was bitterly opposed to the demolition, as we have said, but when he proposed defending it to his council of war the emirs rejected the idea. 'He invited the Muslims to lock themselves up at Ascalon to defend it.' So wrote Ibn-al-Athir. 'No one responded to this appeal but they all said: "If you wish to defend it, go in with us or have one of your sons go in with us; otherwise not one of us will lock ourselves up here for fear of what happened at Acre."' There could hardly be more telling proof that without Saladin the achievements of the 1180s would have been impossible. After Ascalon, a number of fortresses in the southern part of the former kingdom were destroyed – there were just not enough troops to hold all these strong points the year round.

For the moment Richard held the initiative, but he also had problems. With Philip of France back in Europe, Richard feared for the security of his own vast French domains. He was also beginning to have doubts about the quality of his army. Guy had been sent back to Acre to round up the deserters with little success and soon Richard himself would have to go there to roust them out. Even the troops who remained loyal to the colours saw themselves as pilgrims. If they could fight their way to Jerusalem and visit the Holy Places they would be content. They were unlikely to stay on in the East to hold the conquered lands. On 17 October Richard opened negotiations with al-Adil. Saladin was not prepared to compromise his dignity and bargaining position by a meeting with Richard, but agreed that his brother might communicate with the enemy commander. The two had struck up such a close understanding that Richard looked on al-Adil as a 'brother and friend'. At Richard's request al-Adil sent his secretary to discuss preliminaries.

The first stage was the statement of extreme bargaining positions. Pointing out that the war was a wasting sickness damaging both sides equally, the king proposed the time had come to put a stop to it. Then, as the price of peace, he demanded Jerusalem, all the lands between the coast and the River Jordan, and finally the True Cross, 'which for you is simply a piece of wood with no value, but for us is of the highest importance'. Since these were the very three points at issue in the war it is hardly surprising that Saladin, his army still in the field, refused outright. What followed was a compromise solution which horrified contemporaries on both sides and has never ceased to fascinate historians. It was proposed that a marriage be arranged between Richard's sister Joanna, the widow of King William II of Sicily, and al-Adil. From her brother Joanna was to receive all the lands in Palestine under his control while al-Adil was to be made lord of all the remaining territory at present held by Saladin. Only the places held by the Templars were to be excluded from the arrangement. The couple should rule jointly from Jerusalem. In addition Saladin would hand over the True Cross and there was to be a complete exchange of prisoners.

Before continuing the negotiations on this astonishing line, al-Adil got the explicit approval of Saladin. It was willingly given 'because he knew quite well that the King of England would never agree to such terms'. But he was wrong. Whatever may have been Richard's motives for embarking on the Crusade, we can be fairly sure that religious piety was not chief among them – according to legend his family was descended from the devil. When building the castle of Gaillard in Normandy, he ignored protests from the Archbishop of Rouen who owned the land and is reputed to have replied: 'If the angel of God himself should try to stop this building he would be met by a curse.' If the marriage of his sister to a Muslim would settle the Palestine question and allow him to get back to his own affairs he was willing to consider the matter. However, he fully realised the impact on public opinion. His sister seems to have raised some forceful objections too, but these were less influential than the fact that 'The Christian people disapprove of my giving my sister in marriage without consulting the Pope. . . . Accordingly I have sent a messenger to him. . . . If he authorises the wedding, so much the better. If not, I will give you the hand of one of my nieces.' Saladin refused to consider any bride but the king's sister, though if that could be arranged he was happy to go through with the proposal. It is obvious that he was only protracting the negotiations to win time. Whatever the motives of King Richard, Saladin would never have permitted the marriage of his own brother and an infidel. But with winter drawing on he may have hoped that the end of the conventional campaigning season would give him a breathing space.

And Saladin had another card. Simultaneously with the negotiations with Richard he had received an approach from Conrad of Tyre. The emissary was Raynald of Sidon, who, despite their encounter at Beaufort two years before, was well received by Saladin. Ever since his intervention at Tyre, Conrad's policy had been entirely self-seeking – to extend his own power with little thought for the well-being of the Christian cause as a whole. Philip of France, his strongest patron, had returned to Europe, and Richard was openly hostile to his claims on the monarchy of Jerusalem. He was not the only native Frank who was worried at the way the European newcomers were taking control in Palestine, and seems to have gathered quite a following in addition to Raynald. He now offered to help Saladin recapture Acre if the sultan would guarantee Sidon and Beirut to him and his allies, though he refused a straight answer when asked if he would take up arms against

Richard himself. Courted by both sides from the Christian camp, Saladin consulted the council as to which he should come to terms with. On balance they favoured Richard as marginally the more trustworthy, but both sets of negotiations were continued. Al-Adil, who revelled in the diplomatic complications, would sometimes be seen riding with Raynald past Richard's camp. Desultory talks continued with Conrad, but for the time being Richard saw there was little point in his negotiations.

At the beginning of November, Saladin had to release the eastern contingents. The small winter army could not hope to match Richard in the field, even if the rains and mud had not made serious fighting virtually impossible. Saladin withdrew to Jerusalem. But Richard led his army on towards Jerusalem and occupied Ramlah. For six weeks they camped there, fending off the attacks of Saladin's skirmishers; then, to his consternation, they pushed on still nearer, to occupy the fort of Beit Nuba only twelve miles away. In that first week of January 1192 the hills around the Holy City were lashed with storms that snapped the tent poles in the Christian camp and turned the roads into quagmires. But with the object of their pilgrimage so close the morale of the Christian troops was as high as ever it had been. For his part Saladin hourly expected an assault and began dividing the defence of the walls among his emirs.

A week after the Christians had made their camp at Beit Nuba Saladin's scouts reported that they were marching back down the road towards Ramlah. The decision to retreat had stretched Richard's authority almost as much as the decision to stay had Saladin's. The European contingents were straining to attack, but the Palestinian lords confirmed the king's own gloomy diagnosis. Even if, despite the appalling weather and the Egyptian forces camped in the hills, he succeeded in taking Jerusalem, his pilgrim troopers would head for home when the city was won. The Christian army was bitterly disappointed. Against the odds and against the weather they had fought a way to their goal. Now, through driving hail and snow, over marshes and swamps that sucked down men and horses, they marched away, beaten without a battle. There were many deserters, 'the greater part of the French went off in anger to Jaffa and lived at ease', others to Acre, where supplies were abundant, and some took service with Conrad at Tyre. Now was the time for Saladin to strike. But although Richard had defied the appalling weather to get to Beit Nuba the conditions did put a major battle out of the question. It was not merely a matter of the terrain. Archers were Saladin's main offensive arm and the rain would soon have slackened their bow-strings. In addition his army was depleted by the seasonal leave to half strength and demoralised by the failures of the previous months. To have held them together had been an achievement; now he could only wait for the weather to improve and the troops of Mosul and its region to return. It is an interesting light on Saladin's swelling reputation among his enemies that some Christians attributed his inaction to his chivalry.

Events did not stand still. Richard led his army to Ascalon where they 'could barely struggle through the gates over the heaps of rubble' left by Saladin's labourers. The next four months saw these fortifications rebuilt. All that Saladin had won by the agonised decision to destroy the place was a little time. By May, Ascalon was once again an effective Christian garrison town. But the enemy could not deploy his advantage. Conrad refused to join Richard at Ascalon. The French contingent led by the duke of Burgundy was still disaffected, the Pisans had taken over Acre in the name of King Guy and held it against the combined forces of Conrad, Burgundy and Genoa. Once again Saladin's enemies were doing his work for him.

In March he and al-Adil at last brought the negotiations with Conrad to an offensive/defensive alliance, and immediately made a handsome offer to Richard which, shrewdly enough, included Beirut, one of Conrad's prime objectives. In addition the Christians should retain their conquests, have back their cross and be allowed the right of pilgrimage to the Holy Places where Latin priests were to be installed. Saladin had long ago written off his ineffective ally at Constantinople. Al-Adil led the delegation to the plain outside Acre where Richard was working to restore some unity among his allies. On Palm Sunday, 29 March, 'amid much splendour', as a sign of respect for his 'brother and friend' Richard girded al-Adil's son with the belt of knighthood.

The terms were good and should have been acted on. Both sides wanted peace. Saladin was troubled by reports of trouble in al-Jazirah, where one of his nephews was stirring up discontent. Richard was hearing disquieting reports of conflicts between his ministers in England and his ambitious brother, Prince John. He could not afford to stay out east much longer, and early in April called a full council of the kingdom to settle the dispute between Conrad and Guy. Although he had favoured Guy's claim, when the council unanimously voted for Conrad he agreed. It was what the Marquis had been waiting for. He agreed in turn to join the army at Ascalon after his coronation in Acre. Then, on 28 April, Conrad was struck down by two Assassins, sent by Sinan, 'The Old Man of the Mountains'. He had a private grievance against Conrad and may also have recognised that he alone was able to rebuild a powerful state in the Christian lands. But rumour told different stories. Some said that Saladin had asked Sinan to arrange the deaths of both Richard and Conrad; later, rather confused Assassin tradition held that the murder was at Saladin's request. But since it tells how the men killed Richard, it can be discounted. The Christians, remembering the antagonism between Richard and Conrad, favoured the view that Richard had ordered the killing. Since, barely a week before, Richard had at last settled his quarrel with Conrad and had even got his agreement to join the common fight against the Muslims, this is, if possible, still more unlikely. In any case, he made no attempt to rehabilitate Guy. When the people of Tyre acclaimed Henry of Champagne as the successor to their dead hero, Richard again acquiesced. On 5 May, just one week after her husband's death, Queen Isabella married Henry. The speed of the operation raised a few eyebrows in the Christian camp, while Muslim opinion, hardened as it thought to the barbarous morals of the enemy, was disgusted to learn that the marriage had been consummated even though the queen was already pregnant.

During all this time Saladin had been content to watch the confusion of his enemies. The situation in the east was too uncertain for him to commit himself to a campaign and he was still awaiting the return of his emirs. He no doubt thought the provisional agreement with Richard would hold long enough for them to come up. But Richard had now heard reports of Saladin's rebellious family and he may also have heard the rumour that Guy's assassins had hoped to kill him. More probably his military mind saw the chance of a quick, cheap and important gain. In mid-May he advanced by land and sea down from Ascalon to the important fortress town of Darum, twenty miles further on the road to Egypt, and by the 28th it was once again in Christian hands. Still worse from Saladin's point of view was the news that Richard, stirred by the exhortations of his chaplain, had put off his return to Europe yet again.

The eastern contingents were at last flooding back to join the army, but when Richard advanced once again to Beit Nuba Saladin did not feel strong enough to do more than harry the outposts of the Christian force, which stayed in its advanced position for a month. The Christians were as perplexed as Saladin about the next stage of the campaign. The arguments that had persuaded Richard to retreat in January still held good, and now Saladin was stronger. However, another success soon came. A great caravan was making its way slowly up Egypt to the Holy City. We are told by Baha'-ad-Din that Richard himself reconnoitred the position before dawn disguised as an Arab. The result was that his men were able to take the convoy completely by surprise, and only a baggage train belonging to the sultan himself was saved from the disaster – thanks to the heroism of its commander, Aybak-al-Aziz. The military significance of the episode was not unimportant. Among the immense booty the Christians had taken thousands of horses and camels, and once again Saladin's standing with his own people had suffered heavily. Now, he was convinced, Richard would move in for the kill. With a heavy heart Saladin convened his emirs once more to screw their courage to the sticking point of resistance. He called a council of war.

The proceedings opened with an oration from Baha'-ad-Din reminding the emirs of their duty to the Holy War and exhorting them to stand firm. When he had finished the company sat in silence waiting for the sultan to speak. Minutes passed. Then Saladin rose slowly to his feet. 'Today,' he said, 'you are the support of Islam. Only you among the Muslims can stand up against this enemy. If you fail – which God forbid – they will roll up this land like the rolling up of a scroll, and you will be answerable, for it was you who undertook to defend it. You have received money from the public treasury and now the safety of the Muslims throughout the land rests with you.' In that assembly the mention of cash was timely. There was not a man there who had not received richly of the sultan's largesse, who had not at some time had valuable warhorses given him in replacement for the mounts lost in the Holy War. Many of the emirs had already criticised the plan to stay in Jerusalem. The shadow of Acre still hung heavily in the air, and there were plenty of voices in favour of risking a pitched battle rather than waiting cooped up for what they regarded as the inevitable fall of the city. The argument was dressed in specious military reasoning, but Saladin well knew that if once he left the place his cause would be lost. Any garrison left to hold it would fall apart, for 'the Kurds will not obey the Turks and the Turks will never obey the Kurds'. As to the main army, once it was in the open field it would melt away as the emirs looked for safety for themselves and their possessions behind the Jordan.

When he had sat down no one attempted to open up the debate. He was answered by al-Mashtub the Kurd. 'My lord,' he said, 'we are your servants and slaves. You have been gracious to us and made us mighty and rich, we have nothing but our necks and they are in your hands. By God, not one among us will turn back from helping you until we die.' After this Saladin called for the usual evening meal to be served, and when they had eaten his captains withdrew. The whole episode smacks of careful stage management. The uplifting call to the *jihad*, followed by a reminder of the practicalities of the situation, and the whole rounded off by a declaration of loyalty from the leader of the Kurdish squadrons with the hint that defaulters would have them to reckon with. Yet again Saladin had held a crumbling situation together. And for the second time, as if by divine intervention the Muslims were to be spared. Richard, always a soldier first and pilgrim second, saw that the situation was as it had been in January, with the additional hazard that Saladin had poisoned the wells. On Sunday, 5 July, he ordered the retreat, and Saladin, with his emirs, rode out to watch their enemy trudging disconsolately southwards.

Two days later, to Saladin's astonishment, a message arrived from Henry 'King of Jerusalem', demanding the return of all 'his' lands. He was curtly informed that as the successor to Conrad the best he could hope for was the return of Tyre and Acre. In fact, we are told, Saladin was so outraged by the impudence of the demand from an enemy who had completed his retreat that the messenger was lucky to escape unhurt. He was followed by a more diplomatic embassy from Richard, now at Jaffa and determined at last to get back to Europe. He asked the sultan to forgive the rashness of the young king and to consider once more terms of peace that would bring honour to both sides. Saladin's emirs were as keen as Richard to put an end to the damaging and inconclusive campaigns of the past year, and agreement seemed in sight. But neither Saladin nor Richard would yield on the matter of Ascalon. The one insisted that the fortifications be dismantled, the other refused to surrender the one major achievement since Acre.

Richard in fact was so sure that agreement would be reached that he had moved his army to Acre and was pushing along his preparations for departure. Unprotected, Jaffa was too valuable a prize to Saladin for him to let it slip while the final peace was still awaiting settlement. On 27 July he marched down from Jerusalem and three days later his troops were storming through the streets looting and killing. The garrison in the citadel had agreed to capitulate in return for their lives, but this Saladin could not guarantee until the orgy of pillage in the town had exhausted itself. In the meantime the news of the disaster had been brought to Acre, where Richard was on the point of embarking. The exhausted messenger had not completed his report before the king was rallying the fleet and his knights. On 31 July he was sighted off Jaffa with a fleet of galleys. Because of the chivalry of Saladin and his officers the garrison were still safe in the citadel while their enemies tried to pacify the rioting soldiery. When they saw help at hand they took up their arms prepared to hold out until the king of England came to their aid.

There were already Muslim banners on the walls of the city, and for a time Richard hesitated. Then a soldier from the garrison made his way to the king's ship and told him the place was still being held. Waiting no longer, Richard, still wearing his sailor's deck shoes, plunged into the sea followed by some eighty knights and, under the astonished eyes of Baha'-ad-Din, who was still acting as negotiator between Saladin and the garrison, cleared the harbour of the Kurdish and Turkoman soldiers. The king was followed by a force of Italian marines, and as Saladin sat in his tent trying to clinch the final surrender terms the flood of panicked soldiers and refugees crowding the streets told him all was lost. As usual, he, with a small band of loyal troops, tried to rally the cowards round the standard – but the case was hopeless. The courage and decision of Richard had made Jaffa once again a Christian city.

Nevertheless, Saladin knew how weak his enemy was and he refused to concede the position. In the dawn of Wednesday, 5 August, a Genoese sentry in Richard's camp heard the sound of horses and the chink of armour beyond the lines. He alerted the commander. Still dragging on their armour and reaching for their swords, fifty-four knights, led by the martial king, dashed to the perimeter, defended by a low palisade of sharpened tent pegs. They were joined by some two thousand Italian crossbow men. The knights, shields on arms, stood in pairs, their lances pointing towards the oncoming cavalry, and behind them the archers. Saladin had 7,000 horse in the field, but they could not break down the opposition though their attacks came again and again until early in the afternoon. Now, seeing his enemy tiring, Richard and his knights mounted and hurled themselves at the Muslim cavalry. The battle was turned by their gallantry. Richard's horse was shot under him, and al-Adil, who was with the host, sent him a replacement. It was a bad-tempered animal, and Saladin's brother watched intrigued to see whether the king would be able to break its spirit. But Richard had no time for such chivalrous by-play and ordered the Saracen groom back to his master with a wry message not to set traps like that. With the defenders of Jaffa so heavily committed at the camp some of Saladin's men attempted to storm the place, but they too were driven back. Once again Saladin had to retire to Jerusalem and once again he prepared to stand a siege. But this time Richard had no intention of carrying the war to him. Seeing that this last superb victory had exhausted the Christian champion, Saladin was soon back in force at Ramlah. The final round of negotiations began. Richard was forced to give up Ascalon, his suggestion that he hold it as a fief from Saladin in the Frankish manner was turned down. The coast from Acre to Jaffa was to remain in Christian hands and the troops in Richard's army were to be allowed to make their pilgrimage to the Holy Places. On 9 October Richard, desperately sick, went on board at Acre. His last message to Saladin was that when the three-year truce was over he would return to take Jerusalem. The chivalrous reply came back that if Saladin had to lose his lands to any king there was none more worthy to win them than the king of England.

By the 1190s the balance between the Muslim world and Western Christendom was very much in the Muslims' favour. They were in the ascendant in the 'crusading' wars, which, of course, they won with the eviction of the Franks from Palestine in 1291. Theirs was also the dominant culture. Communications across the linguistic divide were in Arabic; the negotiations between Richard and Saladin's brother al-Adil were conducted through the young Humphrey IV of Toron, one of the Franks fluent in the language. Arabic sources, impressed by the dedication of the Franks to their religious cause, criticised Saladin for warring against Muslims – in fact, lordships outside his control showed little interest in the threat from Europe. Genoese galleys en route to provision the Christian army besieging Acre were able to revictual at North African ports; the sultan of Isfahan was indignant when Saladin refused him help against local insurgents.

With the death of Baldwin IV the Franks lost their last notable king; the leprosy that wasted his body never infected his will, dedication or mental powers. The days of Jerusalem as capital of a Christian kingdom were numbered. Saladin had forced its neighbour states into an encircling alliance that would last long enough to ensure the recovery of the city for Islam – a settlement not challenged for some 760 years.

# Chapter 14

# The Death of a Hero

During the weeks between the signing of the peace at Ramlah and the departure of Richard, hundreds of Europeans seized the chance to visit the Holy Sites, as allowed by the treaty. Some fanatical Muslims were angered that infidels should be allowed into the city, and Saladin ordered patrols on the roads to protect the Christian pilgrims from the enthusiasts. Vindictiveness was no part of his nature and he was perfectly willing to permit the defeated enemy a last gesture of piety. Perhaps he regretted that King Richard refused to make the pilgrimage from shame that he had not been able to win the city back for Christendom, but he entertained his emissary, Hubert Walter the bishop of Salisbury, magnanimously. He 'sent him many gifts of price and even invited him to a conference in order to see what kind of a man he was in appearance. He had the Holy Cross shown to him, and they sat together a long time in familiar conversation . . . he enquired as to the habits of the king of England . . . and asked what the Christians said about his Saracens.' At the end of the interview, he invited the bishop to ask any favour he wished. The next day, having begged time to think over his request, Hubert Walter returned and asked that Latin priests be allowed to celebrate Catholic rites at the Holy Sepulchre, Bethlehem and Nazareth.

Saladin's agreement to this request was natural in his generous nature. It is equally likely that he saw political advantages from rival Christian establishments at the shrines. Tension between the Catholics and the Syrian churches had been a permanent feature of the Christian kingdom. In fact Hubert Walter had been prompted to make his request because, in the words of the Christian chronicler, 'he had found the services only half celebrated after the barbarous Syrian fashion' and wished to 'inaugurate a fitting service to God'. Saladin was closely informed on the weaknesses of his opponents and would have been well aware that the arrogance of the Latins had long deprived them of the cooperation of a large body of fellow Christians in Muslim-occupied territory. The new arrangements for the guardianship of the Christian holy places could be expected to keep ill feeling alive between the two communities. Even his friendly agreement to allow Christians from the army up to visit the shrines had had an element of calculation. He knew that the bulk of the newly arrived Europeans had come on Crusade only to fulfil the pilgrimage and once they had made it these Franks would be eager to depart.

The Ramlah agreement on pilgrims seems to have been negotiated by Richard as an opportunity for him to reward his own men with the special passports which were stipulated. But Saladin ordered that all pilgrims should be let through, and soon received an angry message from the English king; he was particularly irritated that the French, who had refused their help at Jaffa, were being given the same treatment as the English. But Saladin gave 'honourable entertainment to such as he chose . . . receiving them at his table and letting them know that by doing so he would incur the reproaches of the king. He ignored the prohibition he had received from Richard with the excuse: "There are men here who have come from afar to visit the Holy Places and our law forbids us to hinder them."'

Saladin remained at Jerusalem until he had received the news that Richard had finally sailed. He had been discussing the advisability of making his own pilgrimage to Mecca. He was anxious to fulfil his long outstanding obligation to the Faith; although only in his early fifties he was aware of the toll that his relentless work schedules had taken on his fragile health. Following his doctor's orders he had often had to break the fasting duties of the month of Ramadan and now, to the dismay of Baha'-ad-Din, he was beginning to pay off his debt to religion by fasting on uncanonical days. It seems obvious that he feared that he might die before he had completed his religious duties. Yet his advisers raised practical objections against making the pilgrimage at this time. Their chief fear was that the peace with the Christians was not firm enough to guarantee the new territories and that if Saladin were to leave at this moment, even for the few months needed for the journey to Mecca, the enemy might mount a new attack. They urged him to make a tour of the frontier fortresses. Their fears were no doubt exaggerated. After a year and a half of intensive campaigning under the dynamic leadership of Richard I and reinforced by European armies, the Christians had failed to win back Jerusalem and had been held to a narrow coastal strip. The prince of Antioch was friendly to Saladin and the armies of the kingdom were in no position to launch a new offensive. Nevertheless, the Muslim high command had seen too many instances of emirs reluctant to fight to be confident of their resolution if the commander-in-chief withdrew.

On 14 October he marched out of Jerusalem on the road to Nablus. There he inspected the fortifications and on the morning of Saturday the 16th he held court, rendering justice and distributing largesse. He heard many complaints against the governor al-Mashtub and fixed a date for a full hearing. It was one of the most serious criticisms of Saladin's rule that he was too indulgent to the faults of his officials. Perhaps with the great goals of the religious war at last achieved he planned to take a firmer hand in the government of his now massive empire. He continued his northward march to Baisan, where he again made a thorough inspection of the fortress, which was now standing empty. He concluded that the place should be put back into commission and thoroughly repaired, and then went on to examine the nearby stronghold of Kaukab, formerly Belvoir. After examining its defences Saladin decided it should be razed to the ground, being too close to Baisan for the practical purposes of Muslim defence and a standing invitation to the Christians to recapture as a counter-fortress.

On the evening of Tuesday, 19 October, he arrived at Tiberias just as a storm was beginning to blow up. That night and the following day torrential rain swept down on central Galilee, churning up the roads and swelling the rivers. But Saladin continued his tour of inspection with the fortresses between Tiberias and Beirut, which he reached at the end of the month. There, on 1 November, he held a great reception for the Christian prince of Antioch, Bohemond, called the Stammerer. Saladin's conquests had isolated his small state from the kingdom, and the Third Crusade had not restored the *status quo*. Bohemond was looking for a deal and left with quite a favourable one. In exchange for homage and the recognition of Saladin's overlordship he was invested with a robe of honour and granted lands in the plain of Antioch to the value of 15,000 gold pieces. Armed with this satisfactory arrangement he returned to his capital, while Saladin proceeded to Damascus.

On 4 November, after four years of absence, he entered his capital to scenes of tumultuous enthusiasm. It was a fitting culmination to his exhausting, at times dangerous, yet ultimately triumphant campaigning in the cause of Islam. The time was long overdue for a rest and during the ensuing weeks he devoted himself to hunting the gazelle in the country round the town with his brother al-Adil and his sons. Between whiles he relaxed with his family in the summer pavilions of his palace. One day, when he was playing with a favourite among his young sons, a Frankish embassy was shown into his presence. When the little boy saw the strange figures, with their close-shaven chins, close-cropped hair and odd clothes, he clung to his father and began crying. The great man, no doubt more than a little irritated at having his privacy encroached on in this way, dismissed the visitors to wait until he was ready to listen to their business. Then, turning to his secretary, he asked him to order something to eat. 'Speaking in his usual kindly way, he said: "It is a busy day. Bring us whatever you have ready."'

Such gentle, well-mannered consideration for subordinates and servants was, to many observers used to the arrogance and violence of petty despots, one of the most remarkable traits of a remarkable character. Open access to the ruler, an honoured tradition at some Muslim courts to this day, was something that Saladin insisted on whenever possible, and during these audiences the cushion he was sitting on was unceremoniously trampled underfoot by the jostling petitioners. Even unimportant courtiers could expect a civil response at almost any time of day. As he was preparing for his siesta one afternoon, an old mamluk, 'whom he much esteemed', came into the tent with a petition on behalf of religious enthusiasts serving as volunteers in the army. Saladin, genuinely exhausted after a hard morning's work, asked the old man, who had pushed passed the attendants, to let him look into the matter later. 'Instead, he held it right up to the king's eyes so that he could read it.' Finding himself so unceremoniously cornered, the greatest lord in Islam wryly agreed to the petition, if only to get rid of the petitioner, but observed he could not sign the authorisation until after his rest when his secretary came with the ink. But the old mamluk, who was obviously used to the evasions of the great, pointed out that there was an inkstand on a table behind Saladin's couch. 'By God, he is right,' sighed the king, and reached for the inkstand. The fact that he did this himself, without calling out a servant, was 'a sign of great benignity' to the admiring Baha'-ad-Din.

We do not have to rely on the eulogies of Saladin's admirers. In summing up his career, Ibn-al-Athir, the pro-Zengid Turkish chronicler, wrote: 'He was a generous man, sweet natured, a man of good character, humble and accepting patiently things which displeased him, though perhaps too inclined to overlook the faults of his lieutenants.' One evening, at a drinking bout with his mamluks, a boot was thrown during the horse-play and nearly hit Saladin; instead of disciplining the offender, he turned to the courtier next to him and opened up a conversation. On another occasion, when he was re- covering from an illness, his servants drew his bath too hot. Saladin called for cold water and the bath boy tripped and splashed the king; Saladin called for more and this time the man stumbled and deposited the whole jugful on him. Despite the shock to his weakened system Saladin merely commented: 'My dear fellow, if you aim to kill me, give me due warning.' And that, added Ibn-al-Athir, was his only observa- tion on the incident.

During the weeks of relaxation Saladin made his vow to make his pilgrimage the following year. In February the pilgrims made their return to Damascus, and on the 20th Saladin and his entourage went out to meet them on the road: it was a magnificent sight and the people of the city came out to greet the king. The winter rains lashing down did little to dampen the enthusiasm of the occasion and Saladin repressed the shivers of his body, but he was already contracting the chill that was to kill him. The weather was so bad that the roads had had to be cleared of the floodwater, yet Saladin forgot to put on the padded tunic which he always wore out riding. Baha'-ad-Din hurried after to remind him. 'He seemed like a man waking out of a dream and asked for the garment, but the master of the wardrobe could not find it.' Later it was to be seen as an omen that the king should ask for something that he never used to be without and could not get it. When they had returned to the place that Friday evening he complained of a great weariness and before midnight was prostrated by an attack of bilious fever.

The next morning he was still desperately weak and the fever was still on him. He complained of a disturbed night but chatted easily with his son, Baha'-ad-Din and al-Fadil until mid-day. He was unable to come in to lunch and his son al-Afdal took the place of honour at the table. To many the sight of the son in the father's place seemed a sad omen. On the sixth day of the illness, his anxious councillors sat him up, supporting his back with cushions and calling for warm water for him to drink after taking his medicine. 'He found the water too hot so a second cup was brought; this he found too cold but did not get angry or start ranting. He simply said: "Dear God, can no one produce water at the right temperature?" At this the *qadi* and I left the room weeping hot tears, and the *qadi* said to me: "What a spirit Islam is about to lose. By God. Any other man would have thrown the cup at the man's head".'

It became clear that he was failing rapidly. On the ninth day he lost consciousness and could not take his medicine. By this time the length of the illness was beginning to cause alarm in the city. The death of a potentate was too often followed by rioting while the palace factions fought for the succession, and some merchants began clearing their market stalls. Baha'-ad-Din and al-Fadil found that their comings and goings from the palace were anxiously observed by the crowds who tried to tell from the expressions on their faces how the king's illness was progressing. 'On the tenth day he was able to take a little barley water and the news caused public rejoicing. But the following morning we were told that the violence of his thirst was beyond belief and had caused the doctors to abandon hope.' When al-Afdal was informed of his father's condition he hurriedly convened the chief officers and councillors and ordered them to make the oath of loyalty to himself. He was an ambitious young man, but the precaution was absolutely necessary and contributed to the smooth transfer of power.

He breathed his last after the hour of the morning prayer on 4 March 1193. He was in his fifty-fifth year. 'The *qadi* came into his room just after dawn at the precise moment of his death,' Baha'-ad-Din continues his account; 'when I arrived he had already passed into the bosom of divine grace.' When the divine who was reading the Koran at the bedside reached the words: ' "There is no other God but he, and in him is my trust," he smiled, his face was illumined, and he gave up his spirit to his lord.'

The death caused such genuine displays of grief in Damascus that the physician Abd-al-Latif commented that it was, to his knowledge, the only time a king had been truly mourned by his people. 'It was a weary day; everyone was so deep in his own grief and sorrow that he could pay attention to no one else. . . . His sons went out among the people crying out for pity . . . and so it went on until after the mid-day prayer. Then we occupied ourselves with washing his body and clothing it in the shroud; but we had to resort to borrowing – even to the straw. After the mid-day prayer he was carried out in a coffin draped simply with a length of material procured, like the other materials needed to shroud him, by al-Fadil. Men's grief overcame them and distracted them even from the prayer recited over him by men clothed in sackcloth. Then the body was carried back to the palace in the garden where he had lain during his illness and was buried in the west pavilion. He was laid in his tomb about the hour of evening prayer.'

Saladin's penury when he died, so extreme that his friends had to borrow to bury him, was attested by hostile as well as friendly commentators, and all recognised that it was the result of a life of unparalleled generosity. Ibn-al-Athir recorded that when he died he left only a single Tyrian dinar and forty pieces of silver. He concluded his résumé of the great man whom he had so often criticised with a warmth which, more than anything written by his friends, demonstrates the deep impression this magnanimous champion of Islam made on all his contemporaries. 'In a word, he was the marvel of his time, a man rich in fine qualities marked by his fine actions and by the great campaigns he led against the Infidel, as his conquests proved.'

'God sanctify his spirit and illumine his sepulchre.'

# Epilogue

In 1976, the obvious parallel to draw between the world of Saladin and the contemporary world was that between the kingdom of Jerusalem brought low by Saladin after some 90 years and the State of Israel, then some 28 (now some 60) years in existence. To Arabs, both were intruders, both seen as agents of 'Western' interests. For example, the first reaction of the barons of the kingdom on the death of Baldwin IV in March 1185 was to refer the matter of the succession to the monarchs of the West. The kingdom's champion warriors, the Knights Templar and Knights Hospitaller, were largely funded by benefactors from all over Western European Christendom.

In the Muslim world, religious reformers urging action were often highly critical of those rulers they considered either corrupt or irreligious or collaborative with the Frankish enemy. In the twenty-first century, the comparison with such modern organisations as the Muslim Brotherhood and their attitude to Westernising Islamic governments is thought-provoking. The comparison of Usama bin Laden with Sinan 'The Old Man of Mountain' and head of the Assassins would seem, to Western eyes, obvious: both operating from remote mountain retreats, both credited with immense influence, and both thought to command numbers of fanatical followers. As to Saladin, an honourable man of high ambition but also of religious principle and military achievement, generally respected by his enemies as he was loved by his friends, no candidate springs to mind in our own day on either side of the religious divide. But then, Saladin was remarkable.

# Notes and Sources

## Introduction

The principal Arabic authority for the Muslim world empire from Samarkand to Cordoba in the time of Saladin is Ibn-al-Athir (1160–1233) of Mosul, author of the *Kamil at Tawarikh*, i.e. 'The Perfect [or Complete] History'. Also sometimes known as his *World History*, it was well in advance, in scope and detail, of his Latin contemporaries. He was an eyewitness of many episodes and is also admired for the simple elegance of his style. The article by Ashtor-Strauss on Jews at the time of Saladin, cited in the bibliography, is still useful. In general, despite the restrictions reintroduced by Saladin, Jews preferred Islamic regimes to the Latin Catholic kingdom of Jerusalem. Many left for Egypt. Alexandria had a population of some 3,000 Jews, Cairo of 2,000, served by two synagogues and a rabbi at the head of the community.

## Chapter I Jerusalem

Ibn-al-Athir remains our chief companion, but we also meet the anthologist Abu Shama of Damascus (1203–67), of the next generation. His *Kitab ar-Raudatain*, 'Book of the Two Gardens' (that is, the two dynasties of Nur ad-Din and Saladin), draws on earlier writers such as Imad ad-Din of Isfahan (1125–1201) who was successively secretary to Nur ad-din and Saladin, and whose seven-volume history of Saladin's times, *al-Barq al-Shami*, was used by several writers, notably Abu Shama, though the original text has not survived. Abu also excerpted Shama of Imad's *al-Fath al-qussi fi l-fath al-qudsi*, roughly 'An Eloquent Account of the Fall of Jerusalem', while greatly simplifying the convoluted style. He relies on Imad for information not to be found elsewhere. We owe the account of Saladin's generosity at Jerusalem to the Latin source known as 'Ernoul', edited as *Chronique d'Ernoul et de Bernard le Trésorier* by L. de Mas- Latrie (Paris, 1971; see also the bibliography under Morgan).

## Chapter 2 Across the Battle Lines

Over the decades, Europeans' attitudes towards themselves as well as to the Muslim world could be mixed – or in the case of the Würzburg annalist downright cynical. But, even at the time, a committed crusade historian like the monk Fulcher of Chartres, who died aged about 60 at Jerusalem circa 1125, having settled there in the year of its capture, could be reasonably objective. His *Gesta Francorum Iherusalem peregrinantium* (found as *Historia Hierosolymitana* in R.H.Cr.Occ. III) is a reliable and reasonably objective account of the early years of the First Crusade.

## Chapter 3 The Quadrilateral of Power

After his 'Perfect History' the best-known work by Ibn al-Athir was 'The History of the Atabegs of Mosul'. Often verging on the panegyric and certainly less objective than his principal work, for page after page it rings to the triumph of Zengi's capture of Edessa. A selection in French translation will be found in R.H.Cr.Or. Vol II part ii.

## Chapter 4 Nur-ad-Din and the Propaganda of the Jihad

This chapter is indebted to *L'Islam et la Croisade* by Emmanuel Sivan. It seems that Saladin modelled himself to some degree on Nur-ad-Din's cultivation of a public reputation for piety, though seen from Egypt his motivation seemed more like ambition than religion. Moreover, though the lord of Aleppo might have dealings with the Franks, his propagandists in Damascus represented the people there as yearning for his leadership to the Holy War, while the prince of their city negotiated with the Christians. Damascus's historian, Ibn-al-Qalanisi (1073–1160), who held various posts in the city, was an eyewitness of much he described and was reasonably objective. Translated extracts by H.A.R. Gibb appeared as *The Damascus Chronicle of the Crusades* (London, 1932). The basic source for the history of Aleppo is the *'ta'rikh Halab'* of Kamal-ad-Din ibn al-'Adim (1192–1262), a native of the city.

## Chapter 5 The Family of Aiyub

Interestingly, to the Christian writer William of Tyre (1130–85) Shirkuh seemed 'a hard-working man, avid of glory'. Born in Syria but educated in Europe, and archbishop of Tyre from 1175, William, who had good Arabic as well as Latin and Greek, is noted for his scholarly *Historia rerum in partibus transmarinis gestarum*, 'History of things done oversea'. In addition to Ibn-al-Athir's 'Atabegs' and Abu Shama's 'Two Gardens' this chapter uses the biography of Saladin by his secretary, Baha'-ad-Din Ibn Shaddad (1145–1234). A lucid narrative (translated in R.H.Cr.Or., 1884) based on personal observation, it gives the best portrait we have of Saladin from an admiring but not sycophantic Muslim point of view, and a vivid account of his times.

## Chapter 6 Vizir of Egypt

The rivalries between the Shia and Sunni communities of Islam were one reason why Sunni Baghdad urged Saladin to suppress the Shia caliphate at Cairo; the rivalries of race compounded the disunity of the Islamic states throughout the period. Ibn-al-Athir's 'Atabegs' gives the details of Shirkuh's expedition to Egypt and Saladin's own account of his personal reluctance to go on the second Egyptian expedition. He and Baha'-ad-Din give the telling insights into the Aiyubid family discussions over their deportment towards Nur-ad-Din, and the debates on the same in the councils of his commanders and emirs.

A decisive moment in Saladin's career was the suppression of the rebellion of the Nubian guards in July–August 1169. According to Imad-ad-Din the Fatimid caliphs' Nubian regiments had traditionally been a cause of trouble for vizirs: in the unrest during Saladin's takeover of power they were slipping out of control. Accounts differ as to the exact sequence of events in the uprising. The rebel forces took up position in the great square between the caliph's East and West palaces. Saladin's brother Turan Shah was in command of loyal troops there while Saladin himself and the main force were in the Vizir's Palace quarter. The Nubians were forced down the main street towards the gate Bab Zuwaila and abandoned their action on news that their quarters at Mansuriya were aflame. Either they were given quarter to rescue their families (as Arab historians reported) or they were harried as they fled. In the next days thousands crossed the Nile for Giza but were hunted down and massacred.

## Chapter 7 The Critical Years

As in Chapter 4, Kamal-ad-Din's 'History' is important for events in Aleppo, Ibn al-Athir for general history and events relating to Mosul. Among secondary sources Emmanuel Sivan's work was most helpful. And as in many parts of the book I turned to Andrew Ehrenkreutz's biography of Saladin here, for example regarding the sultan's dealings with the Aleppan regime after Nur-ad-Din's death.

## Chapter 8 Triumph in the North

Thanks to a decade of excavations on the site, described on the Vadum Jacob Research Project website, under Ronnie Ellenblum, Shmulick Marco and Amotz Agnon, the dimensions of the vanished castle at Jacob's Ford and the strategic consequences of its destruction by Saladin's forces in 1179 were given new importance in the early 2000s. Archaeologists were able to trace the construction sequence of the site – existing barely eleven months from the initiation of the works in October 1178 to the razing of the structure the following September. Saladin's letters to the caliph at the time of his difficulties with Mosul are found in Abu Shama. The 'Travels' of the Andalusian-born Ibn Jubayr (also Jubair) (1145–1217), being an account of his pilgrimage to Mecca 1183–85, was translated into English by R.J.C. Broadhurst in 1952. The story of the presentation of a fuller's bowl to Imad-ad-Din, Aleppo's governor, comes in Kamal-ad-Din.

## Chapter 9 Dynast and Hero

I found William of Tyre's comment on the Christian reaction to the fall of Aleppo and much else in René Grousset's *Histoire des Croisades et du royaume franc de Jérusalem* of the 1930s. This magnum opus was basic to subsequent English general histories of the crusades. The story of Saladin's chivalrous conduct at the siege of al-Karak comes from the Latin source known as Ernoul. That of al-Adil, Saladin's brother, consulting with his young nephews before accompanying them to Egypt, comes from Baha'-ad-Din, who records that he had it from al-Adil himself.

## Chapter 10 Oh! Sweet Victory

In this chapter, Ibn-al-Athir's 'World History' along with Imad-ad-Din's biography of Saladin, and quotations from it in Abu Shama, are important sources for our knowledge of events. Charles M. Brand's *Speculum* article of 1962 has still valuable insights on Saladin's relations with the Byzantine empire and their joint opposition to the Third Crusade and is drawn on both here and in Chapter 11. J. Prawer's *Crusader Institutions* (1980) has an interesting account of the Battle of Hattin. The defeat of the Franks at Hattin smashed the kingdom's logistical system. Essentially, the Frankish presence in 'Outremer' comprised garrison settlements, colonies in effect, that depended for their survival on relatively small numbers of heavily armoured mounted men at arms, operating from scattered fortified bases. Even small units of such troops could be effective against large forces in limited engagements. If brought together in a single force they had to win or at least retire in good order; Hattin removed western capability from military calculations in the region for a year.

## Chapter 11 The Threat from the North

We know of Henry II's letters from the chronicle of Ralph (Radulfus) de Diceto, the dean of St Paul's (ed. William Stubbs, London, 1876 ). The Latin chroniclers' suspicions of Byzantium are discussed by Charles Brand. Throughout the negotiations Saladin took care for the status and preservation of Islam at Constantinople and the mosque there. Baha'-ad-Din described the arrival of the *imam* at Constantinople; he also tells us the emperor Isaac grumbled that the only result of his friendship with Saladin seemed to have been to bring down the hatred of the Franks upon his empire. I take the account of Frederick Barbarossa's death and the reaction to it of the emir from Ibn-al-Athir, who also recorded Saladin's debate with his emirs about the Christians in Acre.

It is worth noting that Barbarossa had appointed St George's Day 1189 as the launch date of his crusade. In September 1191, passing through Lydda, home of the saint's cult since the sixth century, Saladin ordered the destruction of the saint's church there.

## Chapter 12 Acre, the City for which the World Contended

The account of the battle games before Acre comes from Baha'-ad-Din, as does the criticism of the emirs for not pressing the advantage before the Franks could consolidate their position. This chapter draws heavily on him and on Ibn-al-Athir in his 'World History'. More than once, they indicate that Saladin was thwarted of success because of lack of support and cooperation from his emirs. The hardships of the Christian forces in the Third Crusade are detailed in the *Itinerarium peregrinorum et Gesta Regis Ricardi* (ed. William Stubbs, London, 1864). Meaning literally 'The travel record of the pilgrims and the deeds of King Richard', its title is a reminder that contemporaries never used the term 'Crusade'. For them these campaigns were armed pilgrimages to the Holy City; the Muslims saw their campaigns as *jihad* or Holy War to recover lands once conquered for the Faith.

## Chapter 13 Saracens and Crusaders

A most vivid guide to life in the overseas territories of the expatriate Franks of the twelfth century is to be found in the autobiographical work of Usama ibn Mundiq, emir of Shaizar, who lived from 1095 to 1188. Called *Kitab al-I 'tibar* or 'The Book of Instruction', it survives in an incomplete manuscript in the library of the Escorial, Madrid. Baha'-ad-Din, Ibn-al-Athir and Abu Shama are, of course, important to the narrative, and among secondary sources the work of the French scholars Emmanuel Sivan and Albert Champdor have been useful. For the Assassins I have drawn on the work of Bernard Lewis.

## Chapter 14 The Death of a Hero

For the fascinating audience Saladin gave to Bishop Hubert Walter of Salisbury, we have the testimony of the author of the *Itinerarium . . . Regis Ricardi*, and for Saladin's reception of Bohemond of Antioch I have followed the account in

Grousset. But the bulk of this chapter relies on Baha'-ad-Din's account of Saladin's last days.

His reputation has not passed down to posterity unchallenged. The deeds of another hero of Islam, Baybars the Mamluk Sultan of Egypt who vanquished both the Christians and Mongols, are still recited in the popular coffee houses of Egypt. Yet it was the name of Saladin that was invoked when President Gamal Abdel Nasser united Egypt and Syria in the short-lived United Arab Republic, and before his overthrow in 2003 Iraq's deposed dictator Saddam Hussein boasted that he, like Saladin, was born in the city of Takrit (Tikrit).

# Select Bibliography

## A note on primary sources.

The first translations into a European language of the principal Arabic histories were published in *Recueil des historiens des croisades: Historiens orientaux* ('R.H.Cr.Or.') from 1872 onwards; this great French series has provided the basic resource for non-Arabists ever since. For English-speaking readers, the most accessible bibliography of these translated texts is to be found in Steven Runciman's three-volume *History of the Crusades* (Cambridge, 1954), specifically – for the times of Saladin – Volume II 'The Kingdom of Jerusalem'. Companion series provided translations of chronicles and commentaries in Greek and Armenian; while the *Recueil . . . Historiens Occidentaux* (R.H.Cr.Occ.) carried Latin sources. Other useful collections include *Storici Arabi delle Crociate* by Francesco Gabrieli (Turin, 1957), translated into English by E.J. Costello as *Arab Historians of the Crusades* (London, 1969).

On the vexed question of changing fashions in transliteration from the Arabic, Yusuf Ibish, in his 1972 edition of numerous earlier articles by Sir Hamilton A.R. Gibb, commented: 'In an endeavour to achieve fidelity to the original texts, the editor has not attempted to unify systems of transliteration.'

## Secondary sources

Ashtor-Strauss, E., 'Saladin and the Jews', in *The Hebrew Union College Annual Journal* (Cincinnatti, 1956)

Atiya, A.S., 'The Idea of the Counter-Crusade', in *Actes du XXIe Congrés Internationale des Orientalistes* (Paris, 1949)

Aube, P., *Baudouin IV de Jérusalem* (Paris, 1981)

Aubin, J., 'Comment Tamerlan prenait les villes', in *Studia Islamica* XIX (Paris, 1963)

Baha ad-Din Ibn Shaddad, *The Rare and Excellent History of Saladin*, trs D.S. Richards (2001)

Baldwin, Marshall W., *The First Hundred Years*, vol I of *The Crusades*, editor in chief K.M. Setton, 2nd ed. (University of Wisconsin, Maddison, 1969)

Brand, Charles M., 'The Byzantines and Saladin, 1185-1192: Opponents of the Third Crusade' in *Speculum* XXXVII (Cambridge, Mass., 1962)

Brundage, James A., 'Cruce Signari: The rite for taking the Cross in England' in *Traditio* XXII (New York 1966)

– *The Crusade, Holy War and Canon Law* (Aldershot, 1991)

Cahen, Claude, 'Un traité d'armurie composé pour Saladin', in *Bulletin des études orientales de l'Institut Damas* XII (Damascus, 1948)

– *Orient et occident au temps des Croisades* (Paris, 1983)

Canard, M., 'Un vizir chrétien à l'époque fatimide: l'Arménien Bahram', in *Annales de l'Institut des Etudes Orientales* (Algiers, 1954)

Champdor, Albert, *Saladin: le plus pur héros d'Islam* (Paris, 1956)

Cresswell, K.A.C., 'Fortification in Islam before AD 1250', in *Proceedings of The British Academy* XXXVIII (London, 1952)

Daniel, N.A., *Islam and the West: The Making of an Image* (Edinburgh, 1960)

– *The Arabs and Medieval Europe* (Beirut, 1975)

Edbury, P.W., and J.G. Rowe, *William of Tyre: Historian of the Latin East* (Cambridge, 1988)

Ehrenkreutz, Andrew S., *Saladin* (Albany, 1972)

El-Beiry, *Les institutions de l'Egypte au temps des Ayyubides* (Cairo, 1971)

Ellenblum, Ronnie, *Crusader Castles and Modern Histories* (Cambridge, 2006)

Fink, H., 'Mawdud of Mosul; precursor of Saladin', in *The Muslim World* XLIII (Hyderabad, 1953)

– 'The Role of Damascus in the history of the Crusades', in *The Muslim World* XLIX (Hyderabad, 1959)

Firestone, Reuven, *The Origin of Holy War in Islam* (Oxford, 1999)

Gabrieli, Francesco, *Arab Historians of the Crusades*, translated from the Italian by E.J. Costello (London, 1969)

Ghali, Wacyf Boutros, *La Tradition chevalresque des Arabes* (Paris, 1919)

Gibb, Sir Hamilton A.R., 'The Achievement of Saladin' (1952) and 'The Armies of Saladin' (1951), both reprinted in *Studies on the Civilization of Islam*, ed. Yusuf Ibish (Lebanon, 1972)

– *The Life of Saladin: From the Works of Imad ad Din and Baha ad Din* (Oxford, 1973)

Goitein, S.D., 'The Sanctity of Jerusalem and Palestine in Early Islam', in *Studies in Islamic History and Institutions* (Leiden, 1966)

Grousset, René, *Histoire des croisades et du royaume franc de Jérusalem*, 3 vols, (Paris, 1933–36)

Hadia Dajani Shakeel, 'A Reassessment of Some Medieval and Modern Perceptions of the Counter Crusade' in *The Jihad and its Times, Dedicated to Andrew Stefan Ehrenkreutz* (Ann Arbor, 1991)

Hamilton, Bernard, *The Leper King and his Heirs* (Cambridge, 2000)

Heath, Ian, *Armies and Enemies of the Crusades 1096–1291* (Worthing, 1978)

Hindley, Geoffrey, *The Crusades* (London, 2003)

Husain Shanaz, *Muslim Heroes of the Crusades: Salahuddin and Nuruddin* (London, 1998)

Karsh, Efraim, *Islamic Imperialism: A History* (Yale, 2006)

Kennan, Elizabeth, 'Innocent III and the First Political Crusade', in *Traditio* XXVII (New York, 1971)

Kraemer, Jorg, *Der Sturz des Königreichs in der Darstellung des Imad-ad Din al-Kitab al-Isfahani* (Wiesbaden, 1952)

Lane-Poole, Stanley, *Saladin and the Fall of the Kingdom of Jerusalem* (London and New York, 1906)

Lewis, Bernard, *The Assassins: A Radical Sect in Islam* (New York, 1968)

– and H.M. Holt (eds.) *Historians of the Middle East* (London, 1962)

Lilie, R.-J., *Byzantium and the Crusader States*, trs. J.C. Morris and J.E. Ridings (Oxford 1994)

Lyons, Malcolm, and D.E.P. Jackson, *Saladin: The Politics of the Holy War* (Cambridge, 1984)

Maalouf, Amin, *The Crusades through Arab Eyes* (London, 1984)

Mayer, H.E., 'Henry II of England and the Holy Land', in *English Historical Review* CCCLXXXV (London, 1982)

Mayer, L.A., *Saracenic Heraldry: A Survey* (Oxford, 1933)

Mercier, Louis, *La Chasse et les sports chez les Arabes* (Paris, 1927)

Möhring, H., *Saladin und der Dritte Kreuzzug* (Wiesbaden, 1980)

Morgan, M.R., *The Chronicle of Ernoul and the Continuations of William of Tyre* (Oxford, 1973)

Mortimer, Edward, *Faith and Power: The Politics of Islam* (London, 1982)

Munro, Dana C., 'The Western Attitude toward Islam during the Period of the Crusades', in *Speculum* VI (Cambridge, Mass. 1931)

Murphy, T.P., ed., *The Holy War* (Columbus, Ohio, 1976)

Newby, P.H., *Saladin in his Time* (London, 1983 and 2001)

Nicolle, David, *Saladin and the Saracens* (London, 1986)

– *Hattin 1187, Saladin's Greatest Victory* (1993)

Pellat, Y., 'L'Idée de Dieu chez les "Sarrasins" des chansons de geste', in *Studia Islamica* XXII (Paris, 1965)

Pernoud, Régine, *La femme au temps des croisades* (Paris, 1990)

Powell, J.M., ed., *Muslims under Latin Rule, 1100–1300* (Princeton. N.J. 1991)

Prawer, J. 'The Settlement of the Latins in Jerusalem', in *Speculum* XXVII (Cambridge, Mass., 1952)

– *Crusader Institutions* (Oxford, 1980)

– *The History of the Jews in the Latin Kingdom of Jerusalem* (Oxford, 1986)

Regan, Geoffrey, *Saladin and the Fall of Jerusalem* (Beckenham, 1987)

Reston, James Jr., *Warriors of God: Richard the Lionheart and Saladin in the Third Crusade* (New York and London, 2001)

Riley-Smith, Jonathan, ed., *The Oxford Illustrated History Of the Crusades* (Oxford and New York, 1997)

Ritter, H., 'La Parure des Cavaliers and die Literatur über die ritterlichen Künste', in *Der Islam* XVIII (Berlin, 1929)

Runciman, Sir Stephen, *A History of the Crusades* (Cambridge, 1951–54)

Sivan, Emanuel, 'Notes sur la situation des Chrétiens sous les Ayyubides', in *Revue de l'histoire des religions* CLXXII (Paris, 1967)

– *L'Islam et la croisade* (Paris, 1968)

Smail, R.C., *Crusading Warfare* (Cambridge, 1956 and 1972)

– *The Crusaders in Syria and the Holy Land* (London and New York, 1973)

Thomas, A., 'La Légende de Saladin en Poitou', in *Journal des Savants* (Paris, 1908)

Thomine, J.S. and D.S., 'Nouveaux documents sur l'histoire religieuse et sociale de Damas au moyen âge', *Revue des études islamiques* XXXII, Cahier I (Paris, 1965)

Throop, Palmer A., *Criticism of the Crusade: A Study of Public Opinion and Crusade Propaganda* (Amsterdam, 1940)

Tibawi, A.L., 'Jerusalem: Its place in Islam and in Arab History', in *The Islamic Quarterly* XII, No 4 (London, 1968)

Usama ibn Munqidh, 'Kitab al i-'tibar', *An Arab-Syrian Gentleman and Warrior*, trs. P.K. Hitti (Columbia U.P., New York, 1929)

Watt, W., Montgomery, *Islamic Political Thought* (Edinburgh, 1968)

# Glossary

*adab* –
the full range of accomplishments, from some knowledge of mathematics and poetry to the arts of conversation and genealogy, expected of an Arab gentleman.

*A.H.* –
*Anno Hegirae*, the latin term for the dating of the lunar years of the Muslim Era of the *Hegira* (also *Hejira*). The term refers to the Prophet's withdrawal from Mecca to Medina on 16 July A.D.622.

*al-Jazirah* –
from the Arabic word for 'island', the region lying within upper Iraq and south-eastern Turkey between the Upper Euphrates and Tigris rivers – i.e. Upper Mesopotamia.

*atabeg* –
a ruler of a city, from the Turkish word for 'a tutor', i.e. originally the regent for a minor, the nominal ruler.

*Hajj* –
the annual pilgrimage to Mecca, enjoined on all pious Muslims.

*imam* –
a leader of the Muslim community, in some contexts the caliph himself. In the Shia tradition the *imams* are leaders of special sanctity and absolute moral and religious authority who have appeared at successive epochs in history.

*iqta* –
a payment in land revenues, to be derived by the holder (*mukta*) from estates, villages or towns assigned to him for the purpose.

*khutba* –
a sermon. For the cultivated Muslim the *khutba* was an exercise in high poetic literary art, followed avidly so that a listener might be able to repeat passages verbatim. Skilled practitioners were much admired. It was an oration that might have political as well as religious significance.

mamluk or mameluke –
a (usually Turkish) soldier of slave origins. Saladin followed convention by recruiting slave corps in his armies in Egypt. In 1250 a leader of one of these corps

seized power, establishing the Mamluk dynasty that was to rule Egypt for the next 250 years.

*mihrab* —
a prayer niche in the wall of a mosque that faces in the direction of Mecca, the *qibla*; the *mihrab* thus indicates the *qibla*.

*minbar* —
the pulpit from which the *khutba* is delivered.

*muezzin* —
the official of a mosque who declaims the call to prayer from the minaret.

*mulla, mullah* —
deriving from an Arabic word (*mawlah*) denoting 'lord' or 'master', *mulla* came be used as a term of respect for a religious teacher.

*qadi* —
a judge in the tradition of the shari'ah law; he came to be an administrator of pious bequests or a guardian of minors and other vulnerable people such as widows.

*qibla* —
the direction to be faced by the Faithful for prayer, indicated in a mosque by the *mihrab*.

*razzia* —
a raiding campaign (original Arabic *ghazia*, meaning 'war').

*rais* —
the senior official of a town administration.

sultan —
originally with the meaning of moral or religious authority as such, from the eleventh century it was used as the title of a ruler.

*tchogandar* —
the polo master, an important court official. The word derives from *tchogan*, 'ball'.

*ummah* —
the religious political community of Islam in which the power of the Faith is vested and the consensus of whose opinions is the ultimate guide to right-doing. An unpopular or corrupt ruler or regime may be considered a parasitic intermediary on the ummah.

*zarf* —
the sense of style, elegance and refinement that should underlie a gentleman's education.

# Index